Eleanor Tee

The Sanctuary of Suffering

Eleanor Tee

The Sanctuary of Suffering

ISBN/EAN: 9783744660501

Printed in Europe, USA, Canada, Australia, Japan

Cover: Foto ©Lupo / pixelio.de

More available books at **www.hansebooks.com**

THE
Sanctuary of Suffering

BY ELEANOR TEE

AUTHOR OF 'THIS EVERYDAY LIFE,' ETC.

WITH A PREFACE BY

THE REV. J. P. F. DAVIDSON, M.A

VICAR OF S. MATTHIAS, EARL'S COURT ; PRESIDENT
OF THE 'GUILD OF ALL SOULS'

'Saints, is it well with you?—Yea, it is well.'
CHRISTINA ROSSETTI.

'And none of them is young, and none is old,
Except as perfect by the Will of GOD.'
CHRISTINA ROSSETTI.

LONGMANS, GREEN, AND CO.
LONDON, NEW YORK, AND BOMBAY
1896

PREFACE

THE subject of the following pages is one which at once enlists in its behalf some of our deepest human interests. For Suffering is universal, and assumes such manifold forms, that whatever sheds light upon it, or tends to unfold its nature and issues, will always touch, at one point or another, the human heart.

The writer, it should be understood, does not profess to dogmatise upon Its mysteries,—the mystery of pain, and sorrow, and the seeming inequalities of the present stage of human life,—but accepting their mysteriousness, to dwell, in the spirit of quiet and practical meditation, upon the various forms of Suffering, and their purpose in the final manifestation of the Divine Love. Such subjects as Pain, in its connection with the Fall, and in its aspects as independent of the Fall, and the Incarnation, viewed as a part of GOD's original Purpose, modified indeed in its character, but not necessitated by human Sin,—and other kindred points are touched with a sympathetic hand, so as to open up sources of spiritual consolation and devout thought, rather than to limit, by mere definition, what lies beyond our spiritual vision.

And in this, I venture to think, consists the great value of this thoughtful and interesting work. For, in moments of great Suffering, men are lifted above the ordinary levels of life and thought, and introduced to that higher Spiritual Region, in which the eye gazes upon the Mystery of the Divine Purpose in its ultimate tendencies rather than on the immediate human aspect, which such Suffering presents. And in that vision, and at the close of the long vista, is seen the Figure of the Man of Sorrows, embodying in Himself at once the acutest forms of human Suffering and the most perfect Manifestation of the Divine Love.

But, as the writer implies throughout, certain conditions are necessary for the due understanding of the Mystery of Suffering, and the fulfilment of its Purpose. Some of these it will be useful just to touch upon briefly.

1. First of all: there is that sure Trust in the Divine Purpose,—in the perfect Love and Wisdom of GOD, which accepts 'the suffering of this present time,' whatever their immediate aspect be, in the certain assurance of their final and permanent issues, as working out the blessedness of the Future, and as 'an earnest of the glory that shall be revealed in us.' This is the real secret of peace in all the sorrows of life.

2. Next, and in close connection with the preceding, is the Remedial View of Suffering. Suffering is not only the penalty of sin. It is, at the same time, its Remedy. Though no doubt a chastisement, it is a chastisement in the hands of a Loving Father, Who corrects those whom He loves, and chastises every one whom He receives. And so, the whole Creation, though groaning and travailing in pain at the present, will, in due time, give birth to the new Order, 'waits for the manifestation of the sons of GOD,' who shall come forth 'out of the great Tribulation,' purified in the fire of Suffering. And the Church is 'filling up that which is lacking of the Sufferings of Christ.' He Himself, the Eternal and the First-Begotten, in His Humanity, as the Representative of redeemed man and of a renewed Creation, is 'made perfect through Sufferings' that the 'many sons whom He shall bring unto glory' may complete, each in their measure and order, that full sum of human Suffering, which shall issue in the perfected Kingdom of the Redemption.

3. To notice a third and very important point: Suffering is to be made effectual not only to our own sanctification, but to that of others. Human Suffering is still, in a true sense, Vicarious. If we are entering into the true purpose of Suffering, we shall be feeling that others are to be helped and comforted by means of those things which we ourselves endure. It is indeed

impossible fully to estimate the power of this Vicariousness. And in the full revelation of all the mysteries of life, it may be seen hereafter that the submission and trustful patience of suffering souls has been a greater element in the perfecting of the elect than all the energy of the most active workers; even as, at the beginning, it was the Martyr rather than the Preacher, who laid the foundations of the Kingdom of GOD. At any rate, when this consideration is overlooked, there is always a danger lest Suffering should issue in selfishness or in a morbid spirit,—in the murmurs or the repinings of a self-centred and then embittered life, which turns its predestined Blessing into a curse.

4. And lastly: perhaps the most comprehensive of all the conditions of sanctified Suffering is, the growing realisation of the Unseen and the Future. For Reason not less than Faith points to a future Order, of which the present is but a scanty fragment, wherein what is now unequal, and imperfect, and but partially understood, shall be set right. And further, the spiritual element in man's nature suggests Realities beyond this visible scene, in which, by virtue of our spiritual being, and in a mystery, we, even now, have part. Hence into that great department of human sorrow,—the loss, or rather the disappearance from this earthly life, of our loved ones,—there enters the real consolation of a conscious spiritual fellowship, which not only sustains,

but even deepens and intensifies the memories and the sympathies of the former existence, and knits soul to soul in a still closer union than had been realised before. Thus even a life-long sorrow may have its consolations and its hopes. It remains indeed, but, remaining, is transfigured with Light from the Unseen World, until the sorrowful one learns to say, in the beautiful words of the Psalmist: 'The Lord my GOD shall make my darkness to be Light.' For, to quote the words of S. Paul, which describe the true attitude and standpoint of the Christian mind in its contemplation of the true Life of man in Christ: 'We look not at the things which are seen, but at the things which are not seen: for the things which are seen are temporal, but the things which are not seen are eternal.'

May the pages which follow be helpful to many a Traveller on the way of sorrows, as a guide to that Rest which awaits him in the Sanctuary of Suffering!

J. P. F. D.

CONTENTS

		PAGE
I.	ENTERING THE SANCTUARY	1
II.	THE APPROACH TO THE IDEAL	11
	INDIVIDUAL PROGRESS	36
	ADVANCEMENT OF THE LAW OF CREATURELY PERFECTION	47
	SPECIAL CALLS	73
III.	'JESUS HOMINUM SALVATOR'	95
	THE MAN OF SORROWS	101
	THE OFFERED SACRIFICE	108
	ATONEMENT	118
IV.	'CALLED TO BE SAINTS'	133
V.	THE ENDLESS LIFE	145
	MOVEMENT OF DIVINE LOVE	158
	TRANSFIGURATION	174
	JOY OF BEING	191

CONTENTS

VI. THINGS NEW AND OLD (BEING A SUMMARY OF GOD'S GIFTS OF 'PAIN' HELD OUT IN THE SANCTUARY) 209

    SICKNESS 219

    POVERTY 236

    MISCONCEPTION 251

    LONELINESS 265

    LOVE 278

VII. THE GREAT UNVEILING 301

    A SOUL SPED TO THE UNSEEN WORLD . . 319

    INTERCOURSE BETWEEN THE SEEN AND UNSEEN WORLDS 329

    THE UNITED LIFE BEYOND THE VEIL . . . 343

I
ENTERING THE SANCTUARY

ENTERING THE SANCTUARY

THERE comes a time in the life of each one of us when the light of our life seems to have gone out, and we remain in a strange, dark place, from which our soul goes forth in a great cry: 'Hath GOD forgotten to be gracious?' And we wait; and perhaps it is long before any true answer reaches our consciousness.

And during the period of waiting, it is with us as it was with Elaine when the beautiful flowers lay over her body, and the poor unconsciousness could know it not. We do not know of the grand life stirring above us.

In the west of England there is an old churchyard where the roses grow in sweet, rich profusion, entwining their branches in and out of the railings that guard the tombs of the dead, where the birds sing joyously, and the sun shines with a peculiar radiance. It is indeed a 'Garden of GOD,' and one's eyes are lifted up to heaven, the soul goes forth, the heart is thrilled, as around these tombs, these graves of dull, dead forms, the lovely life-forms speak of a gladdening resurrection somewhere, of renewed life possible of attainment.

The present writer visited this churchyard last year,

and as she stood quietly in a corner of the beautiful 'Garden,' a special revelation seemed to be borne down to, and born in, her heart and soul : a revelation which drew its full significance, partly from the tombs surrounded by the sweet, rich flower-growth, partly from a message in the bird-songs, and partly from the expression of the wonderful sky above. It was a grey sky: but here and there were bright flashes of gold, and as the eye gazed upon those radiant flashes the grey lost itself in the shining of the gold, and there was nought left impressed on the soul but a vision—in which, as the sun at high noon-tide was diffusing its rays over the whole seen earth, the light of heaven shone forth, and darkness was for ever expelled.

Souls newly drawn into a special sanctuary of suffering see no light, only darkness. They are sensible of an oppression from which they long with their whole strength to be free. It is an imprisonment. They are like caged birds beating their wings against the bars of their captivity; and, as with the prisoned birds, the strength put forth in the direction of a supposed freedom means loss of power, greater suffering, needless pain. What had they done that they should thus have been punished? What had been amiss in their previous mode of living, to call down upon them such a terrible lot? They had been living the usual sort of life, not very good perhaps, yet not very bad : a life composed of many little pleasures and joys, intermingled with streaks of trouble which had hardly had power to rob them of the pleasures and joys that had charmed them. It had seemed to them a very harmless life: one that surely could not hurt any one, least of all themselves. And then this terrible shock had come, and the pleasant, harmless life, not very good, yet not very bad, was at an end. Why was it? What had they done? Again they say this. And it implies a belief that the world has been proved to be a mistake, and GOD at error, not only in His creation, but in His management of it.

There the 'dead' lie in that old churchyard, waiting for the spirit to awaken them to true life. They lie in the darkness, unconscious of the gladness and beauty around and above them: lie still beneath the sod, and the spirit tarries over them. The sun is high in the heavens, but they do not know it: it is all darkness of gloom. The flowers bloom and are sweet, the birds sing their joyous songs of praise; but they have no sense of either: they are waiting for their awakening to fuller life.

With those who enter for the first time definitely the Sanctuary of Suffering, it is death to the old form in which they had known life. They lie, too, in a gloom, from which no sense of life beyond and outside that gloom goes forth, into which no ray of light can penetrate, no consciousness of glory come. It is as though the old form were placed in a grave, over which the sun might shine, the flowers bloom, the birds sing, and draw out no answer, no responsive thrill of brightness and life, of praise to Heaven.

There must be death: there must be the laying aside of the form of the lower life, ere a higher life be gained. And may we not take the death of the body—the earthly 'seeming'—as involving type and figure of that death of the lower self, which is another mode of expressing the burial, the putting beyond sight, the old form in which our life had been lived—the pitiful old form in which life generally is lived until there is a distinct entrance into the great Sanctuary of Suffering, where the 'Man of Sorrows' can be eventually seen and truly known; that is, recognised as the Perfect Type of human life?

We all must lose ourselves, before we truly find ourselves. 'If I lose myself,' said the holy knight—to whom, as the beautiful legend tells us, was earliest accorded the vision of the Holy Grail—'I find myself.' We start by losing our higher self in a perpetual pandering to desires and wants that are not of GOD, but of the evil about us and the evil in our own heart. We seek to gratify what we regard as natural longings: to realise a happiness to which we fancy we have a true right. But all the while we are following a 'will-o'-the-wisp,' which decoys, allures, leads us on and on, and then disappears in a deep, dark morass. It is not true Divinely appointed happiness, any more than a particular sort of pain is a true, Divinely appointed pain; and until we are arrested in this constant pursuit of an *ignis fatuus* we shall never know real happiness, nor understand the beauty of real pain.

Happiness is a word greatly misunderstood, and the haze surrounding it generally is far more nearly impenetrable than is the Mystery of Suffering—though this, indeed, must here remain in great degree mysterious. Never on earth can it be fully understood, because it is of GOD, and all that is of GOD is infinite—beyond the ability of finite man to fathom. But it is certainly not a satisfaction of lower desires and wants, nor is it the complement of a careless, selfish life. 'The harm that I sustain I carry about with me,' S. Bernard once said. We are not aware of sustaining harm in our idle self-living, nevertheless it is there in great measure; and it is, alas! not confined to ourselves, to the personal circle of our life. Not merely do we, then, sustain personal harm, but we spread it broadcast. Others, through our fault, are submerged in error and unhappiness; and though we may say lightly, if we give a thought to the increase of error and unhappiness about us, or even perceive it without giving definite thought to it—It is GOD's will for them: it is well for them that they should suffer! we are then going in direct opposition to true natural bias, as impressed on human life by GOD; and in our light acceptance, seemingly, of GOD's will for them in allotting suffering, and our acknowledgment that it is well for them, also in opposition to the view we take of ourselves and our desires.

GOD's will? No! Such pain is not the will of GOD; such error and suffering are not decreed by Him. GOD is holding out for them something entirely different from what they have been reaping through us. He has been sowing seed in their hearts, and we have been removing that, and substituting other seed; and the result, therefore, is not GOD's, but ours. The pain they suffer is not the righteous, saving pain of GOD's allotment: it is man's, and it has been caused by a disordered state of being, an anarchy of life in which GOD's voice has not been heard, nor His face seen. We have not been still enough to hear the Divine monitions borne down to us, and the turmoil has been creating a cloud, behind which the Divine Form has stood in vain.

And so it was necessary—only GOD knows how sternly necessary—for us to be drawn aside into a stillness of being, where we might stay waiting for such revelations as should be divinely ordered for us; where we might come face to face with the secret of our creation, and be raised to a higher plane of life.

'Often it is in the moment of defeat, of weakness, of crushing sorrow and desolation, that a man first begins to live a life worth living.'[1] The life we had been living was a life really apart from GOD: a condition in which true, lasting happiness was an impossibility, in which happiness falsely so called had often been attained, perhaps through an individual, or individual human beings, but never from the GOD of our origin. If it was happiness, its roots were but in the earth: its growth, and such blossom and fruit as it might have borne, never tending towards heaven, never making for true perfection or lasting life. And all that we had to lose, so that we might escape from our 'hyaline of self,' and find GOD, and such happiness and wellbeing as

[1] *Lux Mundi.*

should minister to a true growth of lasting life, not merely in ourselves, but in all around us. We had to lose our old self, and obtain a new self: a self that might be able to find GOD everywhere, and consequent undying happiness.

Yes, we must all lose ourselves ere we can find ourselves. We must all enter the dark, strange Sanctuary of Suffering, where at first no light can penetrate, no beauty of life be seen and felt. GOD indeed would have us happy, but in the days that now are past we had only been aiming at a chimera; and if we are to be truly happy we must learn that such thought of 'happiness' could but end, as it has ended now, in a chimera.

True happiness, however, does not come all in a moment. It has to be awaited in still passivity. We are, possibly, never more unlike GOD, in His infinite patience, than when, either for ourselves or for others, we expect that the awakening shall come even quickly. GOD *waits* as He has waited from the beginning of 'time': we *beat our wings* and fight the oppressive air about us—and put further off the peace of life which should be ours. Only, sooner or later the awakening comes. There is a faint stir within, which speaks of life returning, and that a higher, better life. In the solemn hush comes a sense of vague movement, and this it is that we must learn to recognise as the herald of a great, grand Life into Whose embrace we are to be wholly drawn.

If we would know this Life, if we would learn truly

the object of our creation, there must be for us an entrance to the Sanctuary of Suffering.

How merciful, then, is the being drawn into a sanctuary of suffering! 'In this loneliness . . . life must find The Life; for joy is gone, and life is all that is left: it is compelled to seek its source, its root, its eternal life. This alone remains as a possible thing. Strange condition of despair into which the Spirit of GOD drives a man—a condition in which the Best alone is the possible.'[1]

It does not seem like life at all, but veritable death of being. Yet from it is to issue greater life—the greatest Life, the 'Best,' which is of GOD's ordaining.

So we enter the great Sanctuary of Suffering. So life comes to us, and that a better life: so The Life courses through our veins, and we go towards the personal acquisition of a perfect growth, derived from the realisation of The Life.

[1] Dr. George Mac Donald.

II
THE APPROACH TO THE IDEAL

THE APPROACH TO THE IDEAL

'GREAT GOD! and what remained then to move Thy heart, and cause Thee to see us from afar in that complete inanity in which we did not even wait for Thee?'[1]

We know that GOD was ever perfect, ever infinite in His Being, and perhaps, at times, we wonder how it was that within that perfect, infinite Being, there could be any sense of what we should term 'want' or 'insufficiency.'

But to wonder thus is to lose out of sight the perfect nature of GOD's love. The Divine love, being of necessity perfect, must act in accordance with all the natural demands of love. It must have an object beyond itself, on which and for which to expend itself. Perfect as the Divine Being was, there could be no scope within It for the exercise of love's functions, and so must there be an outside object created.

GOD, in His love, took counsel with Himself, and saw in the vast realms of His thought creatures made after His image, possessing similar qualities, endowed with like faculties, depending on Him for their existence and bliss, constituting thus objects of love and compassion,

[1] Lacordaire.

demanding of Him ultimately the absolute sacrifice of Himself—first, the giving *out*, then the giving *of*, finally, the complete giving *Himself* for the sake of their perfection. These shadowy beings, separate and distinct, and in one sense outside GOD's Being, promised the only possible satisfaction of the cravings of the Divine love: the longing for Sacrifice primarily, and ultimately for Self-Sacrifice.

And then it was that the 'Word went forth and the worlds were made.' 'By the holy, the unfathomable and stainless movement of Divine love,' chaos became cosmos, dull, dead inertness became bright, living beauty. GOD had longed for an external object on which He might expend Himself, in behalf of which ultimately He might crown His self-devoted action by a supreme offering of Himself for the good of the object in love created. The whole Being of GOD yearned for Sacrifice. There was a distinct sense—if we may so express it—within the Divine Being of 'insufficiency,' of 'want,' because the pervading love had not the satisfaction accruing from self-oblation. A sphere of marvellous beauty, therefore, was evolved, in which was to be manifold life; and the loving-action of GOD exercised in this evolving of an outer sphere, and in further evolving manifold life brought to the Divine Mind some satisfaction. But the shadowy beings made after His Image, and requiring His very essence of life for their evolution and maintenance—those beings for whom the sphere was primarily evolved—were not yet existent. There had been a giving out, a projection, of love into what we vaguely term 'space,' and a positive had thus been created out of a negative. GOD had projected Himself, infused His own active life and being, into 'a mass of homogeneous vapour'; and from this had sprung forth order, life, beauty, infinite possibilities in accordance with the infinity of the Nature so projected, and revealing somewhat of this Nature.

The whole universe bears still upon it a revelation of the nature of its GOD : every part of it declares Him to be love—but more than love. Rather, indeed, should we say, it declares His love to be composed of light, life, order, wisdom, justice, truth. The universe is at once, to us now, the expression and the explanation of GOD's Being, and of the purpose of its evolution. Over the heavens and the earth it is written—GOD is perfect Love. Over the heavens and the earth also is it written: GOD, being perfect Love, is Light, Life, Order, Wisdom, Justice, Truth. They are a grand affirmation of GOD, of the Word that had gone forth into 'space.' Even to us, dim seeing, slow of understanding as we are, they reveal a boundless purpose, as they reveal a boundless life. They speak of that which was, which is, and which is to be. They recall, announce, prefigure, the world's origin, purpose, and destiny.

'Science may resolve the complicated life of the material universe into a few elementary forces, light and heat and electricity, and these perhaps into modifications of some still simpler energy; but of the origin of energy ($\tau\grave{o}$ $\pi\rho\hat{\omega}\tau o\nu$ $\kappa\iota\nu o\hat{\upsilon}\nu$) it knows no more than did the Greeks of old. Theology asserts that in the beginning was the Word, and in Him was life, the life of all things created: in other words, that He is the source of all that energy, whose persistent, irresistible versatility of action is for ever at work, moulding and clothing and peopling worlds. The two conceptions are complementary, and cannot contradict each other.'

This quotation from Mr. Illingworth's essay in *Lux Mundi*, on 'The Incarnation and Development,' is followed in the original (though not immediately) by an allusion to the belief very commonly held that the universe exists, as it was evolved, solely for man: that the only object that GOD had in evolving 'Creation' was to provide a sphere for man, wherein he might truly grow and develop into the divine pattern of Himself, and be blessed ultimately with a perfection of life.

There is so much truth in such a belief that it is often difficult to combat it effectually; but on the other hand there is so much error that the belief is impossible of justification, when thought out carefully. 'We have now come,' the writer of the essay goes on to say, 'to regard the world not as a machine but as an organism, a system in which, while the parts contribute to the growth of the whole, the whole also reacts upon the development of the parts; and whose primary purpose is its own perfection, something that is contained within and not outside itself, an internal end: while in their turn the myriad parts of this universal organism are also lesser organisms, ends in and for themselves, pursuing each its lonely ideal of individual completeness. Now, when we look at nature in this way, and watch the complex and subtle processes by which a crystal, a leaf, a lily, a moth, a bird, a star, realise their respective ideals with undisturbed, unfailing accuracy, we cannot help attributing them to an intelligent Creator. But when we further find that in the very course of pursuing their primary ends, and becoming perfect after their kind, the various parts of the universe do in fact also become means, and with infinite ingenuity of correspondence and adaptation, subserve not only one but a thousand secondary ends, linking and weaving themselves together by their mutual ministration into an orderly, harmonious, complicated whole, the signs of intelligence grow clearer still. And when, beyond all this, we discover the quality of beauty in every moment and situation of this complex life; the drop of water that circulates from sea to cloud, and cloud to earth, and earth to plant, and plant to life-blood, shining the while with strange spiritual significance in the sunset and the rainbow and the dewdrop and the tear; the universal presence of this attribute, so unessential to the course of nature, but so infinitely powerful in its appeal to the human mind, is reasonably urged as a crowning proof of purposeful design.'

The universe, plainly, has great ends: not apart from man—this could not be, for man is bound up with the whole universal scheme—but by its own right in great measure, and as subserving the Divine intentions of Creation. All ministers now to man, yet all is beautiful with its own beauty and for ends devised for it by GOD. Not alone is man to be perfected: the sphere of his present habitation is to realise its own perfection, a peculiar perfection detailed and entire, foreseen ever by GOD, and promising, in some wise, satisfaction of His Love, yearning to spend and be spent outside Itself.

But when we come to man, we arrive at the point from which GOD's Sacrificing Love assumes to Itself the dawn of absolute Self-Sacrifice, and the centre of the universal scheme is shown forth.

Man! What is he? What was he as he stepped forward into the glorious realm of stirring life and beauty which he was to be allowed to inhabit, and in great degree rule and govern? Was he the full development and outcome of a piece of spontaneously generated protoplasm, acted upon, perfected, by means of outer conditions—climatic power and so forth,—by certain circumstances which determined, by themselves, the manner of his being for him? Was it some sort of mere 'chance' or accident that made of him a man? some chance or accidental force which turned the scale for that bit of protoplasm, and carried it beyond the stage at which it had arrived at being a 'cabbage,' and seemed likely to remain in such form? A well-known Professor has informed us that man might very well have continued only at the cabbage stage had not chance or accident decreed otherwise!

What does it matter how much we concede to those who push the beautiful, sublime theory of development to its extreme point, and beyond its extreme point, of reasonable probability? However man grew, he bears upon him unmistakable witness, in his own even silent being, to the thoughtful Mind and Soul of an external Motor and Principle of Life, termed by us GOD. Man developed from, man the result of, countless different forms of life, inorganic, organic, simple, complex, stands out as the most glorious proof that the universe holds of the Life and Being of GOD. Say that he was developed, by slow and gradual process of nature, through many wonderful gradations of life, into an organised being, capable of retaining and expressing a living 'soul'—that he grew from some original particle, bearing upon it no signs of life-capabilities? Then GOD is greater-glorified. And the Bible tells us that man was made by GOD out of the 'dust of the earth.' We could not well go lower than that.

But the Bible does not tell us that it was chance, or certain climatic conditions, that determined the evolution of man from the 'dust of the earth'! Say that man as we know him to have been at the dawn of his life-history was the climax of the Creative Purpose of GOD: that he grew not suddenly, but by very gradual degrees, from the 'dust,' and that then, when he was completely formed, GOD breathed into Him of His Own Soul and man became a living soul. Say that on an ever-ascending scale of being the animation and quickening of that which had been dull and inert grew into a life, first simple, eventually complex with a complexity akin to the Divine complexity, reasonable with the Reason of the Divine Mind, Divine with something of the Divinity as existing in the Blessed Trinity.

Then you have a Heavenly being. Say that he had 'dominion over the fish of the sea, and over the fowl of the air, and over the cattle, and over all the earth,' because he was man, the supreme object of GOD's care and love; and his prior history becomes a vague shadow of almost grotesque unimportance.

What does it matter how man was evolved so long as we know him to be the peculiar object of that Divine movement of Love, which issued in the Fiat: 'Begin!'

'Eternity moved, and said to Time: Begin! Time and the universe obeyed the Will of GOD, as the Will of GOD had yielded, but freely, to the inspiration of goodness.'[1] The history of man, as the history of the 'world' which he inhabits, is that of the constantly advancing evolution and development of the principle of Goodness, placed in the man's heart, and filling the universe about him. And it remains for us to study man in the light thrown upon him in those early pages of the Divinely Inspired Book, and as he stands towards the ultimate perfect conciliation of what we now too often consider a hopeless tangle of irreconcilable antagonisms. In this study alone can we arrive at anything approaching to that reverent attitude towards the great Mystery, which, keeping ever in this life elements of mystery, can yet be so regarded as to serve as the supremely blessed means of drawing souls to their Ideal. And it is for this that our life, surely, is given to us.

[1] Lacordaire.

We require to study the onward progress of man, and of men,—to mark the gradual advance of civilisation and development—as described to us in the Holy Scriptures.

The Bible has been called 'The Book of Development.' It is also The Book of Revelation: the Revelation of GOD to the man He had made out of His Love: the Revelation to man himself of the purpose of his creation, and the office and relation towards the world and to other creatures which he was expected to fill and fulfil, and of the glorious predestination for him in the Divine Mind. There is revealed to us by the Holy Spirit the naturally high dignity of man, the backward step which, by a misdirected will, he took, and the plan which GOD adopted for his recovery and the ultimate attainment by him—despite his own wrong action—of absolute, conscious bliss.

GOD, as we believe, predestined man for an eternity of highest beatitude with Himself. He gave to man of His Own Soul, that man being a living soul, conscious of the origin of this life within him, and the mode of life which by reason of his origin would be required of him, might, by slow and gradual process, grow into fitness for that eternal beatitude when, sublime with the glory of the God from Whose Being he had emanated, he should realise the purpose of his creation and apprehend the fulness of GOD. He was so planned and organised that, not only was he capable of standing forth as a link between the worlds of spirit and matter, but could also at every point of his being touch some

THE SANCTUARY OF SUFFERING

part of the universal creation and scheme of GOD, and so bind the whole in one grand unity, subsisting in GOD, looking to GOD for ultimate perfection of glory. Man is, as Lacordaire expresses it, 'infinitely complex.' ' By his thought he belongs to the intellectual order; by his will to the moral order; by his union to his fellow-creatures, to the social order; by his body to the physical order; by his entire soul to the religious order: and under all these relations, he has received means of attaining his end, which is perfection and beatitude. It is needful then, in order completely to unfold his destiny, to study man himself, and successively as an intelligent, moral, social, physical, religious being; and under these diverse aspects to take account of the roads which Eternal Wisdom has prepared for him, and in which he must walk to avoid perishing.' And the sad point of the unfolding of his destiny is the moment when, in the beautiful garden, he 'fell' from natural uprightness. And when we see, in the Holy Scriptures, man struggling towards the attainment of the end of his mighty, complex life, we notice him as a creature girt about by pain and suffering of all sorts. His life seems involved in a network of pain.

We cannot say what would have been the precise method of man's growth unto perfection had he not fallen from his state of initial goodness; but revealed as he is in the pages of Holy Scripture in his degenerate state he is a creature of many sorrows, distresses, sufferings of mind and body. It seems just one long ' Record of Sorrow,' and our hearts ache as we read the pages, and our souls are sometimes full of questioning perplexity.

Man 'fell' in the 'Garden of Eden,' and we find that ever since his failure to observe the rectitude of being which GOD had ordained for him to walk in, pain has existed in the world. But has it only existed since then? We are in the habit of regarding pain and suffering as natural concomitants of the 'Fall' of man, but are we right in so regarding them?

Thought and study are in direct contradiction of this theory. We know that animals—with their far longer presence in the world than man—are so organised that pain is inevitably a part of their experience. True, they have not the same 'consciousness' that man has, and have not, therefore, the capacity for pain in anticipation, nor can pain ever be to them in any way what it is to man. Still, there is pain, there is suffering; and this, alone, proves that pain was in the world when man, in his primal innocence, came to it, and seems to imply that it has a far higher mission than could be associated with it were it viewed as man's result, of man's wrong-doing. There is a great deal of pain that is merely this, and the evidences of it are ever before our eyes; but taking the subject of pain broadly, we are driven, by thought and study, to see it as a mysterious power, which, quite independently of human error, was intended ever by GOD to hold some sway in the world, the nature of which it is entirely to our interest to examine.

In the early morning of the world, before man was

created (or evolved), pain throbbed and stirred in life. When man came, he drew into his being with his first breath this pervasion of suffering about him. It was in the air, as it were—he could not escape from it. The various forms of properly organised life had been suffering pain through all the time prior to his advent, and had filled the atmosphere with their groans. There never had been a time when pain had been absent from organic life, for its very organisation involved the sometime experience of suffering, as it implied a permanent continuance of suffering in its realm. And this surely emphasises the fact of deduction, from the endurance of pain which we are ever witnessing, that GOD has a provident purpose in pain far beyond, and greater than, the mere punishment of man for his wrong-doing. It does more than emphasise a fact: it establishes beyond question a theory as a fact.

Pain, for some mysterious purpose known only to GOD, has existed ever, and is, we find, independent of the 'Fall' of man. But we have to do with man fallen; and we are forced to consider pain in relation to him, and as it has been revealed to us as working in all these ages since his 'Fall.'

A 'Record of Sorrow,' we have said the Holy Scriptures seem to be; and our hearts ache and our souls ask questions about it, and we are still, many of us, puzzled and dismayed. Yet, how clearly is GOD's Hand seen in this Record of Sorrow, lifting up man, holding him, raising him higher, pointing always onward to something to which he has not reached! Do we not get some faint glimmering of the great truth about pain and its office? As we see, here and there, a conspicuous figure in the holy history, standing forth in new-found goodness, re-dawning majesty—still so far from the ultimate glory of being which awaits him, —do we not grasp this touch of truth :—that he stands forth thus, purged by suffering, strengthened, illumined, ennobled by some strange bond with the unseen Majesty of GOD? He is a prophet-soul, pointing to the Heavenly Jerusalem, telling of man's redemption from evil, of his perfect destiny. 'Eternal GOD! Thy Word is not all fulfilled; Thy thought . . . not all revealed. The ages that are past have but revealed to us some fragments of it.'[1] Not even yet are GOD's Word and His thought all fulfilled and revealed, but we have learned much, and in the light of our knowledge, and by the strength of our faith, we look back on those old ages and see in the prophet-souls, and indeed in the whole long Record of Sorrow, the evidence of things not then—be it but remotely—generally seen, the substance of things hoped for.

Man was to become perfect and to attain to a perfect life. And the revelation that we have in the Old Testament of his growth onwards is that of advance by means chiefly of suffering—and the offering of sacrifice, to which suffering ever points.

Man had to advance towards his Divinely ordained perfection along a path Divinely regulated, and this path, being as we know a *viâ dolorosa*, should prove to

[1] Mazzini.

us that the *viâ dolorosa* must be the necessary way of imperfect man throughout all ages of the world so long as it exists under its present conditions. We are thus taught that the suffering from which men shrink back appalled was not merely necessary for the right development of primitive man, but must be essential for man of all 'time,' as being of 'kith and kin' with primitive man, though having reached, maybe, a higher plane of life. For the sake of the expansion of that original goodness placed by GOD in the human heart, and its emancipation from the evil encrusting, and seeking to corrode and impair, its beauty, suffering must be.

But suffering now, as then, must be for a supreme reason. It, throughout all time, connected the human race with the eternally foreknown Sacrifice of GOD. As it bound the heart of man then to the Christ on Calvary, so does it ever bind the heart of man there. The Holy Scriptures have shown us man as he was growing towards a condition of being in which it could be possible for him to touch and meet, to recognise and take to himself, Christ. And this must ever go on. Along an ever-widening track of sorrow, pain, toil, distress had primitive man and later man to go. One great aisle there was, stretched on from the gates of Eden, to be pressed by tired, way-worn, agonised feet of men, hedged in by altars of sin-offering, burnt-offering, thank-offering ; and this aisle is still stretched out, though altered to us.

Midway in the aisle was to be Calvary, with the GOD-Man, the Divine and Perfect 'Man of Sorrows,' hanging on a Cross, a willing Sacrifice for His people of all ages. And beyond this midway Station, the character of the onward aisle was to be changed. The suffering still should be, but changed: the altars still should be, but changed in even greater measure. At that Station man was to meet his GOD, and be gathered up into His Being. Henceforth the sorrow, the pain, and the offering of Sacrifice would be, of necessity, different.

It is impossible for us, on this latter half of the aisle stretched forth, to understand and apprehend the beauty and the force of suffering unless we look backward over that former half. We see, then, man growing towards his Ideal: witness him emerging from his simple state of barbarism—albeit with many a temporarily backward and perverted movement,—rising to a higher altitude of life, drawing nearer to perfection: in the throes of suffering. We watch him as he advances from that low state to a higher, by means of the only thing which could bind him closely to the Heart of GOD—that Heart from Which had come the touch of goodness in his own heart: and clearly he stands forth as the seeker of an ideal.

He had put his ideal far off from him by exercising his power of free-will in the direction of Evil, and GOD had to recover him from his fall. If something were not done for him he would go through life a stunted atom, the wreck of a thwarted design; and civilisation and progress of the world would be inert, paralysed, dead.

As we view the mighty progress of men towards The

Ideal through the personal growing into a distinctive ideal, surely we come to know something of the great Mystery of Suffering, and to be content that all should suffer. Pain, after the Fall of man, took to itself a complicated agency:—It had to correct in advance, to correct afterwards, to punish wrong, even as it had tried to save from wrong, in the human life. It had to do all this, as well as to impel, direct, foster true onward growth : and all this in union, not only with the Loving Offering of GOD for the perfection of the beloved, but also with the Divine Sacrifice held up to repair the breach of the Law of Righteousness made by man.

Man's sphere was evolved by a movement of Divine Love issuing in 'The Word'; and man himself eventually, by Divine Grace, and the perfect activity of Divine Love, came forth into the place prepared for him. Good? Yes, good as a little child. 'When GOD made the heart of man,' said Bossuet, 'He first placed in it goodness'; and the whole history of the life of man, of each one of us unfolded gradually before our eyes, is, as has been already said, concerned with the development and perfecting of this principle within the life. In the face of the Fall this history, of necessity, assumes a huge import. The development unto full perfectedness has had, ever since the Fall, to be wrought by an agency of twofold power and dual bearing. Man introduced evil into his life, and by this act involved the presence in the world of a corrective and punitive force, by which he might be recovered from the ever-present evil force consequent on his own wrong-doing.

It became essential for man then, as it still remains essential for him, to be 'saved from himself.' And GOD, and the world which He had evolved, were prepared with the means and the scope of man's salvation from 'himself':—given over, by his own fatal choice, that is, to the power of Evil! And it is this thought which should be permitted room in our minds when we would discuss the great Problem of Pain.

Finding that there was never a time when organic life was not bound about by and involved in a law of suffering, that man when he came breathed in with his life-breath a pervasion, as it were, of suffering, we are driven to the conclusion that suffering in some form or another must have been eternally decreed by GOD. Knowing, as we do now most surely from the revelation of the Incarnation of GOD, that 'GOD is Love,' we are certain that the decree must have been a loving decree. When we get so far as the Fall of man we find suffering acquiring a fresh office and a new element and power, and still we are compelled to admit that Love must be behind this fresh office, this new element and power. Pain must, we know, be therefore not of the mystery of Evil, but of the mystery of Good: the Good which GOD, as Perfect Love, is. There is in pain, in suffering, as it presents itself to us now, much that is evil, but as it was allowed originally by GOD there could have been nought of evil in it; and even as it is, perverted and misused, it could not, by reason of the original permission of its presence—and from our review of the work that it has done in the onward progress of the world—

be considered otherwise than as being safely bound up with, and girt about by, that vast Mystery of Love which reigns over our sphere of living. Under no circumstances may we view it, then, as being anything but a grand inherent factor in the Divine scheme by which the world was to reach that realisation of perfection designed by GOD in the totality of His Being, in the perfect fulness of the Love Which He is.

Starting from these premises, we have to think of the Creative Purpose of GOD as entailing on the world, for the sake of ultimate completion, a certain course of what—failing a better word—we must call suffering. And it remains to follow this course and apply to our own lives, to the mystery and burden of sorrow and pain under which we sometimes groan for deliverance, the lessons and the enlightenment that should accrue therefrom.

GOD had made man 'good.' All creation was looking to him for the fulfilment of the purpose which GOD had in his evolution, and, before that, in the evolution of the cosmic scheme. When, by projecting Himself into 'space,' GOD drew forth a sphere of beautiful harmony and order, of gradually throbbing life, of organic life culminating in man, He declared Himself:—'willing to become the Centre of a realm of personalities.'

And it is man as belonging to this realm that we have to consider. The writer of the above phrase goes on to say that 'to this end He called into existence a world of personal beings, in a sense independent of Himself, but destined, in communion and intercourse with Himself, to find and fulfil the law of their creaturely perfection.'[1] But in a secondary way man was so to assert himself in his high energy and capacity of being as to assume—or accept, rather—that central relation towards other creations of GOD which by Divine plan and intention he was fitted to occupy, and called upon to occupy. GOD might be, and indeed must ever be, the Supreme Centre; but man was himself to be a centre, not only of the universe, and of creatures lower than himself, but also of that realm of personalities to which he of right belongs. Man derives his strength and power from GOD, but, by his very nature and origin, he is required to pass on this strength and power to those who revolve about him in the eternal Purpose of GOD. And the history of man is an account, as it must always be an account, of the way in which he fulfilled the purpose of his being—For this is full development of his principle of 'goodness'! We have, therefore, to deal with man and his progress as bound up with a vast question of general good, dependent largely for its right issue on man's own individual action. He had sublime possibilities given to him. How did he use his possibilities?

Man asserted himself, truly! He put out the arms of his freedom and called to Evil to be his. Then Evil came to him, and man, that splendid creation of GOD, 'fell.'

And—reviewing somewhat the ground over which we

[1] Rev. R. L. Ottley.

have already trodden — from that moment onwards suffering as we know it had to be. The Law—the great Law of Righteousness and the lesser law of man's own complex, yet moral, being — had been broken. Man had done despite to the great Law, and the law of his being, and restitution must be made. He had introduced discord into all things, and a fresh, grand harmony must be evolved.

Man had not simply to grow and progress now: he had, as it were, to be re-modelled and re-made. There was anarchy, dissolution, disintegration of his being, and these must be compelled to yield to a higher force and power than man had then at his command. Pain of a certain kind there was in the world for his service, but now, by reason of his own self-chosen action, this was inadequate to his peculiar needs. Pain, therefore, must be endowed with fresh power and vigour; must take to itself a new office in his life. Man had not simply to grow and progress now, as we say. He had great needs, and these needs had to be met; and in the Divine foreknowledge had been prepared the special agency by which he, this fallen being, in his state of disintegration and confusion, might ultimately recover his 'lost principle of cohesion and order.'

Pain, then, became, through man's disobedience to the Law of GOD and of his own life and being, a new and complex force. It was, henceforth, not only to be stimulative and inspiring, but punitive and remedial also. It would, in its new and awful capacity, be of the Divinely foreknown scheme for man's good, but not of the fore-designed and willed scheme. GOD, of necessity, knew that man would fall, and He provided the full remedy; but never may we suppose that He willed the 'Fall of Man.' This was the result of man's own volition. And after this act of pure volition man had to be viewed and considered as a fallen being, and to bend to the circumstances brought about by his conduct. And for this GOD surrounded his life with the best—the one possible—means of his recovery from the power of sin and his eventual attainment of a perfect life. He had to submit to the new force of that agency of suffering which GOD had ready for him. He had to take it in whatsoever form or degree it might come to him, and strive to recognise in its twofold office the most truly beneficent aid that could have been accorded to him. Mightily and wondrously had pain to work in man's life ere man could approach, in however remote a way, his ideal, as contained in The Ideal.

And is it not so, in ever different measure, with us? We want to find our true selves: GOD's special ideal of us. And we can only find this by growing towards The Ideal of the human race. Pain, the pain that purges, develops, drives on, points the way to The Ideal, is the most beneficent influence that could come into our lives. We shrink from it, we are afraid of it; and it is very natural. Yet we must not shrink: we must not let ourselves be afraid. Nor must we stint our holding up of trust. GOD will not send us more suffering than is needful. He never does this. His Love is Perfect :—All-wise, All-knowing. He may send us hard trials. We may be visited with serious illness—physical infirmity and disease,—with poverty, calling for stern self-denial, with a heavy cloud of 'misconception,' under which we lie hurt and wearied, with loneliness, in which our whole life seems nipped and embittered, with a love that causes us supreme pain, involves us in an awful struggle : with many 'crosses,' each hard to bear. Our life may appear to us at times almost harder than we can bear—but it never is—no life ever is—harder than can be borne. And, in the Sanctuary of Suffering, in our special little sanctuary enclosed by the greater Sanctuary, can we not kneel in humble meditation, reviewing the marvellous effect wrought in past ages by the agency of suffering, realising that to us, too, howsoever it may come to us, it is GOD's 'Best' for His children striving after 'happiness'?

'*What our Father does is well.*' There are two simple little lines which occur in a song very well known, and often, it has struck the writer, very lightly sung :—

> 'I prayed to our Father in heaven,
> And our Father kept me brave.'[1]

It will be remembered that this prayer had prefaced the greatest affliction (almost) that could come into any life. Yet it did not take the form of a petition

[1] *A Bunch of Cowslips.*

that the affliction might not come: only that, when it came, it might be borne well. 'And our Father kept me brave.'

May this be so ever with us:—that the troubles which meet us in life overthrow us not, but find us ready: prepared for their coming, brave during the time of their abiding!

It is only by preserving the intimate relationship of suffering with man's needs that we can ever grow to regard it fairly or justly. It is only by absolute and unwavering trust in GOD that it assumes for us that high and unfailing sanctity derived of GOD. Seen rightly, we are able to place no limits in fancy to its beneficent power, and we understand that, mysterious though suffering be in particulars, without its presence in the world, its action on men's hearts and lives, the human race would not have developed into perfection, would not even have touched the robe of The Ideal, in which all lesser ideals lie enrolled.

So we bear our various 'ills'; so we connect them with the past advance of man, and view them in the light of that past.

INDIVIDUAL PROGRESS

MAN had to attain to maturity and perfection of life and being. He was to grow into complete affinity with GOD, because in that lay his only possibility of perfect happiness. How could this end be secured? Man must look to GOD for guidance.

In the Bible, GOD is seen revealing Himself to the man He had made for this glorious end. To the pages of Holy Scripture must we go if we would learn aught of that mysterious advance of primitive man onwards to his Ideal which it is our concern to study.

But in considering the Revelation of GOD to men we must ever bear in mind that it is a Revelation of the Infinite to the finite, and that therefore it can but be partial, and must sometimes tend in the direction of obscurity: that, being adapted to the limited capacities of the recipients, there must always here be mystery involved in it, lessening as time and man's development advances, but still on earth present.

We have a faint analogue of the obscurity produced by accommodation and adjustment of ideas according to the capacities of those towards whom effort at revelation is being directed, in that difficult process of transmission experienced by a man—a merely human being—intellectually (and elsewise, possibly) supreme amongst his fellow-beings, when he is conscious of an anxiety to impart to them the truth resident in himself. There is a great deal in his mind that cannot be conveyed to the lesser minds, and the attempt to convey to them even as much as they are capable of understanding is rendered doubly difficult from the necessity there is of employing modes of conveyance that shall be suitable to the duller perceptions of those lower intelligences. He has to use terms and manners of expression that are not truly descriptive of that which is within him; and hence—though it is the best that can be done in the matter—there is produced a considerable amount of obscure mystery, in which the man is wronged by those who are simply incapable of seeing the full truth, or indeed any material degree of the truth, of his nature and being.

In the Bible, GOD is to be seen revealing ever as much of the Truth of His inner Nature, and of His views and Purpose, as the people of the particular age or time of the message so given were capable of apprehending. But, from the difficulties inseparable from the relative positions of Revealer and recipients of the revelation, the process was extremely slow, and is to us, as we read the Holy Scriptures, apt to raise in our minds perplexity and obscuration of vision. On this ground, that first intimation of GOD's Justice, of His Thought of sin, was not, nor is now with some, taken in its high beauty and integrity, but is perverted into a species of unworthy 'anger,' or *desire* to 'punish' the offender for the wrong done by him. It was—and is still—taken in such a sense as to obscure greatly the Perfect Love which GOD is.

And so, throughout the inspired account of GOD's dealings with man, we find evidence of the peculiar difficulties in the way of full and true revelation of Himself. It is not that GOD would not reveal Himself to man, but that man could not accept the revelation. And until he could do this, there was no true basis of intercourse with GOD possible for him. GOD had to work for him as He best could under the then severed condition of the being and life of man; and the Infinite Patience of the Divine Being is displayed in the long-suffering with man's recalcitrance and slowness of obedience to the prescribed course for his salvation unto perfection.

Sometimes people speak as though Truth itself had developed as man developed. Truth is, of course, an absolute law, and was perfect ever: only it is that man's capacity for receiving the Truth developed, and so more of the ever perfect Law of Truth became revealed. As man grew, his ability of perception and reception increased, and the Truth was more clearly manifested: conveyed to him and revealed through him. It was not, we must always remember, that GOD and the truth of His Being developed—how could this be?—but that man grew more capable of instruction in the Truth, more open to its advent. Thus in increasing ratio was it given to him. In exact proportion to his power to receive Truth was the Truth conveyed to him: in equal advance with the advance of his own development was the progress of the revelation of Truth to his own inner being, and through that being to others of his kind—the extent not any more than the mode of the conveyance being thus regulated.

The Law of Truth in one sense, as we know, applies primarily to the moral nature, but there is also an important sense in which it is bound up with the intellectual part of man, and it is essential just to touch upon it in such connection.

The Truth as it is in GOD must be apprehended in some measure by man, else the mind of the man cannot work in harmony with GOD, and must stray into those paths of error which lead perhaps to total loss of conscious hold on GOD. And even man as an intellectual being claims consideration in relation to that prevalence of suffering with which his life is encircled. The mind cannot be separated from the rest of his complex being, but must bear its part in all process of human growth and development. In his early days man was an intellectual child—a child before GOD, with childish limitations to be thought of and dealt with. And his evolution from this stage required manifold aid. In this region, however, as in all others, there was a supreme and distinctive method of aid, and in the spur which drove him on from his intellectual childhood to seek a higher mental plane we recognise the beneficent agency of pain. Only as his limitations were extended could GOD impart the Truth to him: only then could man take into himself any true idea of GOD, or conception of his own mental powers.

It has been said that true education consists in the drawing out of natural tendencies:—that all education should tend to the evolution of peculiar nascent ability, in order that man may know in what direction to exert his strength and skill, in what field to look for particular results. But there is one point on which all men's education should be concentrated, and that is the knowledge of GOD. All should surely tend towards this, and as the constitution of minds varies in every case, so in every case must there be some differentiation of treatment, so that the understanding, the intelligence, may be truly ready for such species of manifestation as shall be accorded for the eventual apprehension of its ordained measure of Truth. Variance in mode, as in sort and measure, of development had there to be in the early days of man's life-history, just as this has to be now. At the very dawn of man's career, when he appeared with all his peculiar idiosyncrasy upon him, had he to be viewed and trained as an individual. He stood forth with his own needs, not the needs of others, calling for treatment; and GOD was prepared ever with the discipline that they required. Each man had to grow into the Divine pattern for him, and to grow in a Divinely prescribed course, singular in many respects, distinct from that of his fellows.

Yet, there was a course to be pursued generally. There was not only—any more than there is now—the unity and the general proportion of an individual being to be secured and maintained: there was also the pervasive external unity, the universal proportion to be observed and considered. And for this the development of the intelligence of man was of almost superlative importance. Man's faculty of observation had to be developed: the special right and power that each single man possessed, by his particular natural qualities, in his walk through the marvels and beauties of the universe, had to be quickened into vigour and reality. His distinctive mental office required special education, particular development. Truly, each man was a moral being, but his morality would be impossible of actual attainment unless first of all his intelligence, his peculiar mental structure, was in readiness for the perception and inception of moral impulsions from the great Mind of GOD. The development of his heart and conscience must be, but the development of his understanding and power of apprehending Truth must be the precursor of this. All visible things passing before the eyes of man were intended to fix an impression on his mental retina. The phenomena of the universe, above, about, beneath him, presented him with a field for the enlargement of his mental powers, and gave to him an opportunity of seizing the particular point from which his individual development was to advance.

But because the liberty, in great measure, of his understanding made choice difficult, there was needed a spur and guide, so that error in direction might be felt and recognised, and the man be constantly brought back, or carried on, to the point from which he had errantly diverged, or was missing. Supposing he had been conscious of satisfaction under any circumstances, his peculiar bent would never have been discovered; but when a sense of dissatisfaction, of vague distress, sense of failure, met him at some point, then he was driven away from that to look for satisfaction elsewhere. His faculty of thought was at the beginning almost dormant: it needed to be called forth into living, conscious activity. But also it needed to be instructed. He had sublime possibilities within him, but these possibilities had to be expanded and regulated according to a Divine plan for him. He might not grow as he liked, even mentally: he had to follow a prescribed course towards a Divinely preconceived end :—the man's special end. And we notice him thus advancing. His limits were indeed striking, but the greatness of GOD, working through the complex agency of pain, drawing him on, ever on, triumphed more and more over human littleness, and displayed in increasing measure that wondrous *Love* of GOD which had devised for the man the best means of enlargement and development, the only possible method by which man might cease to be a mere childish being, and grow into ability to receive the Truth.

Not alone was the intellectual capacity of primitive man limited to an actually childish degree, but so also was his moral capacity limited, and the adjustment of the truth of GOD's Being had to be proportioned to this simple condition of morality. Certainly, as his intellectual advance went on, his moral ability developed;

but the process was, of necessity, extremely slow. It was only after ages of training and discipline that man could at all apprehend the Law of Justice. The first intimation of Justice had, as we have seen, tended rather to the obscuration than the clearing of the moral vision. The very form which the message had to assume made in the direction of obscurity; and it was only when, by the discipline of dissatisfaction and distress, man's being had experienced some development, that his moral faculties were at all prepared to receive the truth of the interdependence in GOD of Justice and Love for the fair balance of Righteousness :—that Righteousness which finds its only perfect expression in the Divine Nature. A child—such as man in his early days virtually was—untaught, ignorant of discipline, could not apprehend moral truth, any more than he could distinguish his special intellectual message of truth.

But when the training and education of his mental faculties had advanced somewhat, GOD could begin to reveal a larger measure of moral truth to him. By his mental education he had learned to trust, even though he might not fully understand, and this trust formed a basis on which an erection of morality might be truly raised. Man's heart and conscience were open now to receive Divine intimations of the Moral Law. He could better comprehend the 'science of ethics' as GOD spoke to him. He had more power over his will, for his education had led him to use self-restraint, to exert force over certain pushing inclinations. He had learned by correction and instruction to check his desires, to truly direct his choice. He had started with the one instinctive wish to be 'happy.' He might not have been conscious of what his sole aim was, but nevertheless it was this ; and he had clamoured and striven to secure his wish at all cost, at all hazards. And then a strange process had set in. Constantly his enlightened intelligence struck him, smote him there in the path of advancement towards his goal. Some mysterious force opposed him, and drove him away from where he was going. He did not know exactly what had happened to him ; only he found himself compelled to turn aside, to go back and consider what to do next. Then he would make another advance, and again would the same strange power interfere with his course. It was a perpetual warfare between his inclinations and this hidden force. There was no peace for the man. He *could* not find rest nor content.

It was very perplexing. His longings went forth and were stifled, his gaze was attracted, and resulted in his undoing. He yearned ever for something, and before he could get to it, it either vanished, or something else stepped in and hid it from him. He wanted, but he was never satisfied. He directed his energy in a certain way, and then was thrown back upon himself. The granted desire of his eyes proved the discomfort and distress of his—heart? Yes, now his heart was against him. It seemed to have allied itself with that other strange force that had interfered with his pursuit of 'happiness,' checking his advance, driving him away and back from his goal. Everything was against him now. Man indeed seemed 'born to trouble as the sparks fly upward.' Could no one relieve him? Would he never find rest and ease?

There was a voice calling him somewhere. Where? In what direction should he turn to find out what the voice was like, what it was saying, whither it was summoning him? Would the voice deliver him from his terrible state of disturbed unrest? Was there satisfaction to be found anywhere? or would this, too, lead him astray? When he reached it, supposing he could reach it, would it disappoint him? Would there still be discomfort and disturbance within him?

Ah! was not his quickened thought leading him towards the place whence the sound came to him? Yes, he had an indication of the way. There was something beyond that he had not yet known: there was satisfaction somewhere. There was a goal other than that which he had, by different routes, striven to touch. After all, that mysterious checking power had been right. There was something better worth striving after than such as he had aimed at. Through his heart, through his whole being now, there is the ringing of this new voice. There is a thrilling quivering sense within him that he does not understand, but which seems somehow to be pointing upwards and onwards. He is stirred throughout his nature. Certainly this is a fresh unrest, but it has within it something of which he has not before had experience. Surely some change has taken place: an old hunger has been stilled, a new hunger has arisen, whose very presence promises its own satisfaction. There is a foretelling of happiness. There is consciously to himself a power of fresh life, a prescience of something coming to him that shall change the whole aspect of things : alter their proportions, make evil good and darkness to be light.

What is it?

It is love! It is the development of the principle of goodness placed in his heart by the GOD Whose Love he has never yet apprehended. It is the sudden flashing into his moral being of the secret and the real force and grandeur of that being. Nothing else has satisfied him. Love eventually will, for it will teach him GOD and give GOD to him truly. Only Justice, stern Justice, had he been uncertainly conscious of as ruling the universe? Love is supreme, and it is the Voice of Love that he has heard : that has stirred and quickened him into new life and power. He will follow this Voice; and one day surely satisfaction shall come to him.

So did man go forth to seek his Ideal, so had he been driven to seek it. He had had ignorant ideas of GOD, had aimed at false goals. He had experienced disappointment, difficulty, checks. Now he would seek differently.

ADVANCEMENT OF THE LAW OF CREATURELY PERFECTION

WE cannot rightly imagine the world, or the history of man individually, without admitting the presence of some agency akin to the pain that drove him on to seek the higher, instead of the lower, satisfaction of his ignorant longings. It might be wronged by man himself, and might thus in many cases retard rather than advance development and progress unto perfection, but with this GOD had not—any more than He has now in such instances—anything to do. It has been man's own independent action, ever, that has aggravated the true nature and office of pain, and caused it to become often aggressive and offensive towards him. GOD's allotment of pain was—and is ever—just and righteous :—perfectly loving : man's additional allotment, man's accretion, of suffering, errant, non-essential, harmful—until it be made to yield to Divine efforts for the man's recovery from the effects of his action. The Holy Scriptures reveal man to us as growing by GOD's pain, as retarded by his own self-inflicted, self-involved pain. He is seen there advancing towards the end of his life, the realisation of GOD's purpose in his life, in exact ratio to the obedience with which he submitted himself to GOD's 'educatory providence,' and walked in the path marked out for him.

The fact that sacrifice is the law of love entails on us a firm belief in the necessity of the presence of suffering in the world of GOD's Love. The belief that GOD, being Love, had willed to sacrifice Himself—to give *Himself* for the object loved—as the only possible satisfaction of His longings, and that Love involves the acceptance of its sacrifice ere true union of the lover and the loved can be wrought, demands also of us a belief that something like the pain that we know (like it in one sense, other than it in a further sense), as being bound up with the law of sacrifice, would have been essential in order to bind man to the Supreme Sacrifice that was to be offered for him. The Incarnation of GOD would, we cannot but feel, have been of the ordinance of GOD even if man had not 'fallen,' for by that means alone could man secure his perfect end :—union with GOD. It must have been of the Divine Will, for without that GOD would not truly have given Himself to and for man ; and, as ' union (by sacrifice) is the term of love,' GOD and man would not have been in perfect affinity and kinship. Incarnation meant to GOD the Immolation of Himself for the sake of this perfect affinity and kinship, whereby alone the chief object of His Creative Scheme of Love could realise complete bliss. There was to be oneness of life and being between Himself and the man created by Him for love, in which man should experience true bliss ; and this could not be except by Self-Sacrifice and the

THE LAW OF CREATURELY PERFECTION 49

acceptance of the Sacrifice. Therefore we feel that, irrespective of the Fall, suffering must always have been in the world—Though without the Fall it would not have been what now we think of when we use the word suffering; for, as the human will would have been moving alongside the Divine Will, there would have been no bitter sense of pain, none of that rebellion which constitutes its sting; nor would there have been man's own evil and perverted choice and augmentation—even creation —of it. Man, working in humble co-operation with GOD, unhampered by his own recusancy and antagonism, for the great end of his creation, would have rejoiced in the fact of that mighty spur which drove him on, ever on, seeing in it GOD's loving agent for the production of a perfect realisation by him of bliss. His eyes would have been open, his mind ready, his heart and conscience astir with nobly increasing affections and devotion to GOD, and each fresh movement caused by the loving spur would have elicited from him fresh thankfulness and joy.

Suffering, indeed we must feel, was in the world of all living beings that these beings might in certain sense be led to, be bound about by and involved in, the sacrifice of Himself which was of GOD's loving ordinance. There was to be some sort of connection of the entire world with the Supreme Offering of the GOD of Love. Animals prior to man partook in mysterious fashion, and for partially hidden reason, in the general connection. Man clearly and distinctly stood forth as a creature of suffering, and evidences surely to us the cause, the great reason, the need, of his suffering. It was moving about with him ever, because he was the special object of GOD's sacrificing Love. Man had, above all else, in his own individual being to be associated with the great law of Sacrifice. But he had also to be developed into a fit condition for the direct reception of the Sacrifice, and the Benefits of the Sacrifice. Man had to grow, and the pain that impelled him on to seek a higher and better self was not only on the face of it an agent for good, but had within it a hidden force and power over him from the vital union, which existed between it and the pre-ordained Sacrifice, which was to exist eventually between the Incarnate-GOD and the object of the Incarnation.

It will be well here to once more review slightly the old ground.

Pain was the appointed means of drawing out from man his natural abilities and capacities, and of binding him to The Ideal into Which he was to grow. Without its agency man would have rested content with too low a manner of living. He could not, conceivably to us, have made any advance towards true perfectedness, unless, by the spur of what we are bound to call 'pain'—dissatisfaction, distress, disappointment,—he had been driven from his initial self to seek a more developed self. But with the 'Fall' we know that pain would, of necessity, assume a sort of antagonistic virility which could never have been there if man had remained in simple uprightness; and his history, consequently, is the history, not merely of the development of the

THE LAW OF CREATURELY PERFECTION 51

principle of goodness placed within him, but, further, of the gradual expulsion of evil forces, the correcting and punishing of evil longings and inclinations, resident in his perverted being. Suffering, henceforth, was not simply to bind the world to Christ, the Incarnate-GOD, but to bind it to, and involve it in, the Sacrificial Atonement of the Christ Who was to be the essential Saviour and Redeemer of errant mankind. It had a new office, and it derived new power and significance, from its intimate relation to, its vital union with, the Word That had gone forth when the worlds were made, and Whose Atonement for the world had been, by man's own action, rendered necessary. It was to pervade, to interpenetrate, to act in re-sanctification and strengthening of, all things, that the world of peccant human nature might, by force of union, be redeemed from evil and drawn onwards to perfection.

The appointed Climax of the Creative Love of GOD was to be reached. And so, in the pages of Holy Scripture, we trace man's progress as an advance aided by GOD, hindered by himself, in the throes of suffering: suffering which spurred him on, and led him towards his Ideal.

It was the gradual evolution of fallen man from his personally involved condition of slavery to sin into a freer, purer state. We see man, the apex of GOD's creation, growing from primitive savagery of being into a condition of life in which, not alone was he conscious of love and morality as being altogether desirable, but was approaching a plane on which GOD could truly be revealed to him, Incarnate, as Love and Perfect Purity. The early condition of man was such as to fill us now, as we study the pages of its record, with horror and loathing, and we should surely be enabled to view with tender reverence that chief agent which drove him on to seek his better self: impelled him from the corrupt state in which he then was, to an existence in which his GOD-ordained perfection could in initial sense be realised. We are far indeed, still, from having apprehended moral truth in all its fulness, but even with our only comparative acquisition of it those long-ago times are revolting to us, and the extended growth of its acquisition through the countless ages of the past, by the succeeding generations of men and women then living, convinces us of the enormous value of, the absolute necessity that existed for, the prevalence of pain and suffering as a spur of this onward growth.

There was, as there ever is, the One common Ideal of humanity, but there was also then, as always, a peculiar, distinctive ideal into which man must grow; and in his faithful endeavours to reach this ideal—flashed into his being from the Mind of God—in his devotion to the cultivation, the seeking the very best, of his special natural tendencies and gifts, his capabilities, the man marched towards GOD and his own form of perfection. We know that it has been thus with mankind since the first days of human living, and pain must be considered as it relates to the special onward growth. Man's life had to advance towards the

THE LAW OF CREATURELY PERFECTION 53

Divinely ordered goal through a long system of pains and penalties, of sorrows and deprivations. It was his only chance of growing towards GOD, and his own ideal perfection conceived for him in the Divine Mind. 'Our race,' says Canon Gore, 'was created for conscious fellowship with GOD.' And that sigh of the spirit, of which, at one time and another, every man is aware as going forth from his inner being into perhaps a vague region of speculation, is the assertion of his soul of an absolute right to seek this fellowship for which, unknown to himself, he was created. This is of the touch of goodness that was placed within him, and that so long as he preserves in his heart shall form a ground on which the Holy Spirit can work for his ultimate perfectedness of entire being. Only with the utter eradication of that touch could come actual 'death' to the man, destruction of his true being: only with the due development of it could ever have been, or ever be, evolved the perfection, the fulness, of life for which by his origin and organisation he was predestined and planned, and which is best described as fellowship, or complete affinity, with GOD. The spirit of man is deeply conscious of a perfection possible to be attained somehow and somewhere, and the uncertain far-away cry of primitive man finds its larger and more definite utterance in the cry of the civilised being of to-day, who, putting forth his arms towards Calvary, says: 'My Lord and my GOD!' And pain and the agonised throes of suffering form the wondrous agency by which man yearns for the great attainable: turns to his Means of supreme perfection.

A slow process! Yes; it was a slow process, by which man grew: a slow process through which he learned to understand somewhat the law and purpose of his being, to be even a law to himself in order that unity and proportion of general living might be secured and maintained. It was a long time before man knew what it meant, and entailed on him, to be one of a realm of personalities whose supreme Centre was GOD. He knew nought of 'altruism': he was an ignorant individualist, in his thought, his aims, his will and his manner of living. He had lost out of sight the grand fact that there were 'social' claims upon him: that no man can live, any more than he can die, merely unto himself. He wished to be happy then, as he wishes so greatly to be now, and his ideal of happiness—though in many points coinciding pretty closely with many human ideals of happiness in these advanced days!— was not an exalted ideal: it did not, as a rule, approach in any way to his brother's happiness, nor aim at his brother's advancement in the life that he was living. He fought and he struggled for his own fancied good, and in the fighting and struggle it mattered not to him how many of his fellows were wounded. He had his own goal to reach, and he would reach it, undeterred by any.

This was the determination with which man set out in the early days: a determination which was in positive conflict with both the origin and the plan of his being. At every point of this being touching universal order, and intended to evolve order himself, it was incumbent upon him to live ever, and to strive, for the general and highest good. GOD had made him a grand being, but if he would realise the true grandeur of his being he must be driven out of that 'hyaline of self' in which he then was living. He had come forth from the Hands of his Maker, endowed with a spiritual essence, with the power of a great intellect, and with that sublime gift, a free-will. He came forth in beautiful harmony and keeping with the fair world over which he was to reign. He was at peace with the animals beneath him, with the lesser organisms about his path. He was to be a living, active, loving being, moving nobly about his realm, revealing the majesty and glory of GOD, preaching by his nobility and high power, the Life, the mode of Action, the Love, of the GOD from the Heart of Whose Being he had emanated. By every breath he drew, by every word he spoke, by every act he did, yes, and by every tender, holy affection he put forth, he might preach GOD: the Supreme Law of Goodness. But he was not then doing this. He was silent. And he must be aroused from his silence. He had great duties to be fulfilled towards those other personalities amongst whom he was placed, just as he had great, loving rights over the lesser creatures of GOD's sphere. He must be aroused from the dull, selfish torpor of being in which he was desiring to abide, and be spurred on to a noble activity of self-sacrificing zeal, in his own high behalf, for the general good.

Man, truly, had to learn to regard himself as not his own, to selfishly fight for his isolated 'happiness,' his mistaken, ill-fancied 'good.' He had to be spurred and driven on to consider himself a 'social being,' and a widely responsible agent in the world of his being: hedged in, surrounded by, innumerable claims and demands upon his powers and capacities. He was missing the purpose of his life: failing to see in the personalities about him the opportunity for exercise of the 'goodness' which, above all things, made him akin with GOD, the Supreme Centre of all; and forgetting the true relation in which he stood by right towards the lower organisms that moved around him in the providence of GOD: forgetting, indeed, also the part which should be enacted in his inner life by those marvellous beauties of creation before his eyes, and the consequent outer effect in the range of his living. He himself was to grow beautiful and ever more beautiful for the sake of the general harmony and proportion of things.

And there was a special lesson, amid the many lessons, to be mastered by man. He had to learn, what Pascal has put into concise expression, that happiness was neither within him nor without him; but in GOD, both without and within him! He had to grow, to study and weigh outward matters and visions of beauty and wonder, and to find, by constant pain of disappointment, of failure to reach a particular, longed-for end, that, after all, the only end of man is GOD! Man had to find GOD, and He could only be found by the constant proved dissatisfaction arising from contemplation and study of matters whose edge he touched, whose inner force and significance he never seemed really to approach.

There had to go forward the gradual discovery of natural gifts and powers, and the disappointment accruing from the consciousness of human limitations, and the insatiable longing for the expansion of these limitations, drove the man on and on to seek the GOD of his being, and thus to attain to the secret of the only possible perfection and happiness. Through the gradual extension of his boundaries of thought and desire and longings for attainment, through the slowly increasing apprehension of the powers within him—despite his felt limitations—by the growing realisation of the width of his sphere of living, went forward the yearning after GOD; but it was guided and preserved by the spur of pain, and the nursing care of sorrowful experience, of disappointment and ever increasing dissatisfaction with the present lot :—the grasped truth and attainments. Ever something strange acting as a goad to human endeavour, ever a great mysterious vista of half dreamed of possibilities before men's eyes! This is how it was.

And so, one feels, must it ever have been in some sort and measure, if man were to know complete development. Man, indeed, was originally good, but even had he not fallen from his high, simple state, there would surely have been necessary a long process by which his principle of goodness might fully be evolved and perfected, and the limits of his being be extended into free, rich growth. Elsewise, as he was at the first so would he have been always: never any greater, never any nearer to GOD and true happiness.

Only we know that in consequence of man's fall a

very special process, a special course of educatory—and in this case punitive—discipline was essential. Man's powers had to be developed, his great nature expanded, not merely that he himself might ultimately realise perfection, but that the growth unto perfection might be passed on from him to the circle of beings to whom he belonged—that from the individual to the whole, advancement towards GOD and fulness of life might be carried on,—and man started in common error and in added individual error. Therefore, a special course of discipline, corrective, punitive, adequate in fact to meet the error, as well as the simple natural needs, in his heart and life, had to be applied to him. If in the hands of men this course became, as it did—and does still become—perverted and corrupted, we may not imagine GOD at fault in prescribing the course, but must understand clearly how that whose origin is pure may in process of service and personal use be degraded. GOD prescribed the one possible means of the due evolution of man's nobility, and of the general perfectedness: man, in using the means, robbed it of its original integrity, and made of it an impure force, partly good and partly evil. Yet the good was bound to triumph over the evil in time, and perhaps we have nowhere a greater and more sublime lesson on the omnipotence of Good than that which is contained in the sentence passed on the world, whereby suffering was to overshadow and almost seem to submerge all in its depths that the world might be cleansed and purified for the advent of —*The Redeemer*! Suffering of some sort, we feel, there must have been, if the Ideal of the human race was to be apprehended: suffering as we know it to have been through the early ages, as through the later ages also, suffering acute, awful, at times to appearance malignant, is a consequence of the Fall, but yet an additional argument in favour of the Divine Love.

Acute and awful indeed had suffering become. If one takes up the holy record of the sorrow and agony of the people in the past ages, thinking out but the suffering of one of those far-away individuals, it is appalling to the mind: if one studies contemporaneous history, and thinks out individual suffering as revealed there, it is appalling. Yet, what were man without suffering of some sort? And who are we that we should in thought place due limits to this or that sorrow or agony, feeling that GOD—or man either, as may sometimes strike us in our conceited egotistical judgment—had overstepped the boundary where good ended and evil began? How had man grown, how would he ever grow, without the spur of pain to drive him from a low plane of idle, empty, selfish living to that higher plane, whereon he can know the grand freedom of the sons of GOD, and be brought face to face with his Ideal?

'The immediate operation of the Creator is,' indeed, 'closer to everything than the operation of any secondary cause.' And the nearness of GOD to the sighing spirit of the man created by Him, which we know to be the result of experience of great suffering, is an answer— the most satisfying answer that could be obtained—to the questionings of mankind as to whether pain is in its origin pure or otherwise, GOD's or Satan's. We see man suffering, but we see him growing by his suffering. We recognise the lines of pain scored deeply over him, but we recognise also the lines of love that are running alongside, and often at the very same moment erasing them. It matters not that sometimes it is man's pain, and not GOD's devised pain of growth unto full development:—'The immediate operation of the Creator is closer to everything than the operation of any secondary cause!' There is a record—it is one long record, necessarily—of the travail of man's soul, of his body, of his entire being; but it is a record also of the gradual approach to individual perfection, of the advance of civilisation, the growth of the body politic towards the great Ideal. Creation was a sublime scheme of Omnipotent Love, and man was the central point.

This world of ours, then, with its beauty, its mystery, its pain, is to be regarded as the Divinely appointed sphere, and its events, its epochs, its changes, the Divinely regulated opportunities — involved and encircled as these are in the embrace of suffering—wherein and whereby man might reach the Ideal in which his own particular, individual ideal lies hidden. We know that GOD was ever perfect, and to be assured of this is to be further assured that whatever He conceived in the realms of His Thought must have been a perfect conception; and therefore, though man visibly was imperfect, even errant and defaced, he must one day realise perfection:—that Divine perfection, involving

THE LAW OF CREATURELY PERFECTION 61

essentially omnipotence, must ultimately triumph over every obstacle in the way of the realised general perfection of His creation culminating in man. By his own act man had temporarily degraded from the straight path to perfection marked out for him by GOD, and it would require Infinite Love to recover him from his error, his degraded state of being: but Infinite Love, having foreseen the error and the consequent degradation of being, had provided the remedy.

The Bible—the 'Record of Sorrow'—is the great history of the progress of civilisation, as it is the history of the universal development of man's life and being. It is the Divinely inspired account of man's emergence from a simple condition of perverted savagery to a partial realisation of those complex powers through which he was to attain to perfection—his own distinctive perfection—and the responsibilities that the possession of those powers entailed on him; and the most trenchant words in the whole Bible are surely these:—
'It shall bruise thy head.' Here we have the first intimation of the great Purpose of GOD, whereby man's perfection was to be given to him *despite* his wrong-doing, and given to him in special wise *because of* this wrong-doing. The Divine Purpose, involving absolutely the Incarnation, the presentation of Himself in, to, and for man, involved, by reason of the foreseen Fall of man, His coming as the delivering Seed of the woman, so that the power of the Evil One might be slain.

Man had fallen from his initial, childlike goodness, but he had not the power to thwart the Eternal Purpose of GOD: only, in consequence of his fall, the Divine Purpose contained elements that would not have been there had man remained upright and in harmony with Good. He was still to realise perfection: to be in perfect accord with a universal perfection. On and on had man to go, learning by the experience of the way, by knowledge through suffering, how to use, and how to keep in check, the powers with which he had been intrusted, bound and fettered by laws external to himself, arrested and punished for every infringement of the law of his own being by the painful consequences self-entailed: learning thus to be a law in himself, expressing the beauty of his being. It was, truly, a slow and gradual process leading to a definite end, conceived in the mind of GOD, made possible for man by the lasting contact of his heart to GOD's Heart which proclaimed him GOD's, however he might have transgressed against the original law impressed on him. We see man advancing step by step towards the acquisition of his particular ideal in the One Ideal of common humanity, with many a lapse and stumble, many a halt between, yet never alone, never unaided by the GOD Whom he had wronged, and Whom still he doubted and sinned against. Ever the progress was part of a coherent system, devised out of the Love of GOD and leading to an appointed end. GOD saw the end then as He sees the end of every one and of all circumstances, and in each individual case the method of peculiar advance was determined by the call going forth from the soul and being. And it was by the purification and

THE LAW OF CREATURELY PERFECTION

elevation, the right development, of single natures that the whole body of men advanced towards the great goal of perfectedness :—that the general progress of men, that is, went forward from a disordered and barbaric state to a high state of civilisation, in which the knowledge and vision of GOD might be a close and realised fact to them, bearing on and influencing every thought, word, and deed, until these all became permeated with the breath of His Life, and man was holy unto the Lord. It was thus that the gradual fulfilment went on of that 'law of creaturely perfection' which was impressed on man when he issued from the Hands of GOD, and which could only thoroughly be realised when man, by rigid adherence to outer laws, had grown to understand the law of his own being: seeing it as bound up with the sacred ordinances of GOD, for the good of his fellow-creatures, and learning to desire before all mere thought of individual gain, the collective wellbeing of the whole.

And what took place in the early days of man's living has been taking place, and will ever take place, in our own individual lives and in the world around us, until the Incarnate GOD shall have brought about universal perfection. It must be one long record of sorrow: one long account of the emancipation from evil of the human race, the cleansing and perfecting of the world, into the Perfect Ideal wherein lies each single man's ideal. Humanity now, as then, is growing beautiful through suffering, the suffering that binds it to GOD Incarnate. Humanity now, as then, is advancing in apprehension of the great Law of GOD through the gradual and painful apprehension of its own lesser law of creaturely perfection as impressed upon it by GOD, in the throes of that suffering which binds the whole world to the GOD Who made the world out of His Love, and willed to fulfil the Law of His Own Being by the absolute giving of Himself for the object loved. The corruption of our nature must be expurged, and the higher tendencies, of which we are variously, and dimly perhaps, conscious as stirring within us and clamouring for freedom of action, must be liberated from the thraldom of evil, by the personal knowledge and experience of suffering, ere we can at all understand the true purpose and scope of our creation and our being. The spirit is to be rendered supreme within us, and this certainly in the face of the Fall can only be brought about through the slaying of the body of death which is ours by natural consequence. Talents are to be quickened, genius inspired, latent grandeur of being developed—all this as well as the simple securing of the spirit's supremacy,—that the man of GOD's Love and the men of His Love may arise perfect at the last, sublime with a Divine perfection of sublimity: and the end can only be attained through the fellowship of Divine suffering, the being drawn bodily, spiritually, mentally, into the Divine Being and Sacrifice. If we wish, not merely to be 'good,' but to add our appointed quota to the world's advance towards perfection, if we wish to increase by one tiny fragment of true beauty the great aggregate of beauty which is to be the world's

THE LAW OF CREATURELY PERFECTION

answering of Divine Love according to Divine intention and plan, we must submit to that training and discipline of nature which has been the appointed way for mankind since the beginning of life. 'Thought,—true labour of any kind,—highest virtue itself,—is it not the daughter of pain?'[1]

It is only by pain, truly, that we can grow towards Christ, the revealed GOD of our creation: only by the personal identification with Him which suffering readily accepted and endured involves that we can grow to the realisation of that ideal which should be ours in the highest heavens. When GOD shall come to reign, as King of Glory, eternally and universally, over a redeemed kingdom, the true ideal reached by us will have been reached by patient endurance of the suffering which makes of isolated lives GOD's united single lives, blessed by the close blending of the being with the Being of Christ, GOD Incarnate, the Saviour of the world. We are different now from the people of the earlier times, but we are all alike in this: that, whatsoever may be our peculiar needs, there is one great need standing forth supremely:—the need of absolute growth unto, and union with, GOD's Perfect Sacrifice. And suffering impels and draws and points us to This.

There is want and insufficiency, there is actual strife and warfare, within us, and there can be no satisfaction nor peace until, by the drawing out of our proper faculties and powers in the fire and flame of pain, we come to know something of the true life for which we were

[1] Carlyle.

Divinely intended. Only thus can our higher faculties be enfreed, only thus can we become grand and pure and strong for GOD's use and the fulfilment of His Will of Love. There can be no growth, no satisfaction, no genuine expansion of being, there can be no personal realisation of what life means, without the suffering which leads and will bind us to Christ. Discipline there must be: union with Christ there must be, and this is to be attained by the acceptance of discipline, the faithful submitting to the pain whose end is sacrifice.

Who among us is not conscious, both of yearning want within the being, and of actual strife therein? We yearn for something—possibly we know not what it is:—feebly we put forth the wings of our desire:—then strongly, perhaps, some counter-action seems to bear down upon this weak fluttering growth, and crush it. Even the best must be aware of a struggle often going on in his being: of the presence of a longing to attain, and a mysterious force that strives to thwart attainment. The soul goes out toward good: a voice declares loudly for evil. And if the voice be not silenced the good is not reached. A perpetual warfare there is, and whilst this is so satisfaction comes not. A perpetual warfare there must ever be in some measure, but if alliance with Christ be sought and found the enemy of good is slain, the evil voice deadened. And this means the good of the whole circle of beings. Marvellously interdependent are the individual and the world with which he is associated by right of his wonderful, complex being: marvellously acting and reacting one upon

THE LAW OF CREATURELY PERFECTION 67

another, augmenting, perfecting, or detracting from and marring the great scheme of development in which all are involved. A grand advance of individual man, a grand advance of the whole body of men : a growth of general, of universal perfection! This is what is to be brought about by the discipline which, seeming to be a rending of man's being and a defect in GOD's government of His realm of personalities, is actually a reconciler of antagonisms, an agency for the ultimate realisation of a perfect order and harmony of life, in which GOD may be fully recognised and known.

A realm of personalities, acting and reacting one upon another, influencing, yet influenced by, the tone of the vast stirring, throbbing life around them! A world of personal beings deriving their life from GOD, and dependent on their union and intimate communion with GOD for the fulfilment of the law of their creaturely perfection! Ah! we do not think enough about it. We do not realise what it is that GOD is asking of us when He bids us all be holy even as He is Holy. We do not understand that selflessness which should lead a man to think a great deal about himself in order that his life may bear witness of the light and strength which live within him : do not see that GOD in demanding perfection from the individual is considering the perfection of the whole circle of individuals. How often do we hear people say : 'My life is my own, to do what I like with!' And all the while the life of none of us is our own to do what we like with, but belongs rightfully by Divine ordinance to the body of which we are

68 THE SANCTUARY OF SUFFERING

but members. It is a fallacy to say that we have separate, individual rights when GOD made us members of a realm of personalities, gathered round and subsisting on one Common Centre of life and movement. We are GOD's, and we have to do as GOD likes, and this is merely another way of expressing the truth that we have to obey and fulfil the law of general creaturely perfection for the good of the whole circle of life: that we have to devote all our energies of body, soul and spirit, to the acquisition of a perfect life in the great circle of which GOD is the Supreme Centre, that so may be brought about that harmony of purpose and being which is the end of GOD's creative intention.

This was truly the intention of Creation: that, drawing our life from GOD, walking always with Him in conscious fellowship, feeling our heart to beat in union with His Heart, we might grow to look upon every other creature of GOD as bound up with us in the life we are living, and be able to regard the common good as our good, the common needs as our needs; and thus become a part of a universal perfection, realising the beatitude and glory of such perfection. We were meant to attain to an absolute perfection; but we were never meant, nor indeed were we appropriately organised, to realise perfection in ourselves as mere isolated abstractions. This indeed were an impossibility for any one of us. For each man there exists a solitary and distinctive ideal, and towards the acquisition of this his whole being is to be bent; but it is

THE LAW OF CREATURELY PERFECTION 69

never an ideal cut off from, or in antagonism against, the common ideal:—that into which the whole of GOD's Creation is to grow. GOD, we feel, would have a man concentrate his soul on the realisation of the particular ideal which awaits him by Divine decree, and in this see that he is working towards the accomplishment of general good. GOD, surely, would have every individual regard himself as a toiler in behalf of universal perfectedness, an agent in the advance towards completion of Purpose. The first intimation of the man's ideal, flashed to him from GOD, is GOD's call to him to arise and fulfil the law of creaturely perfection, as it applies to him individually, for the good, in special wise, of his fellows. It is the ground on which his holy living is to be carried forward: the ground on which the Holy Spirit will meet him and work with him, and whereon, therefore, personal greatness and nobility shall be cultivated, and a rich harvest be reaped for general succour. A man's ideal is an inseparable accompaniment, is positively an integral part, of the whole vast advance towards GOD. In his progress thus to holiness and ordained completion of life and being is pushed on the progress of the world to completion, to a realisation of entire perfection. We know that the ideal of one individual, of one sex of individual, of one race, one age, is never the particular ideal of another individual, sex of individual, race, or age. We are told this distinctly, and shown it, not only in the pages of history, but in the experience of life related to us by others, expressed in manifold fashion by our ordinary course of living. Nevertheless, it is by the fidelity of each person to his, or her, peculiar ideal that the march of the whole goes forward. This has been the case ever and everywhere, and must continue until universal perfection shall have been attained. The whole course of true living depends on the conduct and action, the faithful, devoted living, of single persons in the vast circle of personalities of which GOD is the Supreme and Perfect Centre.

And can we not understand how, with the needs of the whole circle at the hands of the individual, there is a stupendous discipline requisite for personal development? that the gradual growth and perfecting of individual character, of personal gifts and powers, peculiar in nature, bearing, significance, can only be wrought by a complete submission and trust of the entire individual being, in order that the Holy Spirit may exert just such influence as shall *open* the being to discipline? Unconsciously, both to them and to him, are a man's fellow-creatures waiting for the special revelation of GOD and Divine things that he, by his particular endowments and nascent ability, is designed to give out. There is within each single member of the circle a personal power, to influence, to lead, to guide his fellows, and they are waiting for his help— just as his ideal is waiting for his ready response of being to its claims!

And he will never find, never reach, his true ideal, never be of ordained service to his fellows, unless by the pain of punishment of his lower self he is *driven*

THE LAW OF CREATURELY PERFECTION 71

to look for his higher self. Man has now, as in the early days, to be spurred on from a low plane to a higher plane. With all his grand faculties and powers, his nascent ability, he will never fulfil his mission in life unless he learns by suffering the true discontent of the way in which he is living. He will never extend his boundaries and look over into the Unseen unless seen and already apprehended things hurt him by their failure to give satisfaction. He will never lose his low, errant self without the sting and smart that tells him when what he is thinking, feeling, planning, doing, is wrong.

Ever the spur of pain must be, even now, if man's nobler self is to be evolved, if union and communion actually with GOD through Sacrifice are to be secured: —if general perfection is to be reached.

Man has peculiar gifts and powers. Yes, ever; but he cannot learn their real use and significance, he cannot grow to understand the special secret of his being, the peculiar message with which he is intrusted, until he is driven away from all semblance of satisfaction with a self which is not his, nor GOD's truly, but a remnant of the Fall of Man. Man must find a nobler self; and he will find it through the pain and suffering which seem to meet him at every turn and movement of his low self. There must be the spur of aching dissatisfaction, felt want—there must be outer suffering, bitter travail of sorrow—before he knows that he is not living as GOD would have him live, not delivering the message that he has to deliver. Surely, he begins to feel in the throes of his pain, there is somehow and somewhere another self possible of attainment: another self, though still with his natural idiosyncrasy upon it? He becomes conscious slowly, through dissatisfaction with his present life and daily action, through the throes of his general suffering, of some vague power within him crying for release; and he gropes towards GOD for an explanation of the questions that are disturbing him.

So he finds GOD in His Holiness, and sees dimly outlined the ideal man that he is to be. And this is the true dawn to him of perfection, of fulness of being. If he had not known pain, if it had not come to goad him out of his pitiful state of germinant satisfaction with a low, errant self, his lethargy, his apathetical attitude towards the marvels of the universe, above, around, beneath him—the wonders about his daily path, the secret purpose of his own being,—this ideal perfection, this fulness of being, would never have dawned for him. He would have remained as he was, and never have given forth to the world the revelation of GOD that he had been planned to make, as his quota to the general advance in the real knowledge of GOD.

The world, truly, could not advance if individual men stood still: there would be general paralysis of GOD-given force, loss of GOD-given 'chances.' Man, himself barren, sterile, would pass on the infection of his barrenness, his sterility, until there would be wide-spread torpor: a great waste before GOD and Heaven of grand vitality and natural power.

SPECIAL CALLS

'THE highest attitude of any man's life,' said Bishop Phillips Brooks, 'is to stand waiting for what use GOD will make of him.'

The scheme of perfection is, as we know, a scheme of universal application; yet there is ever special and peculiar application to be considered in our regard of it. There is to be a general advance to the realisation of perfection, but each man's progress must differ somewhat from that of his neighbour, inasmuch as his peculiar ideal is not the same as his neighbour's ideal. It must furthermore, of course, differ for the reason that one's faults and characteristic difficulties are not another's faults and characteristic difficulties. The march onwards is to the same great End, and must be maintained by the same Supreme Means; but in lesser particulars it varies, of necessity, from the very fact of the differentiation of the personal end to be reached. It has been remarked that 'the object of all education and discipline is to develop all the powers of the life to their highest possibilities' '(and then to hold them in perfect mastery!)' And one feels this remark to be in consonance with the subject under discussion. A 'call' is the first note struck of that harmony of life which is intended to result from a certain course whereby the natural tendencies of a human being are to be drawn forth, and that human being be in touch with his peculiar ideal perfection. True education is the cultivation of natural faculties towards the special result which they are intended to fulfil. And GOD's education by suffering tends ever unfailingly in the direction of the end known by Him as the man's special goal. GOD has a use for all of us, however feeble may be our natural powers, and until we are set on the way of this 'use,' this special purpose to be fulfilled, we are not really living in the true sense of the word: merely floating, as it were, on the surface of life and drifting with its stream.

> 'Hast Thou no word for me? I am Thy thought.
> GOD, let Thy mighty Heart beat into mine,
> And let mine answer as a pulse to Thine.
> . . . . . .
> And let Thy own design in me work on,
> Unfolding the ideal man in me!
> . . . . . .
> Lead me, O Father, holding by Thy Hand;
> I ask not whither, for it must be on.'[1]

There should be in us the readiness and preparedness for any special 'word' that may come to us. We should ever, that is, have our whole being opened for the possible reception of the message and earnest of our ideal that GOD at any time may wish to whisper to us. We must be in a state of calm, still passivity, in which

[1] Dr. George Mac Donald.

anticipatory acquiescence in GOD's Will for us may rest. And ever must we remember that such passivity in no way need conflict with the little ordinary tasks of the day, into which our energy and particular ability should go forth, seeing it as absolutely necessary for the eventual discovery to us of the special work and purpose that GOD may have in view for us. 'I ask not whither, for it must be on'—if it be GOD's design that is to be accomplished; and that is all that should concern us.

All that enters into any life, our own or another's, should be viewed according to the part which it is meant to play in the gradual evolution and development of such natural tendencies and powers as may go to form the true ground of our ideal in the Mind of GOD. GOD has a certain kind of greatness for every one to touch and to realise (in some degree and measure) even here, in this life, and we must watch for signs of its dawn, listen for sounds from Heaven intended to herald its approach. There is a particular relation which each bears to another and to others, and should fill well and faithfully, for the good of his neighbour individually, of his neighbours collectively. And so, apart from elsewise need of special discipline, the method and personal route of advance varies. To some, indeed, a course markedly different from the generality of people is indicated, and it is these whom one would at present especially consider.

A special call, then, comes to certain among us; and they stand out conspicuously, as did those prophet-seers of old: and their anointing must be that of Suffering.

All the highest achievements of religious enthusiasm, scientific acumen, literary insight and power, all the grandest attainments of Art in its wide domain, all the beautiful, tender, loving acts, have been wrought through, or in, suffering. Its value is not limited to one field of thought, one sphere of living action: it extends over the length and breadth of every region where the mind of man can roam, and throbs in each form of beauty, each vehicle of holy, gracious influence and power that the soul of man can devise, or would acquire. It has stirred in, and quickened, the whole life of the world with the fire of its Divine breath, infusing into natural talent, nobler aspirations, 'Divine discontent,' until this went forth to seek its designed perfection. Man has to learn to accomplish great things for GOD alone, for his own sake as before GOD, for his fellows as they revolve about him in the eternal Purpose of GOD. He has a Divine mission to fulfil, personal perfection to realise, general perfectedness to urge and push on. There are rights to be obeyed, privileges to be taken up and worked out, a glorious office to find and fill well. Man does not live to himself alone in any respect, or at any moment, of his life. He lives to GOD, and it is essential that he should live rightly to GOD: obeying the particular law of his life and being, feeling himself involved in, and bound about by, the great corporate life around him, for whose sake so largely he must be holy and great, that the whole may advance to perfection.

Pain is needed, as we know, not merely for man's own sake, but for the sake of that development unto perfection which he is bound by his origin and nature to advance. GOD will hold him responsible, in important measure, for the advance of his fellows : hold him responsible in exact proportion to the powers within him, his strength and abilities, his GOD-given opportunities. So man must find his true self, and then lay that self down before GOD to receive His fresh anointing, His special consecration. Then will the human being be in harmony and unity with the Divine Purpose of Creation. Then will the particular purpose of man's own life be truly fulfilled for the good of his fellow-creatures, and they, too, will go forward in the acquisition of that spirit of submission which places any human life alongside GOD and in approximation to its peculiar ideal conceived for it in the Mind of GOD.

For every person born into the world GOD has, as we have said, a distinctive ideal, and all that enters into our life here is to be viewed in the light of this belief: is to be regarded reverently as an agent of GOD's willed evolution and gradual development of what will go towards the realisation of the ideal. But the principal factor, the chief agent, is ever pain :—the personal endurance of pain, and the witnessing, and, whenever allowed, the attempting to alleviate, the suffering of those around us. And, logically, it follows that in persons whose natural gifts and endowments are peculiarly great, or in those in whom there is some special demand for discipline, the need of suffering will be, as a rule, peculiarly great, and will be proportionately supplied in the providence of GOD. We forget too often what we owe to the submission and fortitude of the conspicuous ones of the earth, whose anointing unto suffering has been greatly for our good. We see the beautiful, or the wonderful, outflow around us, but we lose out of sight its true source, fail to appreciate the significance of it all.

Yet what a message is conveyed through this glorious outflow of Divinely inspired and developed genius that so enriches and adorns the world of our experience! The works issuing from man's special anointing by GOD are, singly and collectively, constant opportunities of grace to us, the beholders. We should grow holy unto the Lord and blessed for men even by the contemplation of them; and if upon us has passed an anointing of special significance, requiring us to go forth with a great power of influence in us—if it should be granted to us to be amongst the great ones from whose inner being conspicuous work may go forth,—we should surely go towards our anointing with deep humility, and ready submission to the entire Will of GOD.

Do we go forward thus? Sant' Antonino went to the Altar to receive his consecration with bared head and feet, symbolical of his inward bearing towards the office being given to him.

Donatello—the beloved 'Donato' of his fellows—bowed his head, and said: 'To thee it is given to make the Christ, to me only the *contadini*.'

Do we, whilst awakened, enlightened, called to a

SPECIAL CALLS 79

sense of some special place and work awaiting us, ready for consecration, thankful for the consecration received, yet with humility recognise both the unworthiness in us and the limitations that still must be ours? Or do we feel worthy of the mission intrusted to us, and impatient of aught that seems to tell us of limitations that we cannot surmount, and must not strive to surmount, lest we lose in the ordained purpose of our bestowed talent?

'Thou, O Spirit, That dost prefer, before all temples, the upright heart and pure, instruct me; for Thou knowest. What in me is dark, illumine: what is low, raise and support.'[1]

We want our lives to be holy and beautiful unto the Lord, helpful and lovely to men. We want our imagination to be 'the Eden in which we walk with GOD,' a holy of holies in a temple suited for the worship of GOD and the service of our fellows. We want to meet GOD in our own selves, and learn of Him, and derive from Him power of blessedness for others. We want to live to GOD as He would have us live, to have our being one long pæan of adoring praise, of sacrificial worship, of sanctified service: to have within us GOD, without us GOD. And truly it is only when He abides in us consciously to ourselves that we find our real, full powers, and discover to others the nature of our mission to them: it is only when the life is allied with the Divine Life that the true secret of our life is revealed to us—that we are able, thoroughly able, to decipher

[1] Prayer from *The Cloud of Witness.*

the characters written within us, and to give forth the particular message which we are charged to deliver.

The grand triumphs of civilisation, of Art, Science, Literature, are undoubtedly the outcome, through initial pain and struggle, of Divine influence brought to bear upon the inner life, of Divine Power working within a man's heart, soul and mind. The glorious growth of the world to its predestined state of perfectedness, the beautiful painting, poetry, music, the discoveries of which people mistakenly talk as discoveries *apart from* GOD and contrary to Religion, the writings that stir our souls and fill us with lofty impulse, noble ambition, spiritual longings—all these are direct results of that union and communion with GOD reached through the knowledge, the personal experience, the patient, even glad, endurance of suffering. Pain is at the back of everything great and beautiful, and of real lasting worth, if we would but realise it; for it is ever pain that draws a man out of his old self and gives to him the new self which means GOD reached and his ideal touched.

Surely we see the value of pain when we study the effects wrought through it? Surely we would not, even if we might or could, banish from the world one heart-throb of the suffering that beats for its perfection? Pain, bringing to the being GOD Himself, draws us into the rare, pure atmosphere of Heaven, where we read the secrets of the great universe, and come to know the purpose of all living. It reveals to us ourselves as one day we shall be, as now we may be. It shows us what are our powers, our sublime possibilities, what GOD requires of us, what men are wanting at our hands. It takes the things of the earth, and irradiates and illuminates wholly the darkness clinging around them, making them bright and clear with Heaven's own light. It is indeed GOD's best for the children of His Love.

There is a story told of a celebrated singer, which illustrates, in slight degree, the part that suffering plays in the evolution of natural gifts, and which may, perhaps without undue digression, be introduced here. She had been singing in the early days of her career to an audience who had been charmed with her skill, her execution, but had gone away dissatisfied, having missed something—they knew not what, possibly—that they would have liked to feel, and drink into their inner selves. No, they would not know what it was, most likely, but still the thing was missed. And afterwards a lady from amongst the audience approached the singer's master on the subject. 'It will come! it will come!' he said. And when a short time had passed, the mysterious power of influence had come. When again the singer stood forth and sang, her audience—that same audience—were spell-bound, entranced. She had got the 'thing,' the strange power that had before been lacking to her. She had got the key with which to unlock the door to their souls, and it had been acquired through suffering! A great sorrow had, meanwhile, crept into her life, and when she arose from its gloom she held in her life's hand this wonderful key.

THE SANCTUARY OF SUFFERING

Do not such instances, small though they may be, add ever to the glory and splendour of the great Cross cast athwart the sphere of men's living? Whether in biography we have been told of special suffering—a distinct entrance into what should be a Sanctuary of Suffering — in the lives of conspicuous workers, or whether we only infer it (read the signs of it in their work accomplished) the evidence is surely there, to be read. We know that they received their beautiful consecration and their supreme power through the suffering that bound them, as it had first led them, to GOD.

Sometimes, as in the case of the glorious poetess [1] not long since passed from us, there is not only throughout her work evidence of suffering, but here and there in it a revelation of the particular form that the suffering had taken. Two small poems in her case make this clear to us. And they also reveal that power of expectation which sorrow engenders and teaches, and which illumines so greatly the path of man's advance. Softly and tenderly we find ourselves looking with her beyond the confines of earth, into the vast Unknown: following her in the clear vision that was given to her of the glad fulfilment of the joy whose dawn she had known here, but which had so quickly turned to acute pain.

And surely some period of special trial must have been experienced and passed through nobly by Archbishop Trench ere he gave to the world these beautiful lines :—

'. . . In that hour
From out my sullen heart a power
Broke, like the rainbow from the shower,

---

[1] Christina Rossetti.

> To feel, although no tongue can prove,
> That every cloud, that spreads above,
> And veileth Love, itself is Love.'

It is at such a time that a person first touches the robe of the ideal. There is shot down into the soul then a gleam of light—nay, more than a gleam: a bright radiancy of light—in which is clearly revealed something of the peculiar power with which a special life has been intrusted. It is then that not only does a poet become conscious of the 'Divine afflatus' that is to go forth in noble song, but that a painter knows that he can paint, and what he is to paint, that a musician becomes aware of the fire burning within him and which is to be expressed in special manner, that to a scientist is discovered the wonderful gift of insight, the particular acumen which shall enable him under GOD's guidance to resolve hitherto unfathomable mysteries, obscure phenomena, into the brightness and clearness of day: at such a moment that a man endowed with a natural power of expressing truths that have been impressed on his mental retina, awakes to a knowledge of his mission, his office, towards other men, and is stirred to exert his energy in its fulfilment. And through these media GOD is revealed and glorified, and the world made better: through these mighty, beautiful agencies GOD is brought home to the hearts and minds and souls of His great circle of personalities, and, to the very outermost rim of the circle, salvation and blessing are spread, and the whole is drawn close to its Ideal.

In all glorious works, indeed, can surely be traced

something of Suffering's anointing. Take up, for example, a picture by Rembrandt. How is it that we find ourselves thrilled through and through as we look at it? What gave him his wonderful power of appeal to the human soul? What gave him that unspeakable pathos, that tenderness and force of conception, that intense sympathy with the ills of life expressed so clearly on the canvas? How had he arrived at the ability to deliver the special message with which he had been charged? He had entered the sanctuary of suffering and seen GOD, Incarnate as the 'Man of Sorrows.' He had found out by his personal life-experience something of the meaning of that great burden of sorrow and pain laid on the human race. Every line, every tone, of his art reveals this truth. See his unbeautiful figures, the seared faces, the bent forms! See the crowd of diseased, disfigured, maimed human beings gathered around that Central Figure, the Man of Sorrows, from Whom is being shed forth healing: Whose whole Person stands out in the midst of suffering, aflame and aglow with Supernatural Light. Notice the marvellous intermixing and blending of effects, the startling contrasts of darkness and light, which so often are just associated with the artist as mere peculiarities of his masterly style! Does not his whole art set forth this lesson: 'When man's at his weakest, GOD's at His strongest'? Does not he exhort to the patient bearing of suffering: extolling its office, revealing its End? Does he not, by his flashing lights, his gloomy shadows, his decrepit forms stepping from out the shade towards a Divine radiance, express what he himself, in his hours of sad need and questioning of GOD, had learned, and must give out? He reveals the true destiny of mankind. He takes their sorrows, their wants, their craving agonies, and holds them toward the Christ to receive their appointed illumination and consecration. He binds up the broken-hearted, and gives to feeble age eternal youth, restored vitality. He draws vividly for us the blind 'Tobit,' groping in his darkness, alone, apparently helpless; and makes him stand out as a representative of the human race: and then he draws our eyes to the Incarnate GOD, glorious, perfect, all-seeing and all-strong, the representative of a *perfected* humanity. And, finally, let us think of his 'Death of the Virgin':—the fainting, drooping form, with the last spark of earthly life going out, and above a blaze of splendour, in which Angels are seen with outstretched arms ready to embrace and lift up the 'spirit just born, being dead.' 'Behold, I make all things new' is ringing in our ears!

Could Guido Reni have painted that wonderful 'Ecce Homo,' if he had not known suffering? his 'Christ and S. John'? even his 'Coronation of the Virgin,' with its grand message to the hearts and lives of men?

Could Ary Scheffer have drawn on his canvas that strangely pathetic, yet unutterably beautiful, S. Monica, without his special anointing? Do we not rather feel that, there on his canvas, looking across the sea from the port of Ostia, the saintly mother and son speak of the artist's own consecration: his own hallowing for a particular message to be given to the world? The Beatific Vision plainly reflected on those two faces, and drawing us to Heaven as we gaze upon them, could not surely have been so reflected if the artist had not had his peculiar entering into the Sanctuary of Suffering. In that must there have been accorded to him a high message ere the picture went forth to the world.

See! they are sitting, S. Monica a little higher than her sanctified son of many prayers—the son who had been given to GOD before his actual birth: a little above him whom all generations of men living since have delighted to honour as a foremost Saint of GOD. His man's hand, so strong and powerful-looking, is clasped and held by her two smaller, gentler-looking hands. Her face, enrapt, is turned to the Vision in the highest Heavens, his face, enrapt too, is turned thereto, yet holds within it—something of S. Monica! Who but GOD Himself could have taught the painter such a lesson as is given out thus? And where but in the Sanctuary of Suffering could it have been mastered? The white-robed mother, with her worn, tired, *hurt* face, sitting high in her emblematised holiness and purity of being and shining with a Divine brightness: the son in his sombre garb, relieved only by one glowing touch of scarlet, dwarfing somewhat her delicate, slight, outer personality, yet below her as they face together the Vision of GOD, and owing a part of that bright shining of his face to the illumination of S. Monica's! What a message is given out here!

'The men of sorrows are the men of influence in

every walk of life.'[1] We cannot take up any great work, or indeed be conscious of any little work accomplished, without feeling this. The whole realms of Art, of Science, of Literature, tell out the great truth of the value and beauty of suffering, of patient endurance. It is all holy ground, on which it behoves us to tread softly and reverently, with bent head, with silent adoration of the Lamb slain from before the foundations of the world. Even if the dawn of conscious burning genius, of great and conspicuous talent, comes not at some particular moment, during some special 'hour' of suffering, there must ever be the spending and being spent. All work has been preluded by pain of toil, weary disappointments, stern self-denial, noble self-devotion. We must—all must—suffer, ere anything worthy can be accomplished. In one way or another must there be a consecration by suffering—we must receive a special anointing. But, most often, it is not merely a natural prelude of this sort that leads to great, holy, soul-stirring work : it is rather a distinct entrance into the Sanctuary of Suffering, a marked stroke of terrible sorrow and affliction, that drives us to cry : ' GOD above everything ! ' as Beethoven had learned to say ere his music could go forth with the glow and fire of Heaven upon it.

Where had been the ' Missa Solennis,' the ' Ninth Symphony,' if Beethoven had not received his anointing thus? What had he been without the experience of that awful sorrow, and the affliction which visited his life

[1] Dean Paget.

and opened his eyes to the Vision of GOD? What but these could have called forth so truly the Divine passion of his music: that passion which thrills and uplifts the soul of the listener? 'GOD above everything!' And when the 'Ninth Symphony' was first performed and drew to a close, not a dry eye was to be seen in the audience.

'The men of sorrows,' indeed, 'are the men of influence in the world'; and whether it be given to us, speaking figuratively, ' to make Christ,' or ' the *contadini*,' or whether we can do no task so great as the making of the *contadini*, whether we be 'men' or women, there must be the special anointing of suffering, the special link that binds the life to GOD's Life, if we would at all realise the particular purpose that lies hidden, at first, in the being. She, who bore her cross so nobly, looking ever 'with clear eyes' to the Beyond, where, we trust, she has met her joy, and where she will not 'question much,' but only smile and rejoice—thinking peacefully of the corn-flowers wild, and the singing bird that had witnessed the breaking of her heart in the bygone days—influences the world still by her sanctified offering of beautiful service.

> '. . . I have not often smiled
> Since then, nor questioned since,
> Nor cared for corn-flowers wild,
> Nor sung with the singing bird.'

Only she had borne the Cross, and served others in the bearing of it.

> '1 take my heart in my hand—
> I shall not die, but live—
> Before Thy Face I stand;
> I for Thou callest such:
> All that I have I bring,
> All that I am I give,
> Smile Thou and I shall sing,
> But shall not question much.'

How reverently we think of her, now in Paradise!— 'The night will pass away and the darkness will disperse, and the light will take its place.' Ay! with a far greater splendour than aught on earth could give.

The night will pass away! The true Light will come! Throughout the world, with its mystery and its marvel, be the subject of our consideration Nature or Art, all is the vehicle of this truth. GOD is ever teaching it to us. But man does not see nor understand these things—this great truth—until his soul is awakened, his heart and conscience and his intellect are astir and quickened by suffering, and the consequent union with GOD.

'When I consider Thy heavens, the work of Thy fingers; the moon and the stars which Thou hast ordained;

'What is man, that Thou art mindful of him? and the son of man, that Thou visitest him?

'For Thou hast made him a little lower than the Angels, and hast crowned him with glory and honour.

'Thou madest him to have dominion over the works of Thy Hands: Thou hast put all things under his feet:

'All sheep and oxen, yea, and the beasts of the field;

'The fowl of the air, and the fish of the sea, and whatsoever passeth through the paths of the seas.

'O Lord our Lord, how excellent is Thy Name in all the earth!'[1]

[1] Psalm viii. 3-9.

THE SANCTUARY OF SUFFERING

Until man has suffered greatly he does not apprehend the truth behind the marvels above and about him. If he has a peculiar faculty for study, and in some degree, explanation of natural objects, he does not find this faculty without pain. These wonders exist largely for the use and benefit of the human race—though, of course, being great with a peculiar greatness, as going to form the completion of the Divine Creative Scheme. —Through the contemplation and study of them, man's spiritual, moral, and intellectual strength is increased a thousandfold, and he comes, under the guidance of the Holy Spirit, to know more of the GOD Who had heretofore seemed remote from his consciousness. The stars in GOD's heaven, the tiniest flowers on the earth, the Angels in their immortal essence, the beasts that perish (as we are told):—all these, whilst contributing to the perfection of the universe, yet exist greatly for the advantage of man. They draw out his soul, they touch his mind, they develop his heart-power: they open gradually, by GOD's help, the eyes of his inner vision to the glory and magnificence, the tenderness, of the Divine Being. Above all, they teach him that humility which is the only true ground of righteousness and intercourse with GOD.—'What is man, that Thou art mindful of him?'

Where would civilisation as we know it, where would general development, culture, upward flight of being, have been without the spur and incentive of the pain that draws a life on to find its natural powers: that binds a life to the GOD of its being? Where, and what, would the world of man's living be but for the spur that has goaded him out of low satisfaction to high discontent and new longings, and the sense that he was coming short of something that GOD had designed for him? GOD is at fault in His method of governing His world, we would say. And all the time, before us, and within us, is the proof of the perfect wisdom of His government. The development of individual character, of individual powers, the advance of civilisation, we owe alike to the force and power of this pain whose continued presence in our midst we would regard as an occasion for complaint against the ruling providence of GOD. Our best feelings, our highest thoughts, noblest acquisitions, are due to the strength of pain's discipline.

To pain's discipline! As in the old time, so now:—Man does not live to himself alone, but acts on the life about him, and by his own loyalty and fidelity to Divine inbreathings, makes to grow and spread true devotion to GOD amongst his fellow-personalities. Each man, in his proper and distinct person, is to radiate light and heat to others. We know this. We know that the whole course of life is a process towards GOD, through the life first of individuals, then of the mass of individuals: that every man, therefore, is a force in his spiritual, moral, mental economy before GOD. There is ever going forward a gradual realisation of power and grace of being, an increase of spiritual vitality, a large awakening to the general possibilities and the wide purpose of living, and it issues from the faithful living and devotion of individual men.

The majority of persons walk along a path alike in many particulars, but to some, as we have seen, a special course, a special route, is indicated; and they, with a ready and hearty submission to GOD's Will, must undergo the particular system of education that is necessary for them. There must be an absolute fidelity to the trust committed to them.

'He will teach us to know that, beneath all that is poor and fleeting and imperfect in our visible life, there is a principle of eternal life by which we, through the infinite grace of GOD, can claim fellowship with Him.'[1] But we must suffer ere we know. We must thus be developed and consecrated, either for great deeds or little deeds, conspicuous manner, or retired, unobtrusive manner, of living. Life will not shine out for us with a true Heavenly beauty and significance otherwise.

Of those to whom much has been given much will be expected: where GOD has sown richly He will look to gather richly. But where only little has been given' little will be demanded: where there has not been such rich sowing GOD will not look for so rich a gathering. Yet must there ever be a life so lived that, in its beauty of tenderness, its gentle, helpful ministry of others, its passion of devoted love, it may be linked to, and bound up for ever with, that Supreme Figure Whom soon in the Sanctuary of Suffering will be met: Who was neither painter, nor musician, nor poet, but Who never-

[1] Dr. Westcott.

theless lifted up His days, His hours, His minutes, in one long Sacrifice to Heaven, and brought blessing on the earth beneath: Who left behind Him a special message to those not intrusted with any peculiar, conspicuous talent or genius, exhorting all men to draw nigh to perfection, whatever their gifts might be.

So, when we find that Figure, do we learn to be content if GOD has not specially endowed us with gifts. So are we glad to be 'ordinary' if He sees fit that we should be so. For each of us there is, we have come to know, an ideal, always different in some way from our neighbour's ideal: for each there is a peculiar sort of excellence to reach, a special word to be delivered to the world. And therefore we can never truly be ordinary: never, as we would put it, be 'lost in the crowd.' We stand out conspicuously and clearly in GOD's sight, and the powers within us, though not brilliant nor great, may be made to shine with a brilliancy not of themselves, but by right of their glorious, patient submission to GOD for the particular blessing that He would bestow on them.

Always, most surely, must there be a spending and being spent, ere life's purpose and mission can, in each one of us, with our relative greatnesses and littlenesses, be discovered and fulfilled. The whole life must be passed through the fire of suffering if its true grandeur is to be evolved.

Happy are they who, like our two great modern poets, can pass from earth to Paradise with nought of their work that they need wish undone. And happy, too, in equal measure—nay, perhaps in greater measure —those who, without great gifts, have striven to live their lives, humbly and far-off though it be, like the holy Prior[1] who, people said, was 'made to live by love'; striven to live them, that is, simply towards the Christ:—The One Ideal of the human race!

Sant' Antonino.

III
'JESUS HOMINUM SALVATOR'

'JESUS HOMINUM SALVATOR'

THE whole purpose and the meaning of life to us are the finding of Christ. In Him, indeed, is life, and in Him alone can be seen the solution of the great problem of suffering. He is the answer to, and the satisfaction of, that sigh which has ever gone forth from the tired spirit of man for more than this world can give him. In Him is the only possible parallelism of those diverse questionings which have disturbed man from (almost) the beginning of his life. The Incarnation of GOD as Christ reveals that Love and perfect Wisdom out of which man was created, and by which he is upheld and led in the way of his life. Seemingly antagonistic verities are here reconciled one with another, and the questions and doubts, the disbelief and the unbelief, of man are alike laid at rest.

Yet, this presupposes a correct and moral view of the Divine Incarnation, and the Atonement for man wrought through, and by means of, the Incarnation. It is possible, we know, to hold a view which is so incorrect as to cause it to lose its right position in our minds, and so unmoral (to adopt a term greatly used in a certain well-known weekly paper of high standing) as to obliterate wholly to us its real beauty and glory. If we were to take away the subject of the Divine Incarnation from the pages of Holy Scripture we should render them chaotic and meaningless ; but if we retain that great truth and conceive a false estimate of its nature and its bearing on our daily living we do more than this :—we make these lives devoid of any right GOD-ordained purpose and method of progress, and malign the integrity of GOD.

The Incarnation, and the Atonement therein wrought for man, explain the 'riddle of the painful earth' as nought else can explain it ; and they hold up in clear and splendid glory the perfection of that Love and Wisdom of GOD which men had so often doubted and had ever so little known. The whole course of civilisation, and the progress generally of man, led up to this point ; even as this course and this progress now derive their strength and force from contact with it. The Life and Death of Christ, the GOD-Man, were at once a fulfilment and realisation of ancient prophecy and anticipation, and a prophetic utterance of the marvels to be wrought in and through humanity, ere 'the trumpet shall sound and the graves give up their dead.' Humanity gathers round, and is concentrated in, the Incarnation of GOD. It was, as we have already seen, the Supreme point to which creation in the Mind of GOD necessarily led up. His Love and Wisdom, evidenced now to us clearly, if we will, in his Incarnation and the entire Sacrifice of Himself, foresaw, before man was made, the only Means by which he might attain to the perfection of being for which he was designed. This perfection of being could not be realised, GOD knew, short of such a Sacrifice of Himself as should make actual participation in His Life and Being possible to the man created. Hence the Incarnation, and the ordained—and thus made practicable—attitude of man towards GOD, and his acceptance of the Fruit of the Incarnation.

Apart from the sin of man, foreseen and foreknown —though not, for one moment may we suppose, willed —by GOD, with all its terrible need and its awful train of circumstances, the Incarnation, we feel, was in the Mind and intention of GOD for the man who was to be in perfect affinity of life and being with His Life and Being. But with man's sin an undoubted fact, the Incarnation means also a Via Dolorosa and a Cross of Shame held up! And in the recesses of the Divine Mind this must clearly have been seen when man walked there, a shadowy being with sublime potentialities. For we must not forget that the foreknowledge of man's Fall involved a fore-provision of the remedy of that Fall. All along, from the dawn of humanity in the Divine Thought had GOD seen Himself, not merely Incarnate in human flesh, but burdened with a flesh corrupted and weakened by human wrongdoing. He saw Himself thus for man's sake; and His Thought reached on to the Hill of Calvary, where He could lay the body of sin down, that man might be freed from his self-made bondage to Evil.

And in considering carefully the Bible as the 'Book of Development,' we come to see how marvellously each step of the march of civilisation and general progress—brought about always, humanly speaking, by the faithfulness of a small body of men working for the good of the whole circle!—prior to the Incarnation and Atonement was a leading up to this point. We see man walking with GOD :—growing slowly according to the Divine scheme, advancing with many a halting step, faint, stumbling, then driven on again by the pain of his stumble, learning wisdom, reaping experience, making his ventures, winning successes, developing in intellect, expanding in morality, sometimes rebelling and murmuring, then instructed again by the happening of the way—towards Jerusalem! We see GOD ever revealing more and more of Himself and His great Purpose as man's capacity for perception and reception increased. We see the opening out of the Law of Righteousness, the illumination of Justice beneath the light of Love, in exact proportion to the clearing of man's mental and moral vision. Then we come to the supreme moment of the Incarnation!

THE MAN OF SORROWS

PEOPLE, as we know, wonder sometimes at the length of time that was allowed by GOD to elapse before He revealed and vindicated Himself as Love Incarnate: wonder why countless generations of men should have lived and died in darkness when light might have been given to them. But those countless generations of men did not live and die in veritable darkness. They had as much light as their eyes were able to behold, and this light pointed ever to Calvary. They suffered, but they suffered always in anticipatory—though perhaps it were unconscious—union with the Christ, the Saviour of the sinful world. There was never a life untouched by Christ: never a life, therefore, lived beyond the pale of Calvary. The whole of humanity was gathered into the Divine Arms outstretched on the Cross, and its great mystery of suffering was pierced by the bright rays from the Cross.

And Christ came in the 'fulness of time.' He came as soon as He might come. The world was not ready for Him before. The march of progress had not gone forward enough. 'The Record of Sorrow' was in too initial a stage: the heart of pain had not throbbed sufficiently long in the world for that world to be capable of understanding how truly it beat with the great Heart of Love. Man had to go further along his little *viâ dolorosa*, offering up his constant sacrifices, before he could at all apprehend the meaning and the end of the way and the offerings. He had, through not merely one generation, but many generations, to draw into his life the complex law of suffering and sacrifice ere he could understand why Christ must come, and how and to what purpose His Sacrifice was being made. We are too apt to lose out of sight the significance of that length of time which preceded the Incarnation. We forget that the whole of the Old Testament, from the book of Genesis to that of the prophet Malachi, is but a record of man's emergence from a state of primitive barbarism, both of life and conduct—by the experience of illuminative (and punitive) pain and sorrow, by the offering up of innumerable faithful sacrifices for his sin and shortcoming—*towards* that condition in which alone GOD could 'tabernacle' with him :—could at all be revealed in His Perfect Love.

It is an account of human development under Divine guidance in the direction of a Divine end :—a description of how GOD led His people on towards a plane where He might meet them Face to face, clothed in the flesh in which they were clothed, living the life that they were living (according to its conditions, that is). It was primitive man growing slowly to the acquisition of his forfeited, yet so lovingly preserved, Ideal : driven, spurred on, by the pain that hurt him—the 'spike of human progress and a loftier, truer way';—and by the continued sense of necessity for offering sacrifices willingly in expiation of his wrong-doing, and as a form of thanksgiving to, and worship of, GOD:—a means of union with the GOD of his being. 'The Lamb was verily fore-ordained before the foundation of the world; and Redemption was the Keynote of Creation.'[1] And we see, in the Old Testament, man advancing towards the moment when GOD could reveal His Purpose in Creation, and show to him the height to which he might aspire, and by what means he could attain to the perfection of living thus made manifest.

And, though the physical world, as the sphere of man's living and the appointed 'theatre' of his redemption, was capable of receiving the Incarnate GOD, yet it had to pass through certain preparatory phases before this might be. Relatively with the man inhabiting it, its advance of development had to go on, its boundaries to enlarge, its artificial chaos to be restored to something of that calm regularity and peaceful order which it was destined to realise in the purpose, and by the mode of, its Creation, in the Mind of GOD. It was then, like man, embarked on a unitive way, and could both receive and retain, and spread around, the marks of its new consecration:—the signs of an ideal destiny conceived in the eternal Thought of GOD.

It has been said that the Holy Scriptures 'stand alone among ancient literature in presenting the idea of gradual progress, gradual education, movement onwards

[1] Dr. Hugh Macmillan.

to a climax.'[1] And truly there we are able to view man and the world in which he dwells as advancing certainly towards a preconceived, pre-ordained end, and on special lines laid down, yet always very 'gradually,' and not with uniform purpose and progress. And it becomes quite clear to our perceptions, enlightened as these are by a greater progress in the knowledge and love of GOD, that although suffering and the offering of sacrifice were appointed by GOD as the unitive way, this way was not preserved and maintained in its purity and directness by man, but was perverted and diverted from, and made to seem almost a parody of GOD's original plan, by the moral obliqueness of human vision and by the corruption of the human heart and life. The account of the progress of man and the development of the sphere of his living, presented to us in the Holy Scriptures, reveals him to us as errant, captious, wilful often against GOD; and thus hindering his own advance and that realised condition of things in which the clouds that had overhung the march of progress and darkened the onward way might be pierced through, and ultimately dissolved, by the Sun of Righteousness.

Clouds had, undoubtedly, overhung, and shed gloom upon, the path of man's and the world's advance. Prior to the Incarnation, the Mystery of Pain had been oppressive to the men walking beneath its shade. Men's hearts had fainted within them; and, though the range of their capacity, the development and gradual enlightenment to some degree of their spiritual power

[1] Canon Gore.

and vision, were increased and intensified, this did not take place with sufficient rapidity to enable them to see through the folds of the veil to the great Divine truth and reality beyond. The course of progress was impeded and retarded, both by wilful error and by the involuntary error of man's vision impaired by his Fall. It was a development hindered in a twofold manner by man himself, and only going forward by the omnipotent grace of GOD towards a right consummation.

Then came the drawing aside the veil of the oppressive Mystery; and the pain under which the whole world, the realm of GOD's personalities, had groaned was seen to have been the 'very beating' of that Heart of Love Which had sought man, and guided and led him, throughout the whole of his suffering course.

GOD had been indeed misunderstood, even as He had been maligned in the life of His people. He had been misunderstood through all the ages of the world: had been regarded as a hard, stern Master, Who delighted in the bondage and pain of His servants. But now He was to be revealed as Perfect Love, bringing release to the *self*-made captive, grander freedom to the sin-bound will. With infinite patience He had waited till this might be: bearing the wrongs, the injustice, the malice of His people: teaching them, leading them, schooling them for the great revelation of Himself. All the way He had led them: through the desert of their complaining; along the road of captivity, where, by the waters of Babylon, they sat down and wept; past the altars to Baal and Chemosh, before which they would halt and do service; on through the heathen groves where these altars were built, and where they tried to linger; across strange lands, where they turned aside from a straight path and took up their abode with idolaters, eating in their temples, marrying with them, adopting their habit of life. In weariness and sorrow He drew them until they might know 'the things which belonged to their peace'!

And then the Light of the World shone out clearly! Men's feet had carried them away from the path illumined by rays of this Light as they pierced through the clouds above, and only with difficulty had they been brought back to the right path; yet always the Light had shone down, and always GOD had pointed to It. Did a Joash erect an altar to Baal? Then a Gideon arose at GOD's bidding and destroyed it, erecting in its place an Altar whereon might be laid a sacrifice typifying the Light that was to come for men's salvation from error and darkness. GOD was, indeed, never without witness of Himself, and the Advent into the world visibly of Himself as its Saviour and Redeemer was but the complete Light and Revelation of Which there had ever been flashes and adumbrations along the unitive way of sorrow and sadness, which was the decreed path of human progress. Since the dawn of the ideal man had there been cast down from Heaven rays of that Light in Which he was to see the realisation of his ideal: the perfection of life and being for which GOD had made him.

And how did GOD appear? He appeared as a 'Man of Sorrows and acquainted with grief.'

THE MAN OF SORROWS

Christ came as the Palingenesia of the world. He came to give to it a new birth unto righteousness: He came to set right all wrongs, to raise earth to Heaven. He, GOD of GOD, Light of Light, was the Climax of the human race, the perfect Representative of a race, self-perverted from right then, but destined by the Love and Power of GOD for a condition of absolute perfection. And, standing there, the Link between two worlds, GOD, yet Man, He held forth to every man who should be born after Him the pattern of his life. Burdened He was with suffering, afflicted, smitten with grief, bruised, stricken, tortured with agony, yet so holy that, as has been said, men have tried to expunge Him from history, lest, having given credence to the fact of His Life, they should feel called upon to submit themselves to the might and influence of such a Life.

He was, at all periods of His perfect Life, 'a wonder, a portent, an enigma,' yet entirely human and natural, fitting into the place designed for Him, coming as the Climax of Humanity: Incarnate GOD, representative Man, holding sorrow and suffering within Him, perpetuating by His own Supreme Life and offering the great Law of Sacrifice, pointing backward and forward, saying: 'Look on Me, and ye shall be saved.' Be ye holy as I am holy—I will *make* you holy.

The Centre of the world, the Link between earth and Heaven, the past and the future: the seen Climax of Humanity! And He is known as *the* 'Man of Sorrows!' How great reflections are these!

THE OFFERED SACRIFICE

IN the Person of Him Who was truly the Man of Sorrows, pain—suffering of all kinds—became a Divine thing. If in the ages preceding the Incarnation, the Life and Death, of Christ the GOD-Man, pain could conceivably have been regarded as of the mystery of evil wholly, as Satan's agent and not GOD's, such a method of regard were now an absolute impossibility. As a matter of fact, pain never was of the mystery of evil wholly, never was Satan's agent and not GOD's. Even if it be not held that pain would have been a factor in the general economy and progress of the world had man not retrograded by his own choice of action, fallen from his religious and moral integrity of being, the experience of life and the study of past ages reveal surely as a fact the value of suffering, and point to a belief in its being GOD's Best for His people: His circle of personalities acting and reacting one upon another, interchangeably, interdependently. And in His Incarnation and Sacrificial Oblation of Himself GOD made pain absolutely His Own. He held it to His Heart, bore it in His Bosom, lived with it, died in it; and then gave it forth again to man to be held and borne after Him in union with Him, to be loved by

THE OFFERED SACRIFICE 109

him, reverenced and cherished, as being essentially indeed the 'very beating of the Heart of Love' for him.

> '... Thine arrows stick fast in me,
> And Thy Hand presseth me sore.
> There is no soundness in my flesh because
>   of thine indignation;
> Neither is there any health in my bones
>   because of my sin.
> For mine iniquities are gone over mine head:
> As an heavy burden they are too heavy for me.'[1]

That cry preceded Christ's Advent, and only found its answer in the Divine Life and Being, and the Divine Sacrifice.

But the history and the method of man's progress seem clearly to imply, as has been already said, that, independently of the Fall, each step of man would have led him to that moment when GOD would come to tabernacle in his flesh and dwell with him for a time, and leave behind Him a Means of constant communion with, and *participation in*, Him, in order that there might be perfect affinity between GOD and man. And it seems reasonable to believe that death of some sort would have been the natural end of Christ's earthly life—For death, the early theologians tell us, is, by the very nature of man's physical being, an inevitable law of that being, and GOD in taking human flesh upon Him would be submitting Himself—or the Bodily part of Him—to this law. It is only that death as it is known to us in our present state is not man's natural, inevitable dying, but is the natural and inevitable penal result of the sin of man. S. Augustine, in par-

[1] Psalm xxxviii. 2-5, R.V.

ticular, stated unmistakably the inevitableness of some sort of death as being the natural passage from one state to another state, but represented it as being quite other than what we now mean by the word. But, however we may view this question, the Death of Christ, even as His Incarnation and His Life, was affected, necessitated thus, by the need of fallen man for restitution to the transgressed Law of Righteousness, and his redemption from the power of that evil which he had made his by law, and so by nature.

'I see another law,' said the Apostle of later days, 'in my members, warring against the law of my mind, and bringing me into captivity to the law of sin which is in my members.' But he thanks GOD through Jesus Christ, in Whom, as he knows, has been wrought the deliverance whereby he is able in some measure to serve the law of GOD. 'So then,' he goes on, 'with the mind I myself serve the law of GOD, but with the flesh the law of sin.'

And this expresses in a figure the distinction between death with its sting removed by the Sacrificial Death of Christ, and death as it was to fallen man before Christ came. 'Death'—penal death—'hath no more dominion' over us, for Christ has triumphed over it. We must all die—even as a punishment it is not remitted to us—but Christ has borne the punishment with us in His Own Being, and therefore, though in one sense it continues with us, and to a certain extent triumphs over us, yet in another and a higher sense it is 'abolished,' and the ultimate victory is ours—'through Jesus Christ.'

'The Death of Christ,' it has been said, 'is, in the first place, to be regarded as propitiatory. On the one hand there is man's desire, natural and almost instinctive, to make expiation for his guilt; on the other there is the tremendous fact of the wrath of GOD against sin. The Death of Christ is the expiation for those past sins which have laid the burden of guilt upon the human soul, and it is also the propitiation of the wrath of GOD. As we have seen, over against the sense of sin and of liability to the Divine wrath there has always existed the idea of sacrifice by which that wrath might be averted. Man could not offer an acceptable sacrifice; it has been offered for him by Christ.'[1]

And the passage is a brief exposition of the meaning of the Atonement effected by Christ in His Death, and leads the way to a loving and tender recognition of the Incarnation as being not only the Loving-Sacrifice of a loving GOD for the supreme good of man, but also the means of reconciling man with the transgressed Law of Righteousness—the only possible conciliation of the then antagonism in man's being, and the restoration of harmony between GOD and the man, errant and sinful, yet created from, and by, Him. Man had done despite to the law of his own being in that transgression of the great Law of Righteousness which was for the right government of the world of which he was a member. There was a double anarchy, and it was into the midst of this anarchy that Christ stepped :—GOD descended from heaven to bring about peace and harmony of life

[1] Rev. and Hon. Arthur Lyttelton.

and being. 'GOD was in Christ,' the Apostle tells us, 'reconciling the world unto Himself.' The wrong done by man had been against the GOD of his being, for the Law of Righteousness was GOD's Law. Yet GOD came to pay the penalty of the breach made. He Who knew no sin was made sin for us, 'that we might be made the righteouness of God in Him.' GOD, as 'Christ,' stepped into the breach of man's making, and assumed his sin, in order that He might justly pay the penalty of it: not remitting to man the natural consequences of his sin, but enabling him by close union with Himself, the Sacrifice, to offer perpetually a sacrifice that could be accepted of GOD, and could avail for the ultimate obliteration of the sin.

None but He Who represented—and indeed actually was—GOD and Perfect Man (though clothed then in flesh weakened by man—not in His case contaminated) could have brought about complete harmony between the Divine and the human, GOD the Creator and man the created. None but He, wholly Perfect, could offer perfect restitution and satisfaction; for the perfection of the Law required a perfect offering. The only Sacrifice that could obliterate man's guilt, and enable him to appropriate to himself the privilege and the power of offering acceptable restitution to GOD, was the Sacrifice of GOD-Incarnate. In Christ alone could alienated man meet, and be welded to, the GOD Whose Arms had, nevertheless—despite his wrong-doing, that is,—ever been open to receive him. GOD was not angry with man as man counts anger, but man's sin had induced that wrath of GOD which is a part of His perfect Justice, and even, of necessity, a part of His Love. The transgression of the Law of Righteousness had been bad for man in every possible way: its consequences were far more widely reaching than man himself could conceive. Man in transgressing the Law had made himself essentially *apart from*, set over against, GOD; and in GOD alone lay the possibility of his realising perfection and bliss of being.

So Christ was born and lived, and died the Death of the Cross: so He drew pained, suffering Humanity to His Bosom, and stilled and transformed the pain and suffering under which the human race was groaning.

We talk so erringly and unadvisedly of the wrath of GOD, as though it were the same pitiful travesty of just and holy wrath that ours is. We do not realise how different GOD's so-called 'anger' is from our own ebullitions of small temper. GOD's wrath, GOD's anger, is remote from all this as the Heavens are remote from the earth. Nay, this is indeed not a true figure:—GOD's wrath cannot be measured nor typified:—GOD's anger is remote from all human thought and conjecture, impossible to represent by any metaphor. His wrath, His anger, even as the Justice which is the cause, is simply and absolutely inseparable from His Love. It has to be viewed as being bound up with, and as participating in, the general perfection of His Being—that Being wronged and sinned against by man's action—; and, in demanding restitution for the wrong done to His Perfect Being, GOD was but declaring and revealing the quality of His

Love, which could not be satisfied with anything short of man's perfection. And man could not know perfection so long as there was that rent in the seamless robe of his nature, caused by his transgression of the Law of Righteousness and his consequent apartness from GOD. He must once more be made in consonance with the Law.

And so GOD came to earth :—came to offer the one Perfect Sacrifice that could be offered, in Man, for Man. And by this Sacrifice Man was placed alongside of Him, and recovered his 'lost principle of cohesion and order.' GOD's Arms had ever been open to receive the human nature again into their embrace, but so long as that nature was in opposition and antagonism to His Own this could not be. The Divine Forgiveness was ever held out for the human sin, but when the sinner was turned from GOD the Forgiveness could not be received. Man's being was closed against all reception of Forgiveness because it was in a state of enmity against GOD's Being, and he could only become susceptible of pardon by an offering of his whole being in a condition of perfectedness :—that is, in a state corresponding to, and in complete alliance with, the Law of Righteousness which he had broken. And in his imperfection and disintegration of life and being man was not able to make such an offering. Thus it behoved GOD in His Infinite Love to repair the breach for him, and so fulfil all righteousness in his behalf.

Man had sinned, and was alienated from GOD : GOD would rectify the sin and draw man to Himself. Man had broken the law of creaturely perfection impressed upon his being by GOD, and the great Law of Righteousness, of which this law was an integral part, must be satisfied: else would the fading, languishing life of man drag on a weary existence apart from GOD.

GOD came to satisfy the claims of perfect Justice and Right bound up with the great Law, and to give to the fading, languishing life a new germ of perfection:—to re-give the original touch of 'goodness' placed in man's heart by Him, and surround it with an accretion of perfection. Man had put out the arms of his freedom and called to evil to be his, and evil had come to him and been held to his bosom. GOD came to unlock those arms, and not only draw, but hold, man to His Own Bosom, so that he might receive a new freedom and a new strength to use the freedom rightly. It was the second distinct movement of Divine Love for man's perfection of being. It was Love working still for the realisation of that Ideal conceived before the birth of actual man; and, as at the first, it issued in the immanence of Himself into that which was chaotic, that cosmos might fully be realised. It had all been one vast Scheme of Love. Man's first freedom had been given to him that he might draw near to GOD, and in GOD find perfection of life and being. And though he used his freedom wrongly, GOD's Heart was not turned from him, but was ever the same, yearning over him, and longing for him with an intensity no human heart can fathom. Always was GOD seeking the love and devotion of man, and this for the man's own good.

Always was the Divine Forgiveness ready for human recusancy and disloyalty: always were His Arms open to receive man. But the sin lay at man's bosom, and closed the door of his heart!

So the man must die, and the death must be a perfect death. He must die for his sin, and that the evil clutched so firmly to his breast might lose its vital power of obstruction in the way of his union with GOD. Until this was done man himself was as one dead in trespasses and sins, and the GOD of his original being was not his.

There must not only be a Perfect Life lived in human flesh, but also a Perfect Death died in that flesh. And so Calvary and the Cross were reared for Man to die thereon. The Hill of Shame and the Sign of Disgrace had to be, that Man might expiate his fault, his awful transgression of the Law which meant his safety. Man alone, man as he was then, in his fallen state, could not hang thereon, but GOD would do it for him, dying as Man, pure and holy, the Representative and the Offering of the entire human race. There, in perfect obedience to, and accordance with, the great Law, He would die the death of the sinner, that the body of evil lying at man's bosom might be slain, and man be at one with his Maker. There, in His Cross and Passion, would the GOD-Man hold up the body of sin and the body of evil, a willing sacrifice by the virtue and merit of His Own pure willing Offering. There would He, as Man with GOD, offer the only Pure Offering that could be, the only possible Means of reconciliation between the Law transgressed and man the transgressor.

Christ was truly the Forgiveness of the Law, broken by man's disobedience; inasmuch as the Sacrifice of Christ was not merely the perfect confession made by man of guilt, and an acknowledgment by him of the Justice of GOD in requiring expiation of the guilt, but also the actual, positive, sufficient expiation required, and thus the removal of all obstruction in the path leading to man's heart and soul of GOD's Pardon. The 'Lo, I am come to do Thy Will, O GOD,' and the doing of that Will, were 'a perfect Amen on the part of Humanity to the judgment of GOD on the sin of man.' The Cross was GOD's judgment of the world: the Death on the Cross was at once the recognition and acquiescence of the world in the justice of the sentence passed upon it and the payment of the penalty demanded of it.

Thus Forgiveness reached man's heart and soul, his whole being; and the harmony of the two worlds was restored.

ATONEMENT

Now, with the peace between GOD and man, were Heaven and earth at one. And by reason of the union of the Divine and the human in the Person of Christ the God-Man, spirit and matter became allied in that perfection of unity which was the destined condition of man's living, and which is to be for ever and ever wrought out and completed in us by the action of Christ in our lives: by actual communion with, and participation in, His Life:—The Fruit of the Incarnation and Atonement.

For the Sacrifice offered by Christ—that Sacrificial Atonement of His Life and Death—involves distinct movement and acceptance on our part-: involves self-identification with, and appropriation of, Its benefits. Only thus can the end for which GOD created us be fully ensured. 'Our race was created for conscious fellowship with GOD, for sonship, for the life of spirit.' But, although Christ lived and died that we might recover our forfeited possibility of fellowship, and receive still greater power of fellowship, with GOD, there is co-operation required of us in His action: as there had been at man's creation co-operation in Divine action required.

And as, in this later Divine action, a far higher work was effected than man's creation had been, so the demand for human co-operation will be more considerable, more widely extended. 'As the Lord in putting on the body became Man, so we men are made gods by the Word, being taken into Him through His Flesh, and from henceforth inherit life eternal.'[1]

Infinitely more is required of us now that our flesh has been lived in by GOD. A far higher standard of life, of purity and holiness, should be ours than the standard of men to whom the flesh had seemed merely their own, to do with almost as they liked. Christianity makes its appeal to the whole nature and life of man. 'The spirit of man is the seat of his personality,' but there is to be not alone perfection of the spirit but perfection of the body also. From the spirit which we chiefly are goes forth power to produce eventually the harmony of being which was thought of by GOD, and evidenced in the Incarnation, in Which He moved as Perfect Being. But the power of the spirit must be exercised universally in man's nature, else that nature is not, nor can be, perfect according to GOD's design of perfection. And nothing short of this is consistent with our aims as Christians. There must be the gradual appropriation, first throughout the spirit, thence through the universal being of man, of Christ as the re-creative Force of Life. Thus only can the flesh receive its crown of perfectedness.

The world in which we now live is instinct with

[1] S. Athanasius.

Divine Love. The living principle of the marvellous scheme of order and beauty before us, surrounding our daily walk, is this Love. The Life Which evolved all things and beings by the Word sent forth, evolved them from chaos by Love; and this Supreme Force would ever evolve a universal perfection from the chaos in our midst. *But*, there must be co-operation! There must be first the willing passivity and receptivity, and then, when the action of GOD has gone further in the designed work, there must be moral and mental activity. We are in the habit of calling ourselves Christians without any true conception of that to which we are thus binding ourselves. We forget what was the real mission of Christ, the whole purpose of His Advent:—forget what the Incarnation and Atonement involve to us in the realm of our living. Christ came that we might be re-consecrated to GOD, and live a new life. The old life—the life that man lived in the flesh ere Christ came to it—the life that he lived when evil was held to his bosom—is incompatible with a profession of Christianity. Christ came that we might live a 'perfect' life: a life, that is, in harmony with, and making ever more entirely and earnestly for, GOD : a life sustained by, and regulated in accordance with, the 'law of creaturely perfection' impressed upon it by GOD. When GOD became Incarnate He took our nature to Himself and made it His. How holy, then, should this nature be! But man has the power, by wilful disobedience, of alienating his nature from GOD; for man has still a 'free will.' It is only by ready, humble co-operation in Divine Agency that his received sanctity and ability unto perfection can be maintained. Man must make Christ's attitude his own. He cannot 'do what he likes with his own life,' as he has so often arrogantly averred. He cannot—may not, that is— do aught but what GOD likes in the matter ; and that means the man's salvation and safety. His life has to be attuned to the Spirit of GOD, Who once resided, and wills ever to reside, in him.

Truly, after the Incarnation and Atonement all sins committed—and repented of—are, if we believe in Christ and His Sacrifice for us, and make His attitude really our own, taken, not as isolated facts unredeemed from their natural evil, but as being involved in His Life and Death, and thus expiated for us by Him and made righteousness unto GOD. Every Christian bowed before the Altar of Righteousness on earth is seen by GOD as being in Christ and of Him. But the point is: What is it to be a Christian? Is it a bare taking upon the lips the Name of Christ? Is it a saying: I believe that Christ lived and died for me, and rose for me, that He might draw me to GOD and bind me to His Heart? Or is it a movement of heart and soul, of will, affection, desire, towards Him? a taking upon one's self the Nature which He created and perfected for us, holding It up before the Father for His glad beholding?

If we place in the light of Christ's Life on earth and His atoning Sacrifice our own daily living, we shall then find how far short it comes of the right standard: how deficient we are in that grace and devotedness

THE SANCTUARY OF SUFFERING

of being which distinguished His Life, how wanting in that willing obedience and gentle humility that found ultimate expression in the Death on the Cross, and which therein were held up, not only to be seen of the Father, but by man himself, to be made man's own.

'The Gospel doth not only represent the doctrine of Christ to be believed; but also the Life of Christ to be followed: nor shall any have Him for their Advocate and propitiation but such as are willing to have Him for their pattern and example, to copy out and imitate His humility, patience, purity, benignity, and self-resignation. None shall be benefited by His Death that are unwilling to live His Life.'[1]

And the first step to conscious union with Christ is a submission of the whole moral being to the Will of GOD: an utterance, above all else, to this effect: 'I will *suffer* what I ought!'

S. Paul thanked GOD through Jesus Christ for his known deliverance from the thraldom and slavery of sin, and upheld ever the beauty and glory of Suffering and Sacrifice: seeing in these a perpetual reminder of, and a means of union with, the Suffering and Sacrifice on Calvary. 'I thank GOD through Jesus Christ' meant with him a recognition and acceptance of the privilege of suffering with Him and of offering sacrifice to Him. And it further meant the oblation of heart, soul, mind, in union with Christ, on Calvary first, and then on the Altars set up in commemoration, and for a continu-

[1] Dr. Worthington.

ance and presentment, of the Sacrifice offered on Calvary, once for the sin and the sake of man, always for the sin and the sake of man. In Christ he saw himself reaching, growing to, Perfection, through the more than recovered 'lost principle of cohesion and order' within him, and reaching it, growing to it, by means of continued union with the Christ Who had *suffered* for him, even to Death, that he might live. Offering to GOD his sins and shortcomings ever in union with the One Pure Offering held up for his sanctification and salvation, he knew himself to be accepted of GOD; and, in the life that he was enabled to live by the communicated power of Christ's Endless Life within him, knew himself also to be verily 'a supplementary Gospel of the Incarnation' and a visible glorification of Pain: a vindicator of the genuineness of its union with Love!

'The great Vine left its glory to reign as Forest King.
"Nay," quoth the lofty forest trees, "we will not have this thing;
We will not have this supple one enring us with its ring.
Lo, from immemorial time our might towers shadowing:
Not we were born to curve and droop, not we to climb and cling:
We buffet back the buffeting wind, tough to its buffeting:
We screen great beasts, the wild fowl build in our heads and sing,
Every bird of every feather from off our tops takes wing:
I a king, and thou a king, and what king shall be our king?"

Nevertheless the great Vine stooped to be the Forest King,
While the forest swayed and murmured like seas that are tempesting:
Stooped and drooped with thousand tendrils in thirsty languishing;
Bowed to earth and lay on earth for earth's replenishing;
Put off sweetness, tasted bitterness, endured time's fashioning;

Put off life and put on death : and lo ! it was all to bring
All its fellows down to a death which hath lost the sting,
All its fellows up to a Life in endless triumphing,—
I a king, and thou a king, and this King to be our King.'[1]

GOD had, indeed, worked for man's perfect good throughout all ages; though it were to most men—to men generally—an incomprehensible way. And always He had pointed and led the advance to Calvary that it might be as the Climax of Suffering and Sacrifice : the explanation in some measure of the world's riddle, the 'Mystery of Pain.' Many had seen Calvary vaguely outlined. Most had looked for the Messiah. Yet all had failed to think of GOD as purely, wholly, Perfect Love. David, the sweet Psalmist of Israel—the chief of the Psalmists—had sung of Him with tender and thrilling devotion, had addressed Him with passionate emotion, as seeing Him differently from the way in which His 'enemies' saw Him. Others had sung praises to Him : Prophets and Seers had magnified His Name and told of marvellous things that should be on the earth and in the heavens. Yet, none knew Him as He is, and as He revealed Himself on Calvary to be. None knew Him as His Incarnation and His daily living in the flesh had displayed Him :—the tenderest, most loving of all men, that is ; the readiest to heal, to comfort, to assuage suffering where this might be, the strongest to bear suffering both in Himself and for others, where the suffering meant the needed good of man. None knew Him thus : yet all previous life and

[1] Christina Rossetti.

ordering of life had led to this revelation and declaration of His Nature. Even His 'wrath'—that which was, as we know, a part of Love—led to the Sacrifice of Himself, the complete expression of His Love. He hated the sin, but loved the sinner ever; though with a Love that the sinner could not comprehend. He could not, loving the sinner, tolerate in him any blemish, or any shortcoming of the perfection and happiness of being that might be his: He must love him unto absolute perfection. Therefore must He draw the sinner and his sin, and above all his suffering and need of sacrifice, unto Himself, and then give forth for him His Own Nature and Being, and the Suffering and Sacrifice perfected. Else could the man never know perfection.

'GOD was in Christ reconciling the world to Himself.' Christ came to draw the estranged hearts of men to the One Great Heart That had yearned over them through all ages of the world. He came to be the Salvation of human life, the Re-Consecrator of the world. He was made Man, associated with men, lived a life bound about by, and subject to, all the laws of which and to which man is bound about and subject; that, triumphing over, and crushing, the power of evil under whose sway and thraldom man then was lying, the whole human race might be lifted to the Bosom of the Father, of Whom He was. He was made a little Child that even the hearts of little children might be Deified: He consorted with 'publicans and sinners' in order that the blackness of sin might be light in Him. He did all things, went along all ways, so that nought could be unknown to Him, outside nor beyond Him. He saved us by His Life, not merely by His Death. He drew us to Him as He walked in the streets of Jerusalem; as He raised the widow's son; as He sat by the well and rested, weary with the burden and heat of the day; as He held the little child in His Arms, and said: Be ye like unto it; as He fed the multitudes, healed the sick, comforted the sorrowful, pitied the weak, cured pain where He might cure it, bore it when He might not—and, ah! yes, as at the end of a hard day spent in toil and grief for others, He went into a place apart, and, kneeling before the GOD of the heavens Whose stars looked down in blessing on the earth, cried all night that the earth might be, even as the heavens, GOD's Own holy kingdom.

This lonely Figure kneeling in prayer to the Father was the Form of GOD Himself! He Who taught His followers to say: 'Our Father Which art in heaven,' praying Himself to the Father, was but continuing the work of Love that had ever been going on for men at His Own Hands! He went about in all things like unto what He would have us be. He lived His Life truly, even as He died His Death, for us. He, going about, bearing the burdens of others—either for them or *with* them,—suffering their infirmities, subject to human laws, bound by human limitations, was GOD, though Man; and, whilst transcending all by the greatness of His Being, conscious of the GOD-head within Him, conscious of His Oneness with the Father, yet prayed and lived and died for us, leaving His Spirit to be the Supreme Rule of our life. 'I came not to do Mine Own Will' [simply, that is] 'but the Will of the Father.' 'My Father worketh hitherto, and I work'— 'The works that ye see Me do are of the Father.' 'I and My Father are One.'

Christ was the Saviour and the Sacrifice of and for men. He was the Lamb appointed to be slain. But oh! how much beyond these things was He, too! He was as the Life of the world, the Light of the world; the Means whereby new life might be given, new light be shed. He lived a Life of pure Sacrifice:—offered up a Perfect Life in the flesh that all flesh might be brought into union with GOD, that men might ultimately be redeemed and delivered wholly from their base slavery of corruption, and be brought into the glorious liberty of the sons of GOD :—that each man might one day look fearlessly into the gaze of GOD, and say, I am Thine; utterly and entirely Thine!

The Death on the Cross has indeed great import for us, but we must not forget the power and efficacy of the Life of Christ. His Life truly was an Offering for us, even as His Death was an Offering. That Holy Life lived in man's flesh was as essential to our salvation as was the Holy Death died in the flesh. The Atonement wrought for us by our Blessed Lord was not, could not have been, wrought unless Calvary had been led up to by a daily living and walking on this earth of man's preparatory discipline. The end of the Life was the culmination of a series of events, each bearing within it elements of tragic solemnity, and pointing to Calvary. The Life was part of the ordained Sacrifice for man (and was, we feel, of the eternal ordinance of GOD for man's full development into perfection):—In it the human flesh received its redemption. And the Death did but consolidate, as it were, and complete, the Scheme of the Incarnation devised in man's interest by the GOD he had wronged. This was the passage to that true Life which was to result from the Scheme of the Incarnation.

In His Death Christ held up to the Father a perfected Humanity, and in this completion of the Scheme of His Life on earth in human flesh, made it possible for man to receive into his being the holy Means of perfect living, not merely in spirit but in the flesh, too. Communicated grace of being was thence to flow into the dual nature of man, that man might meet his power of perfection and be GOD's entirely. In this truth lies the real justification of the phraseology by which we imply that the Death on the Cross was the *completion* of the Scheme of the Incarnation. On that great Altar He died that man might fully live. It was the One Pure Offering to Which all previous offerings had pointed and led up: It was the culmination of His Personal Life of Sacrifice; but, beyond this, It was the culmination of all lives of sacrifice:—all lives, that is, of willing suffering and glad holding up of Divinely ordered sacrifices on lesser altars in GOD's Name. It was the crowning of the reconciliation of man to His Maker, the path to man's recovery from the effects of his own wrong-doing. But we must not, surely, go further than to describe It as 'a path' to this recovery.

Christ offered a representative Sacrifice. He lived a Perfect Life and crowned it with a Perfect Death. But what does all this really mean to us? Is there nothing more? nothing entailed on us?

We may not resolve this great Scheme of Love into a supreme manifestation and expression of GOD's Will for us without examining somewhat the nature of true love, and so learning the bearing that this manifestation and expression of GOD's Love has on our own selves. We regard the Love of GOD, as we regard the love of man :—with no apprehension of the reality of its nature, the mode of its action, the purpose of its being. Possibly we are a little afraid of going deeply into the subject, lest there should come to us a revelation that would be unwelcome. We shrink from fathoming the depths— or attempting to fathom the depths—of love, because on the surface it is so fair and beautiful, and accords so tenderly with our sense of pleasure as the *summum bonum* of our desires! It is such a restful thing viewed thus, and we do not wish to disturb the calm, soothed feelings that then are ours.

And all this shows that deep in the heart of each of us lies the unbidden consciousness that the whole meaning—the action, the being of love is pain: that love can neither be revealed, accepted, nor known without pain: that pain, working ever in the world as it has and will do, is the 'very beating of the Heart of Love' —that if the Incarnation, Life, Death, of Jesus Christ were a perfect revelation of Love, so also were they a perfect revelation of pain, and the involved necessity of pain, in the economy of GOD's world. There can be no love unless there be pain : there can be no union with, nor partaking of, love without the pain that leads *compulsorily* to sacrifice.

And herein lies the great meaning to us of the Sacrifice of Christ for us. We must suffer: we must offer sacrifice. There can be no approaching GOD truly without the sting of that suffering which is of Him: there can be no union with, nor partaking of, Him without sacrifice. And in this case of GOD with man, the sacrifice must be not merely of oneself, but of oneself in and by Him.

A perfect manifestation of Love : a perfect expression of the nature of Love !—an involved Sacrifice !—this is what At-one-ment truly signifies.

' He came to seek in the grotto of Bethlehem for the love of little children, in Egypt for the exile from fatherland, in the workshop of Nazareth for the labouring man, in the desert for the solitary, in the crowd for the busy traffickers, in the temple for the priest, in the synagogue for the student, by the seaside on the grassy flats for the hungry, on the shore to which the disappointed fishers drew their empty nets, for hearts heavy with failure ; at the marriage feast for the light-spirited, by the gate of Nain for the bereaved, on the mountain-top for the ascetic, by the well for the weary, in the garden for the agonised soul, in the palace for the calumniated and misunderstood, on the pavement for those whom men deride and maltreat, on the stairs for those whom men reject with contumely, on the Cross for those in acute bodily suffering, in death for those at their last gasp.'[1]

And all the while was there a visible glorification of pain and suffering, as being bound up with the very law and nature of Love.

'Union is the term of love.' How shall union here be effected? Through Sacrifice.

Christ has lived and suffered and died for us. And He has left us a Means of union with Him.

With the Incarnation there came into the world a new Life, and a new Power whereby man might be made wholly GOD's, one absolutely with Him. It is the Life of Christ, the GOD-Man, perfect in righteousness. This Endless Life was offered finally on Calvary in Death, that It might be for ever on earth communicated to us, until, by Its Power, we shall have been assimilated entirely into perfect Beauty. Christ came to this world to leaven all unto righteousness; and He left us the sure Means of its accomplishment.

[1] Rev. S. Baring-Gould.

IV
'CALLED TO BE SAINTS'

'CALLED TO BE SAINTS'

'GOD has come into our life, and taken us up with Him, and called upon us to follow Him in the way of the Cross.'[1]

This is what 'called to be saints' means. And we are all called to be saints. Life is to be ever a course of suffering, either directly or indirectly: the endurance of the Cross must always be, whether it lie actually on our own shoulders or hurt us through the pressure of it that is so heavy on other shoulders. It must be a gradual growth and development in the fire and flame of pain.

Christ is truly the Answer to all the spiritual longings and questionings which have ever gone forth, or ever will go forth, from man. In Him, not only was man reconciled to GOD and enabled to see in GOD the true end of all living, but in Him also was, and is to be, given out, and taken from, the Means which shall lead to this End.

Throughout the early ages had there been prefiguring of the Sacrifice whereby man should meet his true Ideal and be made the perfection of GOD. All history antecedent to the moment of the Incarnation had

[1] Rev. and Hon. Arthur Lyttelton.

pointed to the meeting of the human race with its one Supreme Ideal; and the history of the succeeding times points back to that Ideal and onwards to man's gradual appropriation of, and growth into, the Ideal.

Life still 'a course of suffering'? Yes, but it leads to Christ. Not uniform nor consistent may the advance of man be: yet ever the march of men goes on.

'We believe that every man ought to be a temple of GOD,' said Mazzini; and in the temple must there be a Holy of holies, wherein Christ can be offered anew to the Father.

But this can only come through suffering.

'All pain, sickness, weariness, distress, languor, agony of mind or body, whether in ourselves or others, is to be treated reverently, since in it our Maker's Hand passes over us, fashioning by suffering the imperfect or decayed substance of our souls. In itself it were the earnest of hell; through His Mercy in Christ, it is a purifying for Heaven.'

So said Dr. Pusey, and in his words we see, surely, something of the beauty of that suffering which, at times, whether in ourselves or in others—more especially in others, perhaps—is appalling to us. We must suffer if we would be purified: all must be passed through the cleansing fires of affliction and pain before Christ can be really brought near, and the fulness of life be reached. Without suffering there can be no true and vital union with Christ: without such union with Christ there can be nought surely of 'Heaven' within us —nought therefore of eternal significance and beauty.

We want our lives to be beautiful and Heavenly: they cannot be so without Christ.

> 'Does the road wind up hill all the way?—
>   Yes! to the very end!
> Will the day's journey take the whole long day?—
>   From morn to night, my friend!'[1]

It is, yet, a sublime process, because the 'end' is GOD.

For every person born into the world GOD has, as we have repeatedly said, a distinctive ideal; and this lesser ideal, finding its secret of strength and peculiar power for perfection in The Ideal of the whole of humanity, must be reached by devotion to the Cross on which the great Ideal was shown and held forth. Thus only can we learn to live as GOD would have us live, and the call to be saints means the first summons of our lives in this Divinely appointed direction, to the devised end.

Only we are afraid of the word 'saint.' We shrink with horror from the application of the term to ourselves, and we hardly like to apply it rashly to others.

But why is this? Is there not somewhat of affectation, or at least of misconception of the meaning of the word, in this regard?

The matter is very simple, really. We were called to be saints—if we would but recognise this fact—when we were baptized; when the sign of the Cross was made on our foreheads, signifying the power of the Cross within our hearts, to be worked out and realised in our

[1] Christina Rossetti.

lives. We were called to be saints then, when by the consecration of the Holy Spirit, we were enrolled under Christ's banner to fight manfully against the world, the flesh, the devil. 'The mark of a saint,' Dr. Westcott has told us, 'is not perfection, but consecration.' We were consecrated at that moment to the way of the Cross: were baptized *into* Christ's Death, that fullest life might be attained by us. It was an expansion of that touch of goodness which had been placed originally in man's heart, but which had been so defiled and so encumbered that it needed the water of regeneration to flow over it, in order that it might be cleansed, made free to grow. It was the new touch of Christ, imparting to the soul a power of vitality that should lead to the grace and the fulness of life bestowed by Him on the Cross. It was a new birth unto righteousness: an incorporation into that Body of His, the Church, in which are set forth the Supreme Means of perfection, the Holy Mysteries of Eternal Life.

We received in Baptism an endowment of sainthood, and were started on a way, a holy path, whose end is perfection. We were made members of Christ, heirs of Eternal Life, to be given in and through Christ. His Spirit was born within us then: His Spirit, by Whose power we may, if we will, be enabled to live a life on earth that shall be a perpetual holding up of His Life to the Father in heaven, a perpetual presentment to the world of the glory of the Cross: a message of beauty glorifying that burden of suffering, which, laid on the human race and misunderstood by the human race,

'CALLED TO BE SAINTS'

pointed the way to Calvary, and found its explanation—in chief measure—on Calvary.

We are called to be saints. And we are made saints: —sanctified, blessed, that is, in Christ, and set on a way that leads to perfection of union with Him, in the Blessed Sacrament of the Altar and in Heaven. Yet we would, with horror, affected or otherwise, thrust the word from us, and deny our right to its use! Is there not truly something amiss with us? Are we not, somehow, and in some way, coming short of that simplicity which should distinguish the followers of Christ? Is it not that a great taint of worldliness is clinging to us? Do we not need to cry: Lord, give me the heart of a little child?

Yes, surely, we need to get rid of that hampering artificiality, that lack of childlike simplicity, which stands in our way to sincere holiness and devotion of life.

And how shall we combat the difficulty?—how act that the word 'saint' may come to be simply loved and accepted by us?

We must justify our claim to the title. That is the answer. We must justify and prove our right to it, by patient living as Christ our Master would have us live, in the smoke and fire of that battle against evil in which all hearts should be engaged. We must fight down and destroy the power of every evil inclination, every cowardly intention, within us. We, enrolled under Christ's banner, with the visibly impressed cross on our foreheads, the invisibly laid Cross in our hearts, must wage war against the hosts of evil encompassed about these hearts, and triumph over them in the Name of the Lord, calling Him our King for ever. We must personally earn this title of honour and glory and blessedness, by a faithful warfare in the Divine cause against evil; by partaking first in the shame, the pain, the humiliation, which He experienced when evil seemed to be triumphant, but which received a crown of splendid victory when evil was made to recognise its own weakness and feebleness, and was laid prone beneath the Might of the Cross. We must suffer with Christ if we would be glorified with Him, and we would be glorified with Him because surely He wills it. He has called us to be His soldiers and servants, fighting, working always, for the spread of His kingdom of good. We are set apart, enlisted in His service, anointed into a life that He has taught us how to live and will give us strength to live :—a life possible to any man, appointed for all men, held up before our eyes in the Incarnation, given out to us in the Blessed Fruits of the Incarnation.

In the Church, as has been already pointed out, lie all the needed Means of Grace to enable man to live his life rightly, and to realise the Life of God. The gift of grace bestowed on us in Holy Baptism is the initial movement of the Heavenly life, the will subjected is the member's acceptance of the blessing conferred by the granted entrance and incorporation into the Church which is described as the body of the Lord : these two combined lead on to the Supreme Means of Grace. There is, however, the ensuring of much besides ere we can reach to Christ in His very Real Presence at the Altar of the Church. A temple built unto the Lord are we ourselves to be : a Holy of holies therein is to be erected, an altar of personal sacrifice raised. And this must be a fashioning as by suffering. Patiently must the tools of affliction be permitted to carry on the work within us that Christ may come to dwell within us in abiding Presence.

The yielding of the will to GOD which should be the first conscious step taken by a reasonable human being, already baptized into Christ's Church, should be but the presage of a devoted bearing of all the pain and trial that GOD sends for the development of human life, and which *must* be accepted before Christ can really be accepted. Only thus, eventually, can perfect oneness with Him be ensured. Only then can the whole being be quickened and glorified, so that it shines forth as a supplementary gospel of the Incarnation, and is a true expression of rightly developed sainthood. We, as faithful members of His Body the Church, have to work out the grace given to us in Holy Baptism ere we are fit to approach our Blessed Lord in His Sacramental Presence at the Altar, and to be drawn into, even as we receive, that Divine Presence. And the 'working out' has to be beneath the Shadow of the Cross. That is to say, we are only able gradually to attain to the maturity and perfection of saintliness, given forth by Christ thus, when we have fought and lived as He fought and lived.

Every little disappointment that comes in early days,

therefore, every tiny thwarting of the lower inclination within us, every little trial of faith, patience, love, every petty annoyance, or passing cloud of mortification, shame, grief, should be taken as going towards the building of a complete temple where Christ may come to be apprehended and to abide. Each failure to attain that on which human desire had fixed its gaze, each crossing of the lower mood and temper, should point to the Supreme Satisfaction of all worthy desire, of all right inclination and longing. Such should leave upon the life a mark of glory, should aid in the erection of the complete building for Christ. Beauty and true happiness can, we know, only be secured in Christ: are only realisable by us through self-identification with, and self-oblation to, Him. But to reach Christ we must first suffer—and suffer as little children.

We despise childish sufferings, yet to the child they are great; and they are his preparation and building up for the eventual reception into his life and being of the GOD-Man born as a little Child in the midst of suffering. They are leading—*should* lead—him to the Altar of Divine and human Sacrifice. They are, if one may so express it, an extended Baptism unto and into His Death, Who was the Saviour of little children even as of grown men and women. They, like their Master and King, go towards their crowning in the throes of suffering, and though in their case the trials to us may seem small, in reality they are oftentimes positive agony and torture.

So early is the Cross laid on human life, that the

human life may soon meet Christ, and be drawn into perfect union with Him. It is a gradual subjugation of the human will to the Divine Will of Love, by the saving efficacy of the Cross—which, finding an explanation of its power in saintly living, is yet further extolled as it merges into that crown of rejoicing which should go up to Heaven and forth upon earth from the Altar, as Christ is fully born in man's entire being, and infusing that being, heart and conscience, spirit, mind, and body, with His own true Life-givingness and power of perfection.

We are 'called to be saints'? Yes, called to suffering and to Sacrifice. We are enlisted under His banner, Who was the Man of Sorrows: bound up with the Sacrifice of Him Who died upon the Cross of shame and agony, and bequeathed the offering of Himself there—left It to us to be made our own—in order that we might be His in 'body, soul, and spirit.' Thus and Therein may we be enabled to justify our right to the blessed title of 'Saints.' Thus and Therein will the heart of a little Child be given unto us.

So it is that men are sanctified for Christ: that the advance to right maturity of growth goes forth, and man reaches his true Ideal.

V
THE ENDLESS LIFE

K

THE ENDLESS LIFE

IF we had been blind to the part which pain and suffering played before the Incarnation, in the evolution of man and the general advance of civilisation, we can in the contemplation of the truth of the Incarnation be blind no longer. If we had closed our hearts against the inroad of thoughts and feelings that would show the necessity for, and the greatness of, the burden of pain under which the whole Creation had groaned and travailed since the beginning of all things, we are forced to open them wide in the full light of the Redemption. S. Thomas Aquinas said: 'The Incarnation is the exaltation of human nature and consummation of the universe.' The Incarnation brought into the world the Epiphany—the real explanation—of the nature and the office in the world of pain and suffering. It has taught us that the true beauty of living can only be in the patient endurance, the brave looking into the face, of suffering; the walking all the common days hand in hand, side by side, with suffering. Christ lived a Life of suffering, died a cruel Death of suffering, and held Pain up before the eyes of the world as a holy, glorious thing, by which man might meet GOD, touch Him, be drawn into His Being, breathe His very Breath, live His very Life, love with, and in, His Love. 'I, if I be lifted up,' He said, 'will draw all men unto Me.' And the twofold cord by which He draws us is of Love, is of Pain. These lead the way to Sacrifice as being the only possible satisfaction and right earthly end of man. Love and Pain do ever strive for the mastery over the evil of men's hearts and lives : do ever point to the Altar of Sacrifice, whereon a submitted will may be offered, a submitted life laid. All the days of His Own *pure* Life did the GOD-Man walk, burdened by man's heritage, in the shadow of the Cross : always was His Face set steadily towards the place where His Offering was to be made. And He left us a measure to be filled up! Christ lived and died, loved and suffered, not that our life might be smooth and easy, our death of necessity painless ; but that, living and dying, we might come to know the beauty of love and pain, and learn the direction of its trending :—that our whole heart, soul, being might go forth to Him in self-dedication—Sacrifice,—and that so we might come to understand, and to appropriate, ' the things that belong to our peace.'

It is not enough for us that Christ has lived and died and offered Sacrifice : we must live and die and offer sacrifice—by the laying ourselves within and beside His Sacrifice. It is not enough that He loved and suffered : we must love and suffer too. It must be hand in Hand and heart to Heart! This is what the Atonement means. In one sense the Divine Sacrifice was, as we express it, 'instead of' us ; but in another sense it was for, and with, us. As our Substitute Christ truly offered Himself, but as our Representative also He truly offered Himself. There is to be holy living and dying, loving and suffering, elsewhere than in Himself purely. There is to be our sacrifice, blent with His, and held up to Heaven for acceptance in Him. Ever suffering must go on; ever hearts must be rived and torn; ever must affliction, disease, death, seem to hold sway over the world, that the world may be brought to Christ, and see in Him Salvation and satisfaction.

With the Incarnation there came into the world, as we have said, a new Life, and a new Power whereby Life might be secured. It is the power of His Endless Life, Who laid down that Life in seeming weakness, yet actual Supreme strength, and in this same strength raised It again and bequeathed It for man's eternal benefit:— the Power given forth to us now from His Altar.

Christ came to be the Bread of Life on Which man might ever feed, the Cup of Blessing out of which he might for ever drink. He, the Virgin-born 'Son of Man'—yet ever Son of GOD,—willed to be born again and always on earth, in the hearts and souls of men, that humanity might truly be bound up with Him : that in body as well as in spirit we might grow 'holy unto the Lord,' and divine with something of His Divinity. He would come into our being that the effect wrought— yet always to be wrought out—by His Flesh-taking, and His Life and Death in that Flesh, might be developed in us personally. The Life lived and the Death died were to issue in a new life to be lived, a new death to be died, by Christians. The Body and Blood, offered on Calvary, and held up to the Father, were the completion of a Sacrifice which was in Its Entirety to be offered always—so long as man's need should last—for the salvation and perfection of humanity. It was to continue, an Offering for man's sin, frailty, disallegiance, imperfection, that man might become (by gradual steps) holy, strong, loyal, perfect; and the world be re-consecrated to its Maker. Christ had lived for man in the flesh, and He died in the flesh. And though we may not think of His actual Body being intermingled and incorporated with ours, still His Flesh is incorporated in us; and there takes place in our being such a blending of His Life with ours that we can no longer be thought of as being simply ourselves, but ourselves *with* Him. And this, surely, was the aim chiefly, and the End, of the Incarnation and Death of Christ; and Itself explains the main mystery of that burden of sorrow and pain under which the whole Creation of GOD has groaned for so long a time. Suffering points to Sacrifice:—here is the Sacrifice!

Christ came to earth in the fulness of time:—at the moment, that is, when it was possible for Him to inhabit and appropriate human flesh. He lived and died in that flesh: loved and suffered and worked in it. After His Death in the flesh He rose in it, taking it up to Heaven and presenting it to the Father there. It was then a Perfected Humanity, borne by GOD, to GOD. In this Perfected Humanity Christ ever lives in

Heaven, yet He also walks on earth, though not as of old. He comes in the Blessed Sacrament of the Altar in His Humanity, to living humanity. He takes up and assimilates the spirit and the flesh to which He enters, and there ensues a gradual blending of His Holiness and our sin, until by mysterious process the sin is absorbed as it were, and we are made His and live in Him.

Thus ever are His Life of Suffering and His Death of Suffering constantly offered to and for man. On the great Altar of Calvary this Offering was first held up: on the Altars set up in His Name the Offering—the same Offering—is ever being held up. And the end is universal perfection, and beatitude of glory. The vital mixture of His Body and Blood does indeed confer on man eternal life; and souls and bodies, for which He lived and died in dual being, are crowned with a power of perfection, The Supreme Sacrifice of Himself in the streets and lanes, the houses and the synagogues, even as the lesser sacrifices preceding this, pointed and led the way to the Blessed Sacrament, in Which He should give His slain Body and shed Blood for the strengthening, the refreshment, the cleansing and purification, of man in his fleshly life and being. He came to save man, to give to him a super-natural, super-sensuous power, by means of which he could realise his only appointed end. It is GOD entering human life again, and giving to the flesh its power of redemption. Christ is here, Spiritually present in lowly matter; and He comes to be received into the being of each one of us, that we in spirit and in flesh may be sanctified wholly. It is to be the gradual evolution of a life made possible by the first Advent of Christ.

So Christ comes, and gives us That of Which He thought when, with pierced Hands held up in blessing and sanctification of the earth, He passed to the highest Heaven. He comes so that, bearing about within us the living and the dying, the whole Pure Offering, of Jesus Christ, the Son of GOD yet Son of Man too, we may be made Divine in thought and word and deed, and preach to the world Christ Crucified for our sins, Risen for our realisation of perfection. We are conscious, truly, of new life; and we know it to be the power of His Endless Life which would so work in us as to make of us an energising force for the good of our fellows. A quiver, akin to that tender breath of dawn, which in an Eastern town seems to pass over all things ere the full light and work of the day set in, has passed over our whole being, and blessed and anointed that being for the great work of the day to be outstretched before our gaze. We have received our anointing, and are awake and stirred to new life and power. There, before the Altar, we have laid down our dark burden of sin and trouble, and we start afresh, brave for the happenings of the hours before us. There we had thought of Him as bearing the burdens of all tired way-worn souls, all aching hearts, all painful, agonised bodies. We had seen Him gently lifting them to the Father in Heaven, and presenting them before His Throne, that they might be transformed in the light from that Throne, and glow with the splendour of the Crowned Cross.

A means of complete alliance of spirit and matter, an entire welding of the whole being of earth with the being that is of Heaven :—a perfecting power which shall ultimately bring about the crowning of the imperfect with its full, designed glory of perfect being! There can, truly, be no power like this. There is nothing in the world to which we can point as being even faintly analogous to it: nothing that could in any degree compensate us for the loss of it, or act vicariously for it. It is Christ within us, as we say: moving, quickening, stirring our whole being, 'body, soul, and spirit,' with His Own Life-givingness: causing the chaos of evil within to yield its sovereignty to the reign of Supreme GOOD, in order that, as at the first, a grand cosmos of beauty may be thence evolved. It is another movement of the 'Word' by Whom all things great and glorious were made. By means of the Divine Word a universal development into perfection is to go forth in the being into which a Divine entrance has been made. Not a part of us, merely, is to be irradiated and perfected, but the whole of us; and to this end there must be absolute yielding—silent, calm passivity, as it were—of the being to the Word longing to evolve a perfect development of this being.

Christianity has indeed a universal claim upon us, as she has (and had ever) upon the world in which we 'live, and move, and have our being.' And the claim is exerted, specially and primarily, in the Holy Sacrament of the Altar. All the parts of our nature are to be brought into personal contact with Christ, so that He may leaven them and make them His by Divine right and perfect Goodness. Christ's Goodness is to be the motor of our life. He, Incarnate GOD, Perfect Man, would so assert over our moral and spiritual degeneracy, our physical infirmity, His Own Divine and perfect human strength, that the entire being may grow perfect in Him and realise ultimate bliss of life. The human race, individually first, collectively thence, is to be possessed by GOD: this possession can only result from a personal communion with Him, in which individuals receive strength and power so to live their lives that they may be media of communicated grace to their fellows, singly and corporately. Christ comes to us individually, and He comes in material form. He gives both to the spiritual and the material parts of each one of us that Spiritual sanctification which will enable us to be true lights of our generation—He, Spiritually present in matter, imparts to the spirit and matter of which we are composed true vitality and power. He says, through the mouths of His duly ordained priests: 'This is My Body,' 'This is My Blood': 'Take and eat,' 'Drink,'— And this that we may be cleansed from our sins and be endued with the power of His Life. But why? for what purpose? Only that we may be saved and brought to perfection? That others, too, may be saved and brought to perfection, *through* us, *by* Christ: that there may come about the upheaval of humanity to 'Heaven.' The inter-penetrating power and grace of His Body and Blood are exerted in us, that not only may we be 'holy unto the Lord,' but may also draw, by Him, others to a like reception with ourselves.

'Doth any man doubt,' said Hooker, 'that even from the Flesh of Christ our very bodies do receive that Life Which shall make them glorious at the latter day, and for which they are already accounted parts of His Blessed Body? Our corruptible bodies could never live the life they shall live, were it not that here they are joined with His Body, Which is incorruptible, and that His is in ours as a cause of immortality, a cause by removing, through the Death and merit of His Own Flesh, that which hindered the life of ours. Christ is, therefore, both as GOD and as Man, that true Vine whereof we are the branches. The mixture of His Bodily substance with ours is a thing which the ancient Fathers disclaim. Yet the mixture of His Flesh with ours they speak of, to signify what our very bodies through mystical conjunction receive from that vital efficacy which we know to be in His: and from bodily mixtures they borrow divers similitudes rather to declare the truth, than the manner of coherence between His sacred and the sanctified bodies of saints.'

And as this universal pervasion of Christ may be ours, so may we spread it amongst those near to whom we come in our daily living, so in thought and word and act may we cause the world about us to acknowledge the supremacy of the glorified 'Man' Who was GOD too, and in the Light of Whose complete Being men saw the Heavens *re*-opened to them.

We believe that Christ's local Presence is in Heaven, but that belief in no way conflicts with the sure faith we have in His pervasion of us as individuals, and of the world as a body. It is essential to bear in mind the universal Presence of our Blessed Lord, and His action and reaction on the world. He is, indeed, permeating and leavening us individually, but this process is extended mysteriously beyond the limits of our being into the very heart of the life that is stirring and throbbing about us. He quickens unto gloriousness of life the earthly or corporeal, even as the heavenly and spiritual parts of us; and we are meant to spread abroad His Presence in special manner, bringing to His Feet souls and hearts and bodies for which He died. Truly, for our own sakes are we thus sanctified, but for the good of others also. Our whole nature and being, 'body, soul, and spirit,' are consecrated : only it is to be remembered that the action on the bodily part is maintained by the spirit, and in this we have a faint analogy to that indirect working of the grace of Christ, mediately through us to the body—the corporate whole of whom we are members. Our spiritual being, deriving new life and strength and beauty from the Presence of Christ, passes on these graces to the body with which it is involved: we, as a whole, blessed and sanctified, pass on our blessing and sanctification to that greater body with which, in the providence of GOD, we are mysteriously blent.

It is action and reaction, and though we speak of ourselves in the active voice, there is yet entailed on us a holy passivity, in the midst of which Christ Himself works, for us first, for others afterwards through us. It is Christ's action, really, exerted in, and by means of, a being interpenetrated by His Spirit, and making for the complete regeneration of—in each case—a whole, designed for ultimate perfection. As one day there is to arise from the grave a body perfect with a Divine perfection, so also on that day shall there arise a world perfected; and the graces of each, supplied by Christ, make for the universal completion, the realisation of satisfaction and bliss:—the peculiar content and consummation for which individual men and the world were created.

So, Sunday after Sunday, Holy Day after Holy Day —and sometimes more frequently still,—we kneel down and say:—

Come to me, Blessed Lord. Thou, Who art Life and Love, give to me Thy Life and Love, that Life and Love Which Thou art. Make my coldness warmth; my hardness tenderness. Make me all like Thee, that so I may go forth preaching Thee. Gather my weakness, my infirmity, my sins and imperfections, to Thee, and give them back to me transformed as strength, as power, as holiness. I am not worthy that Thou shouldst come and abide with me, but come, Lord, and so abide.

And then the Fruit of the Incarnation is nourishing our lives, and up to Heaven goes the cry: 'Glory to GOD in the Highest'; and on earth: 'Peace to men of good-will.'

MOVEMENT OF DIVINE LOVE

RELIGION has been described as 'Morality touched by Emotion.' But this, we know, is an utterly unworthy and inadequate description of the marvellous force which has worked ever in our world, and thus working has brought the world towards its regeneration—its at-one-ment with the GOD of its origin.

Religion, indeed, describes an intimate moral relationship existing between GOD and the world created by Him. The Incarnation, therefore, supplies the one true Answer to all questions as to what is Religion. Religion, we there find, is the welding of the human with the Divine. And in the Blessed Sacrament of the Altar we have practical evidence of the nature of that bond which is to maintain the union inaugurated at the moment of GOD's taking unto Himself human flesh in all its weakness. 'The Lord hath laid on Him the iniquity of us all.' When we come to consider, not alone the Incarnation, but also the bearing upon our lives of the Incarnation: when we think, not merely of Christ come, but as Christ continuing, then we have a complete solution of that difficult problem of the nature of the bond which connects the world with

MOVEMENT OF DIVINE LOVE 159

the origin of the world. The world was made that men might attain to perfection: this perfection is alone realisable in GOD: GOD was in Christ reconciling sinners to Himself; but this, we are assured, was not all. GOD was in Christ, further, because, by that mysterious union of the Divine and the human, by the Personal living of GOD upon earth, Heaven was brought down to earth and earth bound to Heaven: and this bond has to be maintained, and is maintained in the Blessed Sacrament, wherein GOD is, for ever on earth, invisibly present. From this issues Religion, for Religion is Christ born in the life and soul of man!

It is interesting to observe that even General Gordon, whom we are accustomed to regard as somewhat of a latitudinarian in his views of Religion—that guiding spirit of his noble life—ever thought of the Blessed Sacrament as the Centre of all holy living. It was impossible to him to conceive of Religion without these Media of Grace. 'Why is the Sacrament neglected?' was his cry.

'There is a glory that shall be revealed in us; and here on earth we may so draw near and take it to ourselves that its quiet incoming tide may more and more pervade our being . . . till we are wholly ruled and gladdened by His Presence.'[1]

Emotion is not, can never be, absent from Religion, because Religion is Love, and growth in and by Love; and Love, we know, were incomplete, a mutilated part of itself, without 'emotion.' The body of all true

[1] Dean Paget.

160   THE SANCTUARY OF SUFFERING

love is the morality which means, and strives for, and *is*, harmony, order, sealing of a unitive purpose to be served by complex agency of life and being; and its soul is that passionate thrill and fervour of being, which expresses itself, and goes forth, in the resolution and appropriation to itself of the object loved, yet is not spent there, but yearns still and always for something beyond, something unattained. It has been said that in Christlike holiness there is an 'element of passion,' which would alone serve to distinguish Christianity from all lesser systems of life :—from those almost numberless forms of philosophical conception, for instance, which try to push their way through the world, and ever fail midway in their endeavour! Such systems are bound to fail, because they have no capacity for satisfaction of the sigh of the spirit which goes forth from men, expressing the yearning of their being for something not yet attained: only promising, with vague alluringness, a satisfaction and completion of a being made for a far higher condition.

Religion is the bond between the higher and the lower which was thought of when 'the holy, the unfathomable, and stainless movement of Divine Love' exerted itself in the formation of a scheme of cosmos out of chaos. We read in relation to the evolution of the universe that GOD projected Himself into 'space,' and that thence issued worlds :—a cosmic result of the movement of Love. 'The " Word " (of Love) went forth and the worlds were made.' And as we consider that gradual evolution of sublime order from dull chaos there is presented to the mind a picture of the natural process resulting from love. Love ever works for the development of the beloved object into that which—varying with, and dependent on, differing and relative conditions—is its own preconceived ideal of that object. We know that this world of ours is instinct with the Divine Love Which is its Possessor: that the living principle of all we see, and hear of, and read about, as throbbing and stirring in its vast area is Love: that the Life, having evolved life and activity from dead inertion by power of Love, moves ever through this Love, in evolution, and eventual development, of order, beauty, perfection. We see the chaotic, the crude, the imperfect, yielding perforce to the power of Love as it works towards this perfection.

And as in the world, so is it in the hearts and lives of men. Love is ever evolving life and order and beauty of being from death, disorder, repulsive error of being. Not alone every part of the universal scheme, but every part also of the scheme in man's own being, is an expression of the constant active power and energising force of Love. 'GOD is a pure Act,' said S. Thomas Aquinas; and this is but another way of saying: 'GOD is Love'— Love, as we know, expressing itself and going forth in a selflessness of devotion which involves constant activity in the behalf of its object: the purity of the action lying in the perfection of the self-sacrificial offering. We look back and see the long process towards perfection, of man and of the sphere which he inhabits; and we are of necessity struck by the wonderful way in which the process worked: but sometimes we fail to give due prominence to the fact that it was all towards Christ! The Divine Love was working ever on self-regulated lines towards a certain end ; and that end the perfection of the object loved :—The lines were drawn from Eden to Calvary, and extend now—extended always in GOD's Thought—to the Altars set up in the Perfect Name of Love! We hear much, nowadays, of the science of ethics, as though it were a system beginning and ending in itself. The word ethics is best regarded as describing a part of GOD's scheme, finding its origin in Him, and resolving itself in a harmony of being, in which the sigh of man is satisfied by that recognising thrill of possession which comes to the heart and soul in the reception of Christ in His Blessed Sacrament.

Christianity makes its appeal to the whole world, and to the entire individual being of men ; and contains within itself full power to satisfy all wants, full power to appropriate to itself every disordered element, and to resolve such elemental disorder into a harmony of perfection. And it stands alone amongst so-called 'Religions,' in its office and in its power to fulfil that office. As Professor Monier Williams has said : ' It is the perfect concentration and embodiment of eternal truth scattered in fragments through other systems—the perfect expression of all the religious cravings and aspirations of the human race since man was first created.' And it is 'emotion,' and it is 'morality': but it is a good deal more than these.

Christianity says ever, in the words of its Founder, 'My son, give Me thine heart,' and how indeed should it be otherwise when Christ is GOD, and GOD is Love? It is Christ knocking at the heart's door with the Hand that was pierced and nailed on Calvary: He is making His appeal to us by right of the Cross, and on the ground of the Cross. He, the glorified 'Man of Sorrows,' comes and claims His right to enter the being that He, as Redeemer, has sanctified unto Himself. The 'Give Me thine heart' means: Lay thyself down in union with My Sacrifice, offered in thy behalf: 'Come, for all things are now ready.'

And if we obey Him, if we go, then we know what Religion is. And we cannot know otherwise.

Religion is simply Christ born in the heart and life of man, and thus infusing the whole yielded being, heart and conscience, soul, spirit, and body, with the marvellous force and beauty of His Own Life, the wondrous tenderness and strength of devotion of His Own Love. It is the allowed assumption of man's nature by GOD, so that that nature may become penetrated by a super-sensuous power, rendering the life of the man a beautiful epitome of the Incarnation, a perpetual holding forth to the world of a spirituality Divine even in its earthly fettering and limitation: Divine with the Divinity of Him Who went about in lowly human form, and Who comes now in still more lowly form, in order that the world may be redeemed, blessed, and resanctified unto perfection. 'I am the Vine,' said He—'Ye are the branches.' Here is Religion. Here is that true relationship which should exist between the Higher and the lower, and which so surely puts to open shame any attempt to describe Religion as 'Morality touched by emotion.'

When GOD became Incarnate He did most surely draw human nature to Himself and make it His. The personal, individual, human nature, however, is not His really until it has been placed in Him (obscure as this phraseology is) by the reception into the whole being of the Divine Flesh-taking, offered in the Blessed Sacrament of the Altar. This follows, in GOD's eternal decrees, by natural sequence, upon the Incarnation and, as we commonly express it, Atonement. As a matter of fact, the Atonement is not complete without the general personal reception within the being of the perfected 'Human Nature' of the GOD-Man. Christ gives Himself then, His Body and His Blood, to man, that man may take into the very heart of his being the Redemption offered on Calvary. Personal redemption and full sanctification are not wholly and truly possessed without this, and it is of GOD's ordinance that it should be so. To accept The Redeemer thus is but a simple co-operation on the part of man in the Divine scheme of his salvation; and in this received sanctity of life and nature man goes forward unto the peculiar perfection designed for him out of the boundless and perfect Love of GOD. Each time that, in lowly faith and humble adoration, we go to receive Christ, a fresh note of harmony is evolved, a fresh link forged between the Higher and the lower, a fresh impetus given to that

MOVEMENT OF DIVINE LOVE 165

throbbing life within, which is of His Life. So does the work unto perfection go forward. 'I am come that ye might have Life, and that ye might have it more abundantly.' 'By Me, if any enter in, he shall be saved, and shall go in and out, and find pasture.'

Ever is the Life thus given to us, and more abundantly as we 'go in and out.' 'Find pasture?' It is the blessed Fruit of the Incarnation. Christ was made sin for us that He might be also made Perfect Salvation for us: He was nailed to the Cross, that the Body there slain and pierced, and the Blood shed, might be for us Eternal Life and Perfection. 'GOD, Who is eternal, incomprehensible, and of infinite power, does great and unsearchable things in Heaven and on earth, and His wonderful ways are past finding out.'[1] But the presentation of Himself in open vision on the Cross, and the invisible presentation of Himself now, within the hearts and lives of men, whereby they shall be gradually fitted for 'translation into His celestial Kingdom among the rejoicing Angels,' surpass immeasurably all the wondrous expressions of GOD's Love and Power that have stirred the souls of men, and compelled from them recognition of His providence over them. There, lifted up in heart and soul and spirit—and in body too —to the very Throne of GOD, we come to know more of GOD and His 'ways' than we could learn by any other experience on earth, and the much-giving of our Lord compels from us a fervency of devotion in which the consciousness of the Divine possession of our life

[1] Thomas à Kempis.

stirs us unto the perfection of being for the sake of which He lived and died and rose from the dead.

Without the presence in us of this power and blessing we are as that dull, dead protoplasm which we have so often been asked to consider as our primogenitor. We are dead and cold to ourselves, and useless for others. A barren, sterile existence must then be ours :—an existence, in which there is no capacity for true living, no means of putting forth that growth and development of being, through which greater life is spread around us to the glory of GOD.

'I am the Vine. Ye are the branches.' From Him flows to us the vitality and grace, the rich fruitfulness, that declares the might of Love. So there is in us the power of revelation of His Nature and Life-givingness, the appreciation of, and longing for, sacrifice—the immolation of self for other good,—the rapture of being which knows, even as it responds to, the action of GOD upon and within us, and expresses itself in the fruit of gentleness, tenderness, devotedness to all around us; making, thus, for the production in them, *through Christ*, of throbbing life and goodness, so that the world may turn to its Maker, to its Redeemer, to its Full Perfection of development.

Christ comes to us Spiritually, under material form, and gives both to the spirit and to the matter of which we are composed true vitality and power, full grace of being. Our whole nature is quickened unto the gloriousness of eternal life, the earthly or corporeal part being permeated by the leavening of the spirit.

We are consecrated thereby; and when, at the great Judgment, we receive sentence for the things done in the body, the mercifulness of that sentence will be owing to the interaction of Christ, wrought by means of the Blessed Sacrament received and assimilated here : the after-glory of being declaring the largeness of its debt to Christ. It is through the reception of Christ that the body is made truly to partake in the benefits of the Incarnation ; and by constant reception of Him it is so preserved and maintained in the holiness passed upon it that at the last day a perfect body may arise from the grave, to live with the spirit a perfect life. And the new faculties that will belong to us thereafter—as the fully developed faculties—will be, we believe, not merely of the soul or spirit, but of the glorified body also.

A perfect nature, a perfect reality of being, is truly wrought out for us by the Personal action of Christ, that 'Word' by Whom all things were made through the movement of Divine Love—Himself the GOD Who had seen in His Mind a completed being, and by the impulse of His Omnipotent Love projected Himself into 'space,' and evolved a sphere wherein his education might go forth, his true development be assured.

We should, surely, never forget this connection of The Word in all things: never forget that the Christ Who comes to us in the Blessed Sacrament is He Who created the universe : that He is Love, the Love Which not only created but redeemed us ; and that this is the completion of the Redemptive Scheme, the point

THE SANCTUARY OF SUFFERING

to which everything in life works up, and finds its beautiful Answer given on the Cross fully justified, The Might and the beauty of the Cross now shine clearly forth, and point to the radiancy of the Beatific Vision, in the light of Which a perfect life shall be lived, a perfection of glory realised; and it is all one vast continued Movement of Divine Love. The Life Which evolved the worlds gives here a declaration of Love. It stirs and quickens to fresh activity the being awakened from torpor at the Word of Love: It moves unto perfect life and order the chaotic, the crude, the imperfect: It inflames, with the fire of Divine Love, the realm into which It has entered, and calls forth from the whole being an emotion towards, a longing for, harmony of being:—an 'inward unity of personality,' which alone can lead to the perfection foreseen and devised by GOD in the totality of His Being when The Word went forth, proclaiming that 'GOD is Love'!

And as we consider the wondrous, continuous movement of this Love Which describes the Divine Nature, we come to see how that the Blessed Sacrament is the only logical conclusion of the history of the steps which, from the evolution of the Universe onwards, GOD took for the securing of perfection for the race of beings created by Him. The personal participation and assimilation, in the nature and life of man, of the positive Nature and Life of GOD was essential for the ensuring of that complete affinity with Him which only could render the man perfectly happy. So GOD created a sphere wherein man might be trained and

MOVEMENT OF DIVINE LOVE 169

educated: so He created the man, so He lived in human flesh and died in that flesh: so He gives Himself in extended Sacrifice on the Altars set up in His Name on earth—the designed sphere of man's groundwork of perfection.

It is the Gift of gifts. It blesses and goes forth in blessing: reflects GOD, and brings Him more and more to the souls within, to the lives without us. It is the binding up of the broken-hearted, the healing of their wounds, the soother of their distress. It, the supreme benefaction of GOD, gathers into its embrace all other Divine benefactions, and spreads them around, so that the earth, with its burden of sorrow, its weight of affliction, breaks forth into joy and gladness, and the Cross, ever present, is seen, not merely, as the old artists loved to depict it, branching out and putting forth green shoots of livingness, but glorious with the growth of flowers, golden roses, pure lilies, blossoms full of holy, mystic meaning, making the world a great garden for GOD. It teaches to us all things worth knowing :—It takes of the high things of GOD, and spreads them out, and we grow holy and acceptable to GOD. It comes, and resolves chaos into a grand cosmos of living, stirring beauty. It binds us to GOD as nought else could bind us to Him, and the bond means new life, and fresh and continuing development. It means the spread of GOD's Life, and the development into perfection of growth. It is the instructor and precursor of true self-sacrifice, for in it we find the perfect expression of such sacrifice. It is the instructor and guide of all true love: love resulting, and finding satisfaction, in the immolation of self for the object loved, the giving of self absolutely for the life of that object. All love's offerings must, we know, culminate in the devotion of the actual self that a man is and possesses; and here, in the Blessed Sacrament, this truth is illumined, and should be fully learned. Here we are drawn into the grand empyrean of GOD's Truth, coming face to face with a perfect expression of Love.

'He that shall lose his life . . . shall save it,' the Master said. To place the life unreservedly in the hands of another is to lose it in one sense, but so to find it that it becomes salvation of the high self which is for GOD. The Divine Life is offered to us, and when we accept the Offering we place ourselves alongside it, and find it involved in the Life given to us :—There is the completion of Love in perfect Sacrifice, and the resultant union of being! In the Blessed Sacrament Christ comes, and says:—This is the Perfect expression of My Love for thee. Lay thy will down before Me; yield thy being to Me, that I, by the giving of My Being to thee, may possess thee and bless thee with My Life. Die in Me, that thou mayest live in Me, and realise that perfection of union in which alone thy tired spirit's sigh can find its answer and its satisfaction. And in the death of thyself in Me, the new-given Life shall triumph over the corruption of thy heart, and sanctify thee wholly. So shall My tired Spirit's sigh be stilled and satisfied.

And as our being becomes merged in the pure radiancy of the Divine Light of Active Love, every little part and corner of the life is sanctified; every dark and cloudy place yields to its power, and shines in the splendour of Heaven. (For 'Love—such Love —is Heaven,' even as 'Heaven is Love'!): and the Cross, shining in the perfect glory of the Eucharistic Sacrifice—wherein Christ is offered and we in Him are offered too,—comes truly to be known as the sublime concentration of Suffering, the perfect explanation of the force of the sorrows and agonies of the world. Pain is power, but its real force is exercised in the strength of its union with Christ; and when we have been welded to him in 'body, soul, and spirit'— entire being—we come to see its might and true magnificence, and surely then have learned to regard all suffering with tender reverence, recognising in it that throb of Immortality which stirs unto holiness, seeing that Pain is but a form of Love.

Do we not see now clearly why we suffer? We suffer *towards Christ*. We suffer that we may be united with Him: that into the great solitude within us, clamouring for we know not what, Christ, the glorified Man of Sorrows, may come as to a place prepared for Him: that GOD, as Perfect Love, may save us wholly from our sins, and give unto us Eternal Life in close union with Himself. We suffer, and we are led to the Altar; and there we find the Perfect Sacrifice typified long ages ago by the whole lamb slain—pierced through by spits in the form of a Cross—held up for the eternal salvation of men; and we know that we 'are in Eternal Life now'!

But what of those who have never got beyond the first step towards perfection of life? What if the suffering of their way has failed to lead them to Christ?

> 'When GOD smote His hands together and struck out thy soul as a spark
> Into the organised glory of things from deeps of the dark,
> Say, didst thou shine, didst thou burn, didst thou honour the power in the form,
> As the star does at night, or the firefly, or even the little ground-worm?
> "I have sinned," she said, "for my seed-light shed
> Has wandered away from its first decrees,
> The cypress praiseth the firefly,
> The ground-leaf praiseth the worm,—
> I am viler than these."'[1]

Yet it is not too late to praise God in this acceptance of Him which means our real, full salvation unto perfection. It is never too late, so long as the Holy Spirit can strive with man for his good, and the Holy Spirit is not straitened:—If the life of man be but submitted to His Influence, full light shall shine in the darkness, and lead the way to Christ. It has not been the fault of the Holy Spirit that light has not shone clearly therein so far. It has been the error of the individuals themselves, who have not turned their souls towards the 'true Light Which lighteth every man that cometh into the world'—if the man *will*, into fulness of clear light.

S. Thomas Aquinas said :—' Nor is it the fault of the Word that all men do not attain to the knowledge of

[1] Mrs. Browning.

the truth, but some remain in darkness. It is the fault of men who do not turn to the Word and so cannot fully receive Him. Whence there is still more or less darkness remaining amongst men, in proportion to the lesser or greater degree in which they turn to the Word and receive Him. And so John, to preclude any thought of deficiency in the illuminating power of the Word, after saying "that Life was the Light of men," adds "the Light shineth in darkness, and the darkness comprehended it not." The darkness is not because the Word does not shine, but because some do not receive the light of the Word ; as while the material sun is shining over the world, it is only dark to those whose eyes are closed or feeble.'

TRANSFIGURATION

WHEN Christ went up to the Mount He was Transfigured before the disciples, and they caught the reflection of the glow that was upon Him, and, looking round afterwards, 'saw no man any more, save Jesus only.' Then they descended to the vale—*with Jesus*.

The Altar is to us as the Mount of Transfiguration. There we are over-streamed by the Light of the Divine Presence, and we return to the vale—the vale where we have walked with pained and toilworn tread, with tired limbs and wearied soul—with Christ.

And to us it is ever henceforth to be only Christ that we see. He is to appear to us in the people about us, in all the facts and occurrences of life, in the sadness and pain, the trials and difficulties, both of others and of ourselves. Our whole life is to be a transfigured life: all within and without us is to glow with the Light of His shining Presence, and give us Him; and above all else, must suffering shine out gloriously and generously thus. As we look around and see the maimed and crippled forms, and discern the mind and soul disease, both of which seem to meet us at every turn of life, we may see 'Jesus only.' We may see the 'Man of Sorrows,' passing about the earth, Incarnate still, Incarnate ever, holding to Himself and up to the Father the hurt human lives, the tortured bodies, the seared spirits; and the whole great *viâ dolorosa* is then lit up by a light in which the Cross stands forth with a glorious Crown surmounting it. Christ truly lives amongst men still, and now we see Him living: taking every load of sorrow, pain, trial, and transfiguring it in the Light of His Living Presence. Each form of suffering is as the Angel of His Presence, saying, He is here: He Whom thou lovest and knowest. And as we look there seem to be now visibly to our soul's eyes marks of the nails and spear. Hurt and maimed and disfigured do the sufferers look? The 'Man of Sorrows,' Who was marred more than all the sons of men, is shining forth in Perfect Glory, and He holds them pressed tightly to Him that they may grow into a perfect glory too. Have we no trust? Yes; we can trust them there. They are surely deriving illuminating grace from their close contact with Him; and we know that the 'seeming' which is now so sad to onlookers shall one day shine forth more glorious than it would have done had it never known the defacement and disfigurement of sorrow and agony.

Union with Christ through suffering: the being blent with Christ in the pain which He bore! This is a link between Heaven and earth. This is what makes Heaven near and earth exalted. And we now, in our illumination of being, perceive and declare the might and real beauty of all the agonies, distresses, disfigurements around us, and see in them—'Jesus only.'

It is almost—if one dare think of any such comparison—with us as it was with S. John of the eagle-gaze. It is as though to us had been revealed the glorious Vision of Heaven, and we henceforth saw all in the Light of the Vision.

There is within us, now truly, a sanctuary wherein we worship Christ; and there should grow and bloom and fructify all that, like Him, is lovely and of good report. He has entered these lives, these once little trifling lives, of ours, and therein has formed a source of grace and strength, from which we may draw, and in which find a power of ultimate perfecting. And He holds there the sorrow and suffering which are ours; and so illuminates them that, even from these, bright, shining light is cast upon the great *viâ dolorosa* before our eyes. Knowing them to be transformed and glorified by Him, and ourselves enlightened by them *in Him*, we look out on the world that had hitherto seemed marred throughout by the prevalence of suffering in it, and the whole view is altered. For He has lifted up our eyes and pointed to the 'New Jerusalem'; and gazing there we have seen humanity crowned: seen crippled forms, drawn faces, seared souls, shining and resplendent in glory of spiritual essence.

Yes, whether the Cross now be ours, or that of another—or others,—we can embrace it with ready, trustful arms, seeing Christ there, smiling the perfect

TRANSFIGURATION

smile of Love triumphant over Suffering. We learn to understand the wonderful soul-messages, which at times have been offered to us, and to realise what submission to the Divine Will truly signifies. We get that healthiness of spiritual and moral being that—with humble reverence be it said—so characterised the Life of our Blessed Lord, which He lived amongst men for their example and guide; and which finally declared itself in open vision on the Cross, when He refused the myrrh, yet accepted enough of the vinegar to enable Him to utter clearly and distinctly the cry to the Father which should preach to others the undying victory of faith and devotion, and should seal the great Offering of Life. We learn the 'middle course': the necessity for avoiding the extreme in either direction, which is the mark of a normal, Christ-loving person. We learn, in fact, gradually, the 'sweet reasonableness' of Him Whose now we indeed are, and Who is truly ours. We have seen the Face of the pure and all-wise Love That fears not to let the measure of suffering be according to appointment; and the confidence engendered is strength to us. It speaks in our hearts the message contained in His tarrying on the way when His friend Lazarus was dead, and His beloved Mary and her sister Martha were grieving over His loss. We know now how He could stand outwardly calm, whilst the poor heart-broken mother pleaded with Him for her daughter who was being tortured by an 'evil spirit,' and whose misery rived and tore the human heart of her who witnessed it. And we know also how, before those single instances of His endurance of others' 'ills,' He had been able willingly to reject the offer of 'all the kingdoms of the world,' and wait for Suffering to work its sway, and *thus* bring the world to Him.

We may still, with the Divine transfiguration upon us and upon all, feel our own suffering and yearn over the sufferers about us, but it is not the same with us as it was. We can bear it in different wise now, as seeing in it a direct path to Christ. We begrudge nothing of it; for there is GOD's great Purpose clearly before us.

So we bear that

> 'First of the "Noble Truths"; how Sorrow is
> Shadow to life, moving where life doth move;
> Not to be laid aside until one lays
> Living aside, with all its changing states,
> Birth, growth, decay, love, hatred, pleasure, pain,
> Being and doing.'[1]

And the residue of suffering, left over in spite of all human efforts in its cause, no longer appals us as it did, for the Man of Sorrows holds it in the bright, clear Light of His Shining Presence, and we see it changed.

Even hereditary suffering—that form of suffering which has caused so large a number of persons to question and arraign the Love and Justice of GOD— now looks different from what it once did. What is it, really? It is truly of man's creation, it is man's work; but evil is always checked by good, and here GOD steps

[1] *The Light of Asia.*

in and works upon the evil wrought until it becomes wholly good and beautiful. The hurt lives here are raised on to a plane apart, where they are driven to seek the GOD of their soul-life; where He comes to them and communes with them in a holy stillness, and they receive a special anointing unto ultimate glory. They, in their apartness from their fellows more 'fortunately' (as the word goes) placed, see more than these fellow-beings see; and their lives become, perhaps silent, but not the less mighty, agents of progress and holiness. They learn in their condition of outer infirmity the inherent grace and beauty of being. They can live more easily in grand Personalised loneliness with GOD, their being wrapped wholly into His Being, with a blessedness of union not so fully vouchsafed to those more 'fortunately' (!) placed. Seared, scarred and enfeebled they are; but still aflame with the glory of GOD, preaching the might of suffering in their crippled, hurt lives. This is how it is with them :— these maimed, humanly injured ones.

We see all maimed lives in some such wise now. The distorted and suffering forms around us, the forms scored with the deep lines of pain and disease, the bent bodies, the mis-shapen limbs, are transfigured for us in the Light and the belief of His Presence, to Whom all affliction belongs; and we see the Man of Sorrows erasing the lines of pain and filling up the spaces with His evident Love. We see what *will be*—nay, we truly see what at the present time, behind the suffering, *is*. We see the gloriousness of Divine Love there, and the marred forms, the lines of pain, transfigured already. We see the crown of glory resting on, and lighting up with splendour of beauty, the signs of the Cross upon them.

So we now surely reverence all suffering, whether it be our own or others'. Before our transfiguration we had not seen nor known suffering as it really is; and the suffering visibly around us had been terrible to contemplate. But within us has been born a patient willingness that all should suffer, and so be united to Christ. We know that suffering means eventual holiness, and it matters not to us if the cross be laid heavily —whether on our own shoulders or on those of others— so long as it means union with Christ. We can bear it bravely and trustfully, seeing in it the path to Him. We have learned to keep down the old feverish longing to remove a burden of suffering at all hazards. We can let it lie there, in its appointed place, now that we understand more about it; and perhaps few things stir us more fiercely and painfully in our new enlightenment than questioning and murmuring on the part of some person grieved and oppressed by the knowledge and the experience of suffering. It hurts us to hear questioning murmurings against the GOD of Perfect Love.

There is no doubt that we may not always put forth the strong right arm of help when we see suffering near us. We often have to let the burden lie in its place: to stand by whilst the sorrow, the agony, does its Divine task in the life afflicted. It is easy to have our little ideas about the rightful amount and term of suffering to be endured, and possibly in the old days we had said—as many say :—'Surely he has borne enough? Why should one life be so burdened when another is glad and free?' Yet, who can tell the sufficiency of a burden? Who, either, can declare true gladness and freedom? We should rather trust the new belief that is ours :—that if, when all reasonable efforts at removal or lightening have been tried, the burden remains exactly the same as it was, then it is intended to be there, and is best for the burden-bearer: that so alone with him can real gladness and freedom be eventually, or at any rate ultimately, found. It is a mystery, perhaps, to us why here and there one should stand forth unequally as a sufferer, but surely trust will quite adequately meet any questions in our minds ; and if a particular burden does not yield to our anxious, loving touch, then we must placidly let it lie in its place. For there is GOD's great purpose to be remembered faithfully, and no fretting nor complaining against Him should ever mar the service that we strive to render to others. Happiness-seeking for them needs to be guarded as carefully as happiness-seeking for ourselves—indeed more carefully, for there is with many of us a far greater likelihood of undue efforts in their behalf than in our own. We require to be ever watchful against that spirit which clamours to relieve what GOD would have unrelieved. (It is easy to allow such a spirit to make us slaves to its behests, and then GOD is wronged and others suffer apart from the Divine Will and ordinance.) Though now, in the sanctified view that we take of suffering, we are less liable to fall a prey to such feverish efforts, and the suffering that we find lies beyond our permitted scope should be accepted even joyfully by us, being seen in its inherent truth and beauty, as we let them suffer—as, in perfect wise, GOD can let all men suffer.

So, in place of fretful questionings, is generated within us a permanent resignation to the so-called 'ills of life.' We can be calm in the face of hideousness of suffering. Idle? No, not idle; busier far than ever we had been in the old days of feverish energy: only at rest in the midst of our busy efforts, at rest with a sure and abiding sense upon us of GOD's Perfect, All-Wise Love.

And what of the 'beauty of holiness,' of which the psalmist, in full measure, did but fore-sing? Is it realisable? Was the psalmist right? Yes:—'We have seen the King in His beauty': we have touched the robe of Him Who is our Ideal. Our heart is consecrated to Him, and even the defacing pain of little daily worries and anxieties has no real power over the heart thus consecrated: the contradictions, the crossings of our will and desires, the disappointments, the thwartings, the uncertainties of life, leave no lasting scar upon it. For it is GOD's, and at the first movement of impatience GOD stays it, whispering in His Love: 'Be still, and know that I am GOD.' And the stillness becomes gradually so reflected in the face of a person thus blessed that even that preaches the 'beauty of holiness'; for the power of GOD is seen clearly there.

And Nature? How does Nature appear to us as

we view her from our new standpoint, with the fresh, grand light shed upon her?

Nature now neither grieves nor satisfies us. She says a great deal more to our souls than used to be the case: she fills us with a certain heart-hunger which in itself is beautiful and fertile of grace, increased and intensified glory, within our being. She inspires us with a fresh rapture of admiration and love. 'Whence in our nature does that throb of sympathy arise that answers to the call of the spirit of beauty and truth? ... What is the secret of that power that holds the mind enthralled as the after-glow of sunset fills the eyes? Whence comes that sense of rest and yet of longing, lingering desire as the sight loses itself in that ocean of light? Why no sense of solitude in those awful depths; no fear, but only joy in that sublime infinitude? Why? but for the conscious presence of more there than sight perceives? That glorious sheen of light and colour is but the clothing of a sphere of life into which we pierce and find no strangeness in it.'[1]

Christ within us, and without us! Christ quickening, elevating, drawing the being to Himself! Has it not been our 'Mount of Transfiguration'? When He came to us, did He not pass upon us and upon everything about us a splendour of glory? And when we look on the beauties of Nature we seem to see an altar even there, raised to the great GOD of the Universe! Before this altar countless forms of life and earthly beauty are worshipping Him. Strains of music seem

[1] T. Gambier Parry.

to fill the air; sweet scents blow gently in the breeze that flutters round about us; filmy cloud-forms flit about our heads; the blue vault of heaven is stretched above, covering the earth with a canopy speaking of Eternal Love; life, animate and inanimate, tells of beauty, yet tells also of imperfection. Nature is crying out to Heaven: 'How long, O Lord, how long?' Her whole face seems convulsed with longing. She bears upon her signs of the universal groaning and travailing for the 'Blest new birth,' which we know awaits her as it awaits the imperfect, the vaguely yearning, human lives. She, too, is waiting for her ideal. Before her is perfection, and her longing arms are held outstretched towards it.

'Matter,' said Carlyle, 'exists only spiritually, and to represent some idea, and body it forth.' In all the material part of Nature is the great idea of dawned perfection: are there the signs of a perfection ultimately to be acquired, set forth clearly to our eyes. On her, too, rests a Heavenly transfiguring light, in which the imperfect is seen as perfect: in which the grand and beautiful are visualised in perfect grandeur and beauty; in which her variations, her gloom and her brightness, her revulsions and her peaceful, sweet gradations, of change, are seen harmonised to perfect peace and constancy.

She is insistent on our souls, and she is sympathetic to us.

> 'Oh winter! sad wert thou and full of sorrow!
> Oh soul! oh world, the summer comes to-morrow!
> . . . .

Oh soul ! 'tis Love quickens
Time's languorous feet ;
Oh world ! 'tis Spring wakens
The fair blossoms sweet ;
Fair world, fair soul, that lie so close together,
Each with sad wintry days and fair spring weather !'

Think of the soul-messages here given to us ! Think how Nature calls to us from out the thunder-cloud, the lightning-flash, shading the earth, illumining with brighter radiance the shadowed gloom ! Think of how, from mountain-top, amidst the 'eternal snow' of purity, she calls in the heart of the tiny blossom there to the heart of man in the vale below, telling of Love in the High Heavens above her : how, in storm and flood, in wind and rain, she touches and impels outward the gloom and fight within the tired breast of man ; and then, through brightest glow of sunshine, warms his heart and makes him shine anew : how, in leaf and flower, in ripened fruit, she tells of growth and strength of purpose, crowned by satisfaction of the efforts made ! And yet how, with all her startling contrasts, her phantasies and changes, her phrases and her melodies, she never strikes a false note, nor jars upon the tired, yet tutored, ear that hears her theme, but soothes and stills the spirit sighing for GOD in His Holiness !

Strangely insistent Nature is ? Yes, and sympathetic too. Do we not know what it is to have been dimly worshipping GOD in some temple of His, built by the hands of men : some hallowed place enclosed within—cramped by, it sometimes seems to us—four stone walls, and then come out into the wide expanse of Nature, and feel that now, more than before, GOD is with us, His Soul touching our soul? It is as though a new revelation of Him were being made to us, a new quickening of the spiritual longing within us to live in constant communion with the Unseen, to work in the glory of another 'world,' another 'life,' with the web of this earthly world, this everyday life. We see GOD and heaven, before, above, around us, and so the very air we breathe is lovely to us, and holy beyond expression. GOD! It is all GOD. We have not gone out of His Presence by departure from those hallowed four walls: we have His Presence in new and fuller measure. The temple had been consecrated and set apart for Him. Yes, but the great temple of Nature was consecrated and set apart for Him at its creation. It has ages of Divine consecration upon it; and the sanctuary has ever been there, the sanctuary and an altar. His Presence fills—yes, the very air we breathe. His Love blows upon us in the breeze that stirs about us. 'Lo!' we cry, 'there is no more mortal and immortal! Nought is on earth or in the heavens but Love!'[1] It is all Love, for it is all GOD. And 'Love is heaven, and heaven is Love!' This, indeed, is a temple not made with hands: and here, verily, may worshippers come, and kneel before the GOD of Creation and Redemption, proclaiming Him the only GOD:—our King, our Master, our Lord Supreme.

'The day is Thine, and the night is Thine: Thou hast prepared the light and the sun. Thou hast set all

[1] F. W. H. Myers.

the borders of the earth: Thou hast made summer and winter.' Alike in these GOD is: the light and the darkness, the warmth and the cold, the shining and the gloom; there to be worshipped, there to be *loved*, then there to be known.

A temple not made with hands? A temple whose roof is the broad blue of the heavens by day, the great steely blue arch by night, whose walls are the limitless 'space,' whose floor the earth on which GOD, as the 'Man of Sorrows,' trod, as He passed on His way of mercy to the lost and the suffering. Holy indeed is this temple. Most beautiful and tender are the thoughts that come into our minds, most glorious does the world with its burden of suffering and yearning seem; most truly do we understand the 'riddle of the painful earth,' that once so troubled and perplexed us. We know now her groanings, her strivings, her putting forth towards a high ideal. Does all her beauty speak of loss and the pain of loss, of insufficiency, imperfection? Do we, as we feast our eyes upon her loveliness, drawing in delight of splendid tints and colours, viewing the fading flowers still holding up their heads as death approaches, the cloud-forms passing, passing, far beyond the power of earthly eyes to follow, put out pleading hands to the GOD of the universe, praying Him to stay and still the aching heart? Do we almost ask that on those passing cloud-forms a tired soul may lie, and be borne to the great Unknown? Are we troubled, vaguely troubled? Do we fix our gaze upon the burning glow in the western heavens that tells of a vanished sun, and pray that GOD would let His Kingdom truly come to all? Are we filled with sad thought, uncertain longings ? We turn away, and the leaves sink down in the earth, and the flowers are dead ; and night has come, so that now no more are the white cloud-forms seen.

But the leaves are serving, the flowers are serving ; and the canopy of night-darkness encloses a world of life that needs refreshment, that cannot do with glare of sunshine always. There is another lesson here for us ; and it is a very practical lesson. Dropping one by one, laying down their lives, the leaves are offering themselves, as it were, for a good not their own: serving ends of creation, taking their part in the universal pæan of sacrifice going forth to Heaven for general good. And the flowers, too, die down in beautiful devotion to a common cause. Each leaf, each flower, preaches the beauty of holiness as lying in the offering of self for greater good. And the night coming on ! What does this not say to us ? Earth closes in, stillness reigns, GOD's Voice is heard speaking through the gloom, saying to the soul: Arise ; shine with thine own light. And through the whole transformed being is breathed the whisper:—Through death comes life: through loss a greater gain !

Ah! yes ; Nature now teaches us great lessons, moves us in mighty fashion. She takes her GOD-given treasures, her splendour, her losses, her pains, lays them before our eyes, and says : Thou, sanctified one, live for GOD's use! In all her beautiful movement and change she tells of the true beauty of self-offering, the call for self-devotion. She preaches the significance and the power of Calvary, holding up the Death there as entailing sacrifice. And the signs of yearning for a 'Blest new birth' pass through us a great thrill of emotion, as we think of Christ, Who died and gave Himself in rich, full measure, that the 'Blest new birth' might be for all and everything. Transfigured we indeed are, and the whole world partakes of the light in which we move and walk. All things—even as all people—take upon themselves fresh and prophetic glory of life and being; and we see them in the way in which Jean François Millet saw his art:—but as 'a beginning.' And the Love Which, residing in our soul, blesses ever that soul, so draws us towards perfection, that the transfiguring radiance issuing from it (by reason of the Divine Presence) makes the whole world seem to be blossoming as the rose and giving fruit like the vine, in order that Love may be satisfied in Its Eternal longings, and The Great Ideal acquired.

We see 'Jesus only.' And we see Him as the glorified Man of Sorrows, Who bore in His Bosom the Mystery of Suffering, and pointed to the Great Unveiling.

So we pass along the vale, and though there may sometimes be pained and toil-worn tread, tired limbs and weary soul, we have built our 'tabernacle,' and are content.

There is a holy stillness in the being. And when all is done that can be done, and we sit down conscious that the Mystery of Suffering still abides, that hearts and souls, and bodies too, are torn with many distresses, that suffering speaks even through natural things, through epochs and events about us, that the whole wide world seems but as a *Viâ Dolorosa*, and the Cross never beyond sight, let us—for truly we may—lift our eyes to Heaven, and see Christ 'sitting at the right hand of GOD,' and know that the transfiguration which on earth has come to us is a prefiguring of a glorious perfectedness in the Great Beyond, when we shall be face to Face with the Incarnate Love That made of the Mystery of Suffering, even on earth, a Sanctuary in which Love might be known.

For this we wait, holding up our lives as do the flowers when they turn Heavenwards for the dew to fill their chalices, speaking surely to us in words like these:—

'Fill the chalices of other lives!'

JOY OF BEING

THEN there arises that 'delight in mere living,' which is permanent joy, true happiness: joy and happiness that may exist side by side with intense suffering, and which none and nought can take from us.

It has been said that 'the highest pinnacle of the spiritual life is not happy joy in unbroken sunshine, but absolute and undoubting trust in the Love of GOD.'[1] But we do not attain to this sure trust until we have found GOD in Christ.

GOD made us and intended us to be happy, and all that enters into our life—even this fallen life that now is being lived—has in it the germs and possibilities of perfect happiness, when once we have found Christ, and become allied to Him in a blessed harmony of wish, inclination, and aim. 'Happiness,' says Pascal, 'is neither within us nor without us; it is in GOD, both without us and within us.' When we possess GOD in the being, therefore, we possess eternal happiness.

We are ever seeking happiness and ever missing it, simply because we seek it in a direction opposed to that where GOD is. We seek it within us and without us, and not in that close union and special communion with

[1] Dr. Thorold.

Him which brings Him into our very being, to be a part of our whole life. This alone is certain, true happiness.

It is the highest pinnacle on which a human soul can here live. We know nothing of what may come to us, of what the days, the weeks, the months perhaps, the years possibly, that we may have to live on earth may bring to us, but if we have this 'absolute and undoubting trust in the Love of GOD' which real living with Him involves, then we may be enabled, not merely to possess our souls in patience, but may also experience that grand content and satisfaction which shall render our lives truly well-pleasing to GOD, and of use and blessing to our fellow-men. When once the heart is bound up with GOD's Heart, there is within us a happiness which indeed none and nought can take from us, but which, at the same time, is as distinct from, and other than, the joy of unbroken sunshine as is substance from shadow, truth than the parodies by which men seek to represent truth. It is only now, when we have learned, by personal experience of His Love and Power, to look into the Face of GOD, as it were, and say: My Lord! My GOD! in tender confidence, that we really know true happiness, and can understand in some wise the Mystery of the burden under which creation has groaned, and still groans, in bitter travail. Happiness does not, as we have learned, consist of a satisfaction of the soul's lower desires, but is the absolute answer to, and consequent satisfaction of, that supreme longing of heart, soul, life, which has ever gone up from earth to Heaven, and which, though oftentimes unconsciously to the individual so longing, is the 'sigh of the spirit' after holiness and perfection of being.

In GOD alone can this sigh be stilled. In GOD alone can be rest: the rest for whose acquisition the tired spirit of man, the yearnings of the earth, go forth.

There will still be pain, because pain is always necessary for complete development. But when the whole being is in accord with GOD, willing towards His Will, knowing that that must be best, the agonising sting of pain is gone, and there remains but such suffering as is compatible with true content—so far as earth can yield content.

And this 'content' is our joy in which we may walk always, now in our transfigured life; and by means of which we may draw others to GOD: which shall bear blossom and fruit so long as our life shall last, and when He shall summon this little earthly life and plant it in the garden 'above,' shall still and for ever shine forth in beauty of growth. None and nought can take it from us! The slights and the wrongs of those we love, the wounds and the scars caused by the hands of those who hate us, the 'slings and arrows of outrageous fortune,' the misery, the hardness, the misconstruction of words and acts, the deprivations, disappointments, trials of all sorts—everything that makes up the sum of '*un*happiness'—is taken up into, and embraced by, this great, sure sense of the perfection of GOD's Love and Power, which we have learned through His indwelling our being: is blessed and irradiated by it, and made 'happiness.'

And indeed we had never learned this true joy of being unless first we had sorrowed well and faithfully. Though it sound paradoxical, it is nevertheless a fact that sure, pure joy comes from misery. It was misery that really led the way of our life to GOD. No other experience of life can show GOD to us in Christ. Happiness comes from the misery through the thick, heavy folds of which we have looked and looked until we have seen the ' Man of Sorrows,' and made Him ours. We must in fairness trace it back to its origin. This joy of being which we rightly call happiness owes itself to the ' Mystery of Pain.' It is not a cold 'philosophy,' arising from a sort of schooled natural strength. It is more than this. Philosophy is an element of this new learned happiness, but merely an element. Philosophy will carry a man some way: it will enable him to bear. It will not, however, enable him to *penetrate*! It will not impel him through the encompassing folds of his trouble to the real solution of its mystery. He does not get free from his misery and the sense of it: on the contrary, he then hardens himself to a continuance of his condition. He cannot emerge: he must stay where he is. It is far removed indeed from the 'sweet reasonableness' of mind which follows on the willing and conscious acceptance of Christ into the being, and, following only thus, distinguishes the truly Christian person from all other human beings.

With the consciousness, and by the power, of Christ's

JOY OF BEING

indwelling of the life, there arises that peculiar resignation which is more than passivity in the face of sorrow: which is verily the key-stone of a perfect arch of character. Viewing sorrow as Christ views it, we see ever the inner force and significance of it to the sufferer, and can welcome it, howsoever it may declare itself. It is really a simple prefiguring of the growth that is to be carried on in the Intermediate State, when the will of man shall know even more of the Will of GOD than now is possible, and his heart so readily embrace the 'purging as by fire' that the very purging means satisfaction and 'happiness' to the soul.

Ah! a paradox, a folly, is it to assert that joy comes out of misery? It is a great truth of common experience. In the moments when we are most miserable, most bowed down by suffering, is a basis of perfect happiness being laid within the being :—a foundation on which shall be erected a fair building, wherein can be a sanctuary into which, certain of recognition and acceptance, Christ can come and infuse us with that spirit which ever went forth in willingness to suffer all that should be laid upon it. GOD's pain does lead to the only real and sure happiness : does build the only possible foundation for the Divine temple within us— the temple that shall hold a sanctuary within it!

Only we must be certain that the pain we suffer is GOD's, and not of our own creating. There is a very great amount of suffering in the world with which GOD has nothing at all to do, and which only by His infinite Mercy can ever be induced to yield any true blessing to the individual who causes it and to those affected by it. There are constant examples before our eyes of pain sought and eventually created, not merely by the wickedness of a man's heart and life, but by shortsightedness and by morbidness of mind. All around us are souls warped, disfigured, cramped, by that perverted dread of self-indulgence, or self-idolatry even, which makes them regard natural GOD-sent blessings as devices and snares of the Evil One, to be fought against, downtrodden, spurned and loathed as (supposed) enticing forms beckoning them to hell. There should, of course, as we know, be a very stern inward asceticism, a watchful spirit of self-discipline and self-instruction; but this perverse rending and tearing of the being *against* GOD's *Will*—for that is what such action really is—cannot be provocative of any genuine spiritual health. It is a disease, a canker, that eats into the very heart and life, destroying with its evil fibrous growth the beautiful strength and vigour of soul that GOD would have, and which means His joy, His happiness, for the creature made and redeemed by Him. It may be pleasing to Satan, but certainly not to GOD. In time a man so wrought, so distorted and distracted, will grow to look upon the fairest scene, the most beautiful and the purest object, with loathing and horror. His whole life will be ugly, and the ugliness will extend to, and destroy, his true perception of, his fellows, and the earth on which they move and have their being. Their good will be seen as evil, their truth and honesty as the lies of Satan; and the whole world will appear evil as they seem evil.

JOY OF BEING

We may not—it is an easy development of the learned lesson of submission and devotion to the Cross of Christ, but we may not—seek pain and the permanent mortification of desire whatever that desire may chance to be. It is ever for GOD to give or to withhold satisfaction of the cravings within us. There is to be a ready, willing acquiescence in all that GOD would have us bear of trouble, sorrow, agony of mind or body; but a normally healthy spirit will not forestall Divine monitions, and shape its own cross on which to hang side by side with the Redeemer. To take or to leave as GOD shall will; to enjoy or to suffer, to be glad or sorrowful: this is what He asks of us. And in such an attitude of living does the building of the temple go on, in advancement towards readiness to receive Christ. If we go out of our way to find sorrow and suffering (and surely there should seem no need to do this, in a world where one of old cried out: 'Man is born to trouble as the sparks fly upward!'), if we try to manufacture a cross for ourselves, we lay upon the shoulders a burden which GOD, never having meant to be there, has to devise special means for removing, and which, therefore, entails a going back of the spiritual life, a marked delay on the onward course. And by such personal infliction it is implied that GOD does not know the correct measure of suffering for the gradual perfection of our lives and the offering that these lives should be. There is arrogance in this voluntary searing of the soul's life, though the searer little suspects it. It is a little human parody of Divine discipline.

Yet, how often it is done! How often have we seen a man arrogating to himself GOD's rights in this respect! He sees before him a certain course of action which he knows it would be supremely painful for him to adopt. It promises such intense harrowing of his soul that he feels quite sure the gain to that soul will be great, and GOD proportionately pleased. So he adopts it, and—Satan is pleased. He commences the torturing of himself without justification or need in an earnest endeavour to uproot the effects of Adam's Fall. It matters not, evidently, that Christ, having provided the only sure remedy for, and corrective of, the canker of sin, will apply this remedy and corrective to him personally in just such constant measure as he is able to receive it: he must hang upon a self-devised cross. So he tortures himself, so he proceeds to call black white, good evil, never dreaming that he is getting further away from GOD than he was.

We long to go to such a man with our hands outheld towards him, with our eyes burning and glowing with love, and say:—GOD would have thee happy! GOD would bless thee and crown thy life, thy livingness, with this beauty and tenderness which thou so fearest. But the man *will not*. His habit of renunciation has laid its hands on him and looked at him, and he cannot shake its now baneful influence off. And so he goes on his own way, and we grieve for him, and pray to GOD for him, and have to content ourselves with trying to bring light and blessedness to him in little unseen, unknown ways that GOD teaches us in our hours of

JOY OF BEING

prayer for him. And in those hours perhaps we learn another lesson, a personal lesson:—a selflessness which does not analyse, nor weigh, nor measure, the things that belong to our peace, but lies still before GOD.

And this, surely, we pray may be counted to the honour and glory of him who, out of (a mistaken) devotion to GOD and anxiety to do (what he thought to be) His Will, had created a darkness in which he had but been able to grope for the GOD Whom, all-unconsciously, he had wronged and maligned—the GOD Who would have him happy! He had missed the way. In that darkness there had also been a storm and stress, a state of perturbation, in which the Divine Voice could not be heard directing him, any more than the sad, grieved Face of GOD could be seen. Yet it had all meant devotion, and we would like to think that in that day when GOD shall make up His jewels a radiant crown may surmount his head, and the happiness which he feared here be his in the 'highest heaven.'

But nevertheless should we be on our guard against any such morbidness of will and heart as may lead to the viewing of innocent, GOD-ordained things as evil:— enemies of our soul's life. It follows very naturally in the wake of devotion and self-oblation to the Divine ordinance of suffering as an agent of good in the life, and if not watched against may exert an entirely wrong influence in our being, rendering that being less GOD's than it was before. The Will of GOD, expressed in the ordinance of suffering, makes for the realisation in the personal life, of Christ; and is distinctly against the gratification of low desires. But we must be careful not to strive, in our zeal of devotion, against the also realisation in the personal life of what is meant to augment the natural power and beauty of that life, and render it more susceptible to the willed influence of Christ, our Possessor, as our possessed. We need to love ourselves as GOD loves us. It is customary—and it is a very hazardous practice—to speak of ourselves as though we were unworthy of our loving thought and care. There is a certain love of self, however, which is not unworthy, but GOD-willed; and this is a love which seeks to enrich and beautify the life to the fullest possible extent, because it is GOD's life. He sacrificed Himself for it, and views it ever in the light of Eternity. We must sacrifice ourselves for it, and view it thus. And the sacrifice is the complete blending of our will with the Divine Will, which enables us to take or to leave only as He shall plainly declare to be right.

Shall we not grow beautiful for GOD by all the means that He places at our disposal? Shall we not put forth our energy of being towards anything that has within it capabilities of life-givingness, possibilities for the enhancing of the beauty of natural living? We want to be able to do without the blessedness and the comfort of this or that treasure for which our heart craves; and for this certain very strict—rigorous—self-discipline is essential—and emanates from, even as it fosters within us, a right 'love of self.' But we must not rob GOD of aught that belongs by right to His

Glory. We want to learn the patient abiding at the foot of the Cross, through which we may become one with Him Who gave up heaven itself to hang there for us. We want to live in the shadow cast down by the Cross—yes, but shall we not live also in the light thrown up from the Cross? Shall we not take darkness and light from Him as being both alike:—instruments of His Glory, a part of His Will? We want the habit of renunciation to be the very air we breathe, to be drawn in, wrought into, our soul's life. Yes, but do not let us get morbid: do not let us acquire that sad dread of taking to ourselves a curse in the guise of a blessing; of fancying we see the cloven hoof peeping from under every fair garment:—do not let us refuse the joyous blessedness of a happiness which is not Satan's, nor man's alone, but GOD's for the man He has created and redeemed from evil.

Truly is it right to draw into our life all the beauty and rich development that we can. Whatever tends to enlarge its range, to illuminate its vision, to quicken and strengthen its natural, yet too often dormant, power, whatever shall teach and enlighten the mind, purify, and call into intenser fire, the affections of the heart, whatever may add to the vigour and force of being, whereby GOD may be greater glorified and the diffusion of beauty around us be possible, is to be regarded as ministering to that 'Best' which GOD desires for us, and the attainment of which is an answer to His love of us.

It is nothing to us—or should be nothing to us; and

in a normal, healthy state of spiritual life would not be anything to us,—comparatively with the thought of GOD's glory, that we shall by a certain course of action be 'happy' or 'miserable,' enjoy or suffer. These alternatives are in His Hands, and should be simply accepted, or as simply rejected, according to the monitions which, in stillness before Him, can be felt and recognised by us. But it is a great deal to us that we should obey the Divine Will, and miss no slightest intimation of what that Will is for us at any particular, at every particular, moment and crisis of our lives. We must lose nothing that might bring into those lives fresh beauty and power for others: must let go nothing that would aid us in the great task that is set for us all to accomplish in our daily walk before men :—the acquisition of full beauty in ourselves, and the consequent spreading of beauty around us. We are meant to grow beautiful in soul and heart and mind, and to learn to count our good as the eventual good of our fellows. 'It is in the interest of those to whom I speak,' said Madame de Sévigné, 'that I should read beautiful books.' It is in the interest of all that we should cultivate every gift and power of our being to the fullest possible extent: that our life may expand, may enrich and glorify, the whole great range of being around us. 'Mighty of heart, mighty of mind, magnanimous—to be this is indeed to be great in life; to become this increasingly is indeed to "advance in life" —in life itself, not in the trappings of it. He only is advancing in life whose heart is getting softer, whose blood warmer, whose brain quicker, whose spirit is entering into living peace.'[1]

'*Diem perdidi!*' was the self-reproach of the Roman Emperor, when at night he was driven to see that during the day he had done no good to any one. '*Diem perdidi!*' should we cry if a day has come and gone, and we have not experienced one thrill of the great pure joy of living because we are living with, and to, and for, GOD and our fellows: if the birds' 'sweet evensong' had rung forth and found no answering note of glad, rejoicing praise of GOD in the life that had passed through one more day of great opportunities and seen in them—*nought?* Dull through the day had we been? 'sullen were we in the sweet air?' sad in the bright shining of the sun? deaf to the sounds of music in the air? Deaf now are we to, and incapable of appreciating, that simple bird-choir of praise going forth to the GOD of Creation?

And he, who only lately passed to the higher life, has left to us the legacy of these lines—he who was so stricken with physical malady as to be banished to one small corner of the world, remote from all tender associations, cut off from all ties and familiar delights of life, wrote out his beautiful soul thus:—

> 'If I have faltered more or less
> In my great task of happiness;
> If I have moved among my race
> And shown no glorious morning face;
> If beams from happy human eyes
> Have moved me not; if morning skies,

---

[1] Carlyle.

Books and my food, and summer rain
Knocked on my sullen heart in vain ;—
Lord, Thy most pointed pleasure take
And stab my spirit broad awake !'[1]

Out of that suffering, patient life went this daring cry, and perhaps by none of his great accomplishments did he so greatly glorify GOD as when he uttered it.

And what scope for glad interest there is in this Universe! How richly has GOD provided the heart and life of man with the means of rich development of his being! What joy there should be reigning in the being enlightened by grace to behold deep meaning hidden everywhere: what yearning to fathom the significance of each fresh beauty and wonder of creation that stands arrayed in panoply of glory before the eyes! How can any one fail to be joyful as beauty after beauty speaks to his soul and connects itself with the life that he is living in, and with, and for, Christ?

'What! dull, when you do not know what gives its loveliness of form to the lily, its depth of colour to the violet, its fragrance to the rose ; when you do not know in what consists the venom of the adder, any more than you can imitate the glad movements of the dove! What! dull, when earth, air, and water are all alike mysteries to you, and when as you stretch out your hand you do not touch anything the properties of which you have mastered ; while all the time Nature is inviting you to talk earnestly with her, to understand her, to subdue her, and to be blessed by her!'[2]

---

[1] Robert Louis Stevenson.   [2] Sir Arthur Helps.

And when these marvels are seen by us in the light flashed into our being from the Beyond, where Christ in actual Bodily Presence is, to which we, in and by Him, hope one day to go, how full of glorious meaning are they! Joy in the beauties and marvels of the Universe indeed we may.

And then there is the great joy of service: the joy that comes of ministering to another's happiness, of lightening another's burden of woe. We are never so helpful in the world as when, by the acquisition of the 'delight in mere living,' we have attained to that condition of life which is GOD's Will for us. Flooded as we then are with happiness, there is in us a great power for the sanctification and blessing, for the enriching and ennobling, of other lives. It is not merely that we have been able to draw into, and out from, our being special intellectual insight and power; not merely that certain natural gifts have been developed within us:—we are powerful because we have learned GOD's happiness, and it is as an embathing of our life in Heavenly light and shining. Our lives are illumined, and they must shed upon others something of their illumination. It is indeed the joy accruing from the transfiguration of our lives by Christ, and it must communicate itself in varying measure to all who, according to GOD's Providence, touch, or are bound up essentially with, our being.

We see many persons whose lives—whose faces, even —speak of this twofold joy, and we never see them without being better and stronger for the sight. We catch the light in their eyes, the sound in their voices, which proclaim them the owners of this joy, and we go on our way refreshed and gladdened by them. Of such as these was S. Bonaventure speaking when he uttered these well-known words :—

'There is something in their very presence, in their mere silent company, from which joy cannot be extricated and laid aside. Their influence is an inevitable gladdening of the heart. It seems as if a shadow of GOD's gifts had passed upon them. . . . Somehow, too, all the joy turns to GOD. Without speaking of Him it preaches Him. Its odour is as the odour of His Presence. It leaves tranquillity behind, and not unfrequently sweet tears of prayer. All things grow silently Christian under its reign. It brightens, ripens, softens, transfigures, like the sunlight, the most improbable things which come within its sphere.'

And this joyousness of being may be ours, and should be ours, when once we have found Christ. Natural temperament may interfere somewhat with the full realisation of such glad living, but even this should yield, and we know does yield, before the influence exercised within by the conscious possession of Christ, and the perfect trust which His Presence gives and teaches us. To all it is possible to be servants of our fellows in this manner.

Happiness is undoubtedly GOD's Will for His people, and on those of us whose temperaments are such as to offer no hindrance to the diffusion of joy within, is laid a special summons to diffuse it without us, abroad amongst our 'neighbours.' It is in cases of this kind perhaps the great task that GOD has set us to do for Him. And in the Great Beyond, when we kneel before the Crucified Lord, holding out to Him our poor little sheaf of works wrought for Him, the tenderest blessing of all will be bestowed on us as we unbind and take out the cheering and gladdening of broken lives that we had regarded and held forth to Him on earth as glad and ready offering. Some will have many sheaves, each worthy of great blessing, but our poor little sheaf will receive its crown of blessedness according to the measure in which we have used our talent of special joy-givingness.

Come the sunshine of GOD's Love, or the rain of His Love, we should be happy, with a happiness unknown to one who has not found Christ. All should be happy when He has been truly brought into the life, whatever the peculiar temperament may be. But from those of us whose temperament hinders not, but assists, the growth and acquisition of this radiancy of being which should follow from the inward reception of Christ, must there be a great response of happiness. And on our faithful answer to the Divine call made depends in great measure the pleased blessing that will be bestowed on us by Him Who longs for all men to be happy.

'When saw we Thee an hungered, or athirst, or a stranger, or naked, or sick, or in prison, and did not minister unto Thee?'

Many shall cry thus, but what will it be compared with a contemptible cry going forth from us, individually:—When saw I Thee as the 'Man of Sorrows,' and did not strive to comfort Thee, to cheer Thee, to embathe Thee in my own rich happiness? Might He not indeed then say to us, 'Depart from Me!'

Ah! GOD's happiness in us, the joy of being that He gives us, is meant, not only to lead us on through smiling plains, lovely fields, beautiful groves where the shadow of the trees but serves to accentuate the glorious shining of the sun above us; up steep hills, rugged mountains, whose sides yet are glorious with many-hued blossoms, filling the air with their scent: it makes us look over the summit of the mountains and see the rising of a new day. And on that day, when the realisation of Perfect Life shall be ours, we shall surely see that the happiness that GOD gave us had never been merely for our own sake, for our selfish hoarding, but that we might spread it around and make the earth shine:—make every 'common bush afire with GOD'!

> 'Temper joy with fear
> And pious sorrow, equally inured
> By moderation either state to bear,
> Prosperous or adverse!—so shalt thou lead
> Safest thy life, and best prepared endure
> Thy mortal passage when it comes.'[1]

---

[1] Milton.

VI
THINGS NEW AND OLD

o

THINGS NEW AND OLD

'To each one who, in His Grace, has entered in, that gate is a glorious portal, opening to fields of light and homes of rest, and the company of the Saints and the presence of the Angels, and the sight of those we love, and the commenced Bliss of Eternity, to be perfected then, when our vile bodies shall be made like unto His glorious Body, according to the mighty power whereby He is able to subdue all things to Himself.'[1]

It has been said that 'to follow Christ does not of necessity involve anything new.' Yet each trial of faith and patience, each need for self-denial and the mortification of desire, each pang of sorrow and agony, is to the individual being a new thing: though, in itself, an old thing. Our natures are different one from another, our powers are varied, our faculties greater or less; and so it is that the Cross is laid in fresh wise on every separate person, and from that person is required a new and peculiar manifestation of the glory of the Cross, of the Grace of Christ Jesus our Lord.

What we have to do is to learn the special secret and message of the trouble that comes to us: to strive to fathom its true depths, and then set ourselves firmly to

[1] Dr. Pusey.

obey its peculiar demands on us. Thus ensues the full glorification of what otherwise would bind us down in a dull, heavy monotony of grief wherein we should 'mope, and mow, and strike sparks' to our own sure hurt: thus comes about the finding GOD as He may be found.

There are two questions ever to be thought out by us:—Will the trouble master me? Shall I so master it that it is as an angel of ministration to my wants and needs? And on the answer depends our salvation from self, and the true vision of GOD in His Perfection of Love. Before the trouble came we had been 'isled in a hyaline of self,' far-off really from GOD. We need to be withdrawn from this that we may find Him.

Yes, the passing through the gate of the Holy of holies is to each of us a new and strange thing; and none of us may know from another's experience what awaits us therein, nor in what guise shall come that trial which is meant to evolve in us a higher life, a greater degree of sanctity. Only we must 'enter in'; and in the sure, trustful knowledge that before us are 'the fields of light and homes of rest, and the company of Saints and the presence of the Angels.' And, as the passing through the gates is a new thing and yet an old thing, so shall we find that, once within those portals, we receive from GOD's Hands 'Things New and old': each thing having within it a special beauty and power, each being stamped with the image and superscription of Him Who bore pain in His Own Bosom and made it a thing Divine.

We can receive nothing from GOD's Hand that has not been blessed and sanctified by Himself. No sort of pain can be ours that was not first His: no affliction come to which He is a stranger. 'In all their afflictions He was afflicted, and the Angel of His Presence saved them.'[1]

It was thus in the old days, among the old people; and it is thus in these new days with the new people. In all suffering, through all suffering, of whatsoever kind, Christ *is*: holding the pain to His Bosom, and giving it forth, an old thing and yet a new thing, instinct with the beauty and the glory of His Own Being. It is Pain? It is Love? Who shall say which? It comes forth from the Saviour of the world: it has upon it His image and superscription. It is His, yet it is ours; ours to hold reverently, guard tenderly, use holily. It is the coin of His Kingdom: the gold of the Sanctuary. It is that which will open for us the doors of other hearts: which will purchase for us an entrance there that shall be for the healing and the strengthening, the saving, of those hearts. It is the 'Open Sesame!'—the magic touch before which pride will go down, hardness will melt, coldness will become warm. It is that on the strength, and by the Divine right, of which we too may be saviours of men. It is the power of the Cross, that magnet of the world. By it is there to be shapening and fashioning until upon us, too, are stamped the image and superscription of Christ, and we are 'meet for the Master's use.' We are

[1] Isaiah lxiii. 9.

to go out into the world shining with a new lustre, as 'supplementary gospels of the Incarnation,' bearing about with us a Heavenly message and a Divine right :—the right to enter other lives and make them GOD's.

Knowing this, how dare we shrink from pain as from some noxious thing? How dare we turn away when GOD would give it to us?

For we do shrink, we do turn away, when we see the advent to us of suffering. We put out our hands to keep it off, not noticing the great loving Hand that is holding the pain, the suffering, within Its clasp. The pain we see, but GOD bearing it towards us in the Love Which He is we do not see.

And yet all the time, before the Altar of Sacrifice, is the Figure of Him Who never shrank nor turned away from pain. And on His Face, could we but see this, is that wondrous look which, whilst saying to each timorous, fainting heart: 'Would I could bear it for thee, My child, My child!' says also: Have I not borne it for thee? Is it not Mine that I give to thee? Mine for thy good, for thy blessing, thy strength? Wilt thou not take it from Me, bear it with Me, use it by Me? Wilt thou not grow to be strong for the weak, brave for the timid, patient for all? See! I give it thee, made My Own, warm from My Bosom, pulsing with Love, mighty for others!

It is the day of our visitation, this entering into the Sanctuary of Suffering. Christ is come to us, and He talks to us Face to face. We see Him as the 'Man of

Sorrows,' 'acquainted with grief': and we are thus to learn what Love is and what it will do for its fellows. We are to look now into the vast mystery of the Universe and approach a solution of its mystery: to see the clouds roll away and the sun shine forth brightly. There are the 'fields of light' stretched out before us, the Divine Son of Man being the shining thereof; and we are to see Light moving amidst our darkness, the darkness vanishing around it. Before our eyes is to be unfolded the great Scheme of GOD. GOD will be revealed to us as He has never before been revealed to us; and in the new light of the revelation will come a fresh beauty, a radiancy and sanctification of life and being in which others shall be illumined and made beautiful too. Then it is that there dawns for us the true vision of 'those we love, and the commenced Bliss of Eternity'!

'The commenced Bliss of Eternity'! We sigh for happiness, and GOD draws us into the Sanctuary of Suffering; and the happiness we had—and were not contented with—seems gone, and the sun of our life set. We walk at first as children of a mist, seeing nothing, knowing nothing: only guessing, and that, too often, wrongly. We had cried out for happiness as children cry for the moon, and with all a child's ignorance of the nature of the object so longed for. We reach out our arms to it, and it is as far beyond the reach of these arms as the moon is beyond the child's. We formulate it now as this, now as that, bending our full energy of force towards this or that as it appears to us: and the thing never comes, and our arms drop down by our sides, and we say that GOD—if there be a GOD—is cruel to us.

And then He comes, and in His Hand 'there is a cup, and the wine is red: it is full mixed, and He poureth out of the same'; yet not in wrath, but in exceeding mercy, as giving to us the Best that could be given.

Ah! It is the 'Holy Grail,' for which all the while, though we knew it not, we had been sighing and thirsting. It is the 'commenced Bliss of Eternity.' And as He pours the red wine on our souls there is felt growing within us a new life.

'Things New and Old' GOD gives us, and all of them, whilst seeming to be pain, are actually gifts of Love: born by Him Who is Love, instinct with the breath of this Love, pointing to the reception of That Which shall so quicken, revivify, glorify the being within us, that gradually every part, body, soul, and spirit, shall shine out with a Heavenly splendour: until 'Earth's crammed with Heaven, and every common bush afire with GOD!'

We can, indeed, receive from GOD's Hand no pain that is not of Love, and instinct with the Divine breath; nor which will not, if we let it, lead to that Eternal Life which is to be found through Christ. Many forms, truly, pain bears—in many varying outer shapes GOD's treasures are given forth to us,—but always at the heart is Love, and always does it point and would it lead us to Christ: always is there within it a seed of blessing from which should spring rich growth and fruit. But its supreme power of re-vivification and recuperation of life comes not only from the fact of its alliance with Christ by right of His Personal bearing of it, but also because it leads to the eventual holding of Christ verily within the being, and thus the spreading of Life around us.

Pain, therefore, should bring before our eyes the beautiful vision of the sainted Fra Currado, who saw advancing towards him the Queen of Heaven, holding in her arms the Blessed Child that he might take Him to himself.

And tenderly should we think of these suggestive lines :—

> ' Who is the Angel that cometh ?
> Pain !
> Let us arise and go forth to meet him ;
> Not in vain
> Is the summons come for us to meet him ;
> He will stay
> And darken our sun,
> He will stay
> A desolate night, a weary day,
> Since in that shadow our work is done,
> And in that shadow our crowns are won !' . . .[1]

Then surely we set forth as lamps to light other lives, and so draw them on that eventually they, too, may come to know 'the things that belong to their peace.' Weighed down by the Cross are we? Ready 'to do the Master's work in the Master's way!' For 'all that Christ asked of mankind wherewith to save them

[1] Miss Procter.

was a Cross.'[1]—'Christ's whole life was a Cross and a Martyrdom: and dost thou seek rest and joy for thyself?'[2] Ah! rather the Master's work in the Master's way. We would not have our Easter Morn save through the *Viâ Dolorosa*. We would not have the rest, the peace, the joy, for which GOD made us unless we reached them by His Own appointed way. We would not have them to ourselves :—unshared by those whose weakness calls for strength, whose blindness cries for light. Not alone would we reach the garden whence full glory shall ensue: not alone to us should the rustle of the Angels' wings proclaim the realised Bliss of Eternity ours.

'Leaning o'er the wistful limits of the world,' what is it that we see?

We see a Perfect Life for others and ourselves! And to this Life we strain our every nerve to reach.

[1] Lammenais.   [2] S. Thomas à Kempis.

SICKNESS

THERE is not, in the case of Sickness, as a rule, so great a tendency to bitter heart-rebellion as there is in that of poverty. The tendency here is rather to a collapse of the spiritual being.

Yet in the years, or the months, or the weeks preceding the actual advent of Sickness, there is very often a great and terrible dread of it. Many of us have experienced this dread; many have known others who have suffered from it. In weakness of the disposition towards GOD there has gone forth from the soul a half-unconscious (perhaps it has been half-unconscious: perhaps even wholly conscious) appeal that He would send any other trial than this. We have met with those who have told us that as they felt the approaching advent to them of some awful disease, they have gone about with a sense of utter despair in their minds: every ache or shoot of forewarning pain, every little feeling of unnatural weariness, bringing with it an additional agony of dread of that which seemed to be stealing upon them. And as they thought of the weary days and nights spent in bed—a bed from which, perhaps, they felt they would never rise again in the body—their souls shrank back in terror, as though the trial would be unbearable.

But the pain is generally only in anticipation. When the Sickness comes, it mostly finds us not certainly actively rebellious, not even conscious of such bitterness as had shown itself in anticipation. If it come suddenly it is a hard shock, if it come after general premonitions of its eventual advent it still has something within it of the nature of a shock to us. We are stricken, maybe, with a disease which we know to be a fatal one. We are laid low by a burning fever which does not necessarily involve death, but which may leave serious consequences behind it, and will, in the happiest case, demand great patience. Or possibly the illness is one that will add us to the great roll of permanent invalids, and give us suffering through the whole term of life. Whatever form our Sickness may take, it is ever a great trial. It is so beautiful to feel well: so beautiful to be strong and healthy and active, able to go about with an easy heart and a quick step: so beautiful to feel that for almost any task or purpose there will be the strength to meet it: so beautiful to rise in the morning, awake to the glad light of another day, holding up to GOD one's self with all its powers, to be devoted, in Him, to the ready service of our fellows, who, as the day goes on, may need this service:—looking out minute by minute, almost, for some little opportunity, even if it be but the opportunity of replenishing another's cup with the simple cold water that has run out of it—even if it be that other sort of opportunity, of bringing ultimate help to some one by the causing to be written upon the personal being one more of those lines whose full meaning and completion will be, by GOD's Grace, seen in Heaven. All this is so beautiful.

And there is different beauty of life which many feel chiefly, perhaps: the glad enjoyment of the glorious and pleasant things in the world, the study of matters above, beneath, around the earth on which the life is lived.

'To make some nook of GOD's creation a little fruitfuller, better, more worthy of GOD, to make some human hearts a little wiser, manfuller, happier, more blessed, less accursed! It is work for a GOD!'[1]

There is work for GOD that we may do upon earth, from which shall ever go forth, both within us and without us, an increasing nearness and conformity of soul to Him, an advance towards particular and general perfection, a welding of the seen with the Unseen, a gradual growth unto Heaven of earth. 'Oh! come hither. The earth too is so beautiful!' has Rubinstein told us the music of Schubert ever said? The earth is beautiful, but its beauty borrows most of its charms from the fact of its dependence on Heaven; and herein lies a lesson for us.

Whatever the especial joy accruing from the possession of health may be to the individual, all truly cherish it and fear the removal of this grand possession from their lives. Everything seems to hang upon its presence with us: power of devotion, ability to work, capacity

[1] Carlyle.

for enjoyment of the beauty and delights of the world. If health slip from us, then surely life will be then 'not worth living.' Yet when health does slip away—even if it slips away for ever, and we know it—what is it that has really taken place in our lives? Is life no longer worth living? Have all gladness and bright thrill gone from our being? Let us find the significance of the lesson to us.

At first, as one says, true resignation and submission are not there, but rather there is a dull collapse of the higher part of us, harmonising, as it were, with the lower—the bodily—part. We 'find it difficult to be resigned,' we say. It is not that we are actually resentful or rebellious; only we 'find it difficult to be resigned.' We have lost so much that we can never recover, and at the thought of our loss, maybe, we grow a little irritable and fretful, and we wonder sadly why it should have been allowed to us. It is quite clearly lack of submission that leads us to wonder thus sadly: lack of a submission which richly there would enable us to see in the affliction a 'Jacob's ladder,' on which Angels pass up and down; to Heaven from earth, from earth to Heaven again!

A ladder on which the Angels are passing up and down! That is what Sickness is. By and by, it will become more than this, but ever it is this. By and by a sick-room becomes a holy of holies: a place where Christ ever is, a place more of Paradise than of earth; a spot on which may truly be fulfilled former dreams and visions of good to be done for GOD, of higher service rendered to Him: a place where Christ will give Himself in grand, full measure; where other souls may be helped, other lives strengthened, other hearts redeemed for Him. When we are stricken with disease and infirmity we fancy that the old dreams and visions of still greater things to be accomplished, nobler and more beautiful tasks completed, greater happiness realised and enjoyed, are at an end. We feel the loss of physical power to be a thwarting of all active longings and impulses, and we think that life will henceforth mean for us a still lying on a bed from which our whole self yearns to be free.

But how different it usually is from all our fearsome anticipations! How soon, by GOD's grace and help, we grow patiently accustomed to the lying stilly there! How soon does the room become transformed into a holy of holies!

Yes, very soon we are more than reconciled to the trial that has reached us. We had thought once of attaining to great ends. Nothing could be greater than what we shall realise here, in our new living:— that living which, perhaps, many who did not understand it would speak of in sorrowful tones as 'a living death'! GOD is here indeed about us: Christ is with us in wonderful nearness: the angels, who ministered to Him in His special need, are, by His own appointment, hovering round us. Was the Sickness to us as a ladder on which these holy beings passed up and down, taking our needs to Heaven, bringing strength and refreshment to earth? The Angels, though ever ready to hold up our requirements to Heaven, remain also with us. Almost we can hear the gentle flutter of their wings: surely may there be upon us a soothing consciousness that they, in their perfect obedience to the Lord of all, are helping and serving His afflicted ones with especial love and care.

And should we not, shall we not, learn even of the holy Angels how to worship GOD truly? Christ must ever be the supreme Teacher, but are not they intended as instructors of our life, our will? And here in our sick-room, lying on our bed, is there not a peculiar opportunity given to us of learning from them? See! They serve GOD day and night in perfect obedience, shrinking never, refusing nought. May we not learn a like obedience, though our obedience take different form from that of the invisible Angels? There can be nothing more beautiful than to serve GOD as they serve Him : nothing more beautiful than that true 'consecration of the heart' which should in us respond to the monitions from Heaven, be equivalent to Angelic obedience. It is this which GOD's Saints have ever held forth and up to Him, and which has resulted to them in their glorious sainthood. They have joined their heart-worship with the pæan of praise yielded to Him by the circles of Angelic beings, in devotion, in perfect obedience, to His behests, whatever these may be. There is surely no more fitting offering that we can make than that which has endowed men with sainthood, and linked them with the Angels: no true oblation to GOD even possible that is not prefaced by the offering

SICKNESS

of a chastened, perfected will. This brings Christ within the life and being.

> 'O Lord my GOD, do Thou Thy Holy Will—
> I will lie still—
> I will not stir, lest I forsake Thine arm,
> And break the charm
> Which lulls me, clinging to my Father's breast
> In perfect rest.'[1]

This is now to be the true expression of the 'consecration of the heart' within us. Our activity is at an end: stillness before GOD is to be our lot. We may not murmur: we dare not disobey—lest we lose 'the charm' which lulls us as we try to cling unto our Father's breast? Yes, lest we break away the bond that holds us, the holy link that joins our life with the Heavenly Life!

'I will lie still!' I will to lie still, where Thou hast placed me. I will it, because it is Thy Will for me. And Thou Who art perfect Love will so fill me with love and patience that I may grow like unto Thee by the bearing of my cross with Thee. Thou wilt fill me with Thyself, so that others, seeing the vision of Thee in my face, may be brought to Thee by my sufferings borne in Thee. Unite my suffering with Thine, O Blessed Lord, and give to it, and to me who bear it, the power of a blessed life, strong to save, mighty to heal, perfect in holiness.

When we can say this, surely all sting of the trial is gone. It only remains for us to bear calmly, and as gently as we can, all that GOD shall send us of pain and

[1] Keble.

weariness. There will no longer be that exaggerated self-consciousness which magnifies even in anticipation every pang and smart of pain, and renders it a terror to us. Lying still, racked perhaps with real agony of body, every nerve of that body strung to extreme tension, every limb and every muscle strained, a still small Voice will be rather sounding in our ears :—Even so I suffered for thee : My Body was racked, My nerves thus were strung, My every limb and muscle strained. I knew the weariness that thou feelest. I bore it all, carried it all, for thee. I held thee in My Arms and passed thee to My Bosom when I was tortured with the suffering. Now thou mayest hold Me in thine arms and press Me to thy bosom, and thou wilt only see thy suffering as perfect Love. I would have thee rest with Me a while, and learn the secrets of My Heart ; I would have thee understand My Love, that so thou mayest find perfection. Let me do even here what I will with Mine own. Bear thy pain with Me, resting there where thou art. Learn of Me : learn with Me. Thou art bone of My bone, flesh of My Flesh : thou art Mine, and I, Thy GOD, am thine.

Then truly is our spirit calm. And from the calm ensues a light of ecstasy from which the soul goes forth in glad thanksgiving and humble prayer. There will henceforth be offered in our room such service as not our highest dreams foretold. The odour of incense sent up to GOD and forth for men will bring around us an atmosphere into which none can enter, from which none shall leave without the gain of something Divine in its significance and power. The very breathing of our marred life now is prayer, the very throbbing of the pain within us has the mighty force upon it of GOD's Love. We are Christ's as never before were we Christ's: we are men's as never before were we men's. The odour of devotion and glad self-surrender fills all about us, and rivets the chains that bind the beautiful earth to the Heaven of its origin. Heaven is brought down to earth: earth is drawn up to Heaven. Others see the reflection of Christ's Love on our faces, and they go forth with an illumination upon themselves. They learn much of us, and we—how much we learn of the Blessed Master! As we lie enclasping Him in our being, as it were, and yet are all the while enclasped by Him, how surely do we hear and feel the beating of His Heart of Love! How light does the once blackness of darkness become!

'Speak to Him thou for He hears, and spirit with spirit can meet,
Closer is He than breathing, and nearer than hands and feet.'

'Speak, Lord, for Thy servant heareth.' Now is the evening hour; the temple is still, the lamp burns low, there is a silence from the great stir and 'bivouac' of life. And behind the veil of sense, screened by the holy curtain of 'blue and purple and scarlet,' upheld by the hooks of gold in the silvern sockets, GOD indeed is speaking. We can never be nearer to Him than at this moment. It is a great pause, a grand opportunity. It must be taken now. 'Yield yourselves to His

¹ Tennyson.

Fatherly Hand Who gave it to you, to do to you, in you, through you, His loving and gracious Will.'[1]

It is ever a great opportunity that is presented to us in Sickness, whether it be a form of illness which shall be permanent on earth, or whether it be but a temporary drawing aside from the 'bivouac' of life. In the latter case, the opportunity is one of especially solemn and awful import, for if it be not seized at once, it is missed. Perhaps the thought of temporary illness, rather than of the particular point under discussion, was in the mind when the words were used, 'We can never be nearer Him than at this moment.' It is under this circumstance—the temporariness of illness—that stress should be laid upon the unique opportunity that is afforded to the human will and heart. Beyond doubt such is a unique opportunity. It is a crisis in the spiritual life; and by the way in which it is met will be determined the highest point of spirituality to which the life will ever on earth be raised. If, then, we let GOD do what He will with us, if we stay humbly before the ark of the covenant listening to His revelation of the counsels of His Heart, how great will be the height to which ultimately we shall attain! If we rebel and turn away, how great the depth! Never can there be the same old self that knew and cared so little about GOD. Never this! It is possible that there might be a worse self—one knowing and caring still less about Him; but it is Divinely intended and willed that a new and glorious self shall go forth, illumined by the bright Light of His

[1] Dr. Pusey.

near Presence, made His, sanctified, blessed, strengthened by Him for high service in the world, endowed with the power of drawing other lives to Him, of giving to them, by Divine aid, the clear vision and knowledge of the Unseen.

It is wonderful what we may learn in those quiet days within the holy of holies that a sick-room constitutes: wonderful how strong, and brave, and patient, we may grow. There, where in the dim light we seem to be apart from the world with all its noise and stir, it is as if we were already out of the body. We are surely hearing and seeing things unspeakable, and are face to face with the true realities of life, instead of with their flimsy, unsubstantial shadows. Everything looks different to us: once great things appear small when we are in this holy place. We look backward, and marvel at the earnestness of feeling that we have often bestowed on matters which now we see had no power of satisfaction in them actually. It seems to us as if we had always been foolishly pursuing shadows, and had only been at this late time convinced of what life really signifies. Our whole view of, and attitude towards, our daily living has undergone a change. We no longer see natural objects as they had appeared to us when we were well. We seem to know, as we lie here, that there is much far beyond all ordinary earthly plans and aims, far beyond the limits of which in ordinary living we have been conscious. We can enter better into certain discourses and arguments that we had often heard; and always, when we heard them, despised and put away from us as mere strings of empty words and phrases. We are lifted on to another plane of life; and to this plane there seem no limits.

And, most surely, there are no limits, for it is a spiritual, as contrasted with an earthly, plane, and GOD here reveals His own Infinity and the infinitude of His plans and aims for mortal living. We are caught up to see that life has no boundaries when it rests in GOD: that the limits of earth mean but the vast infinitude of Heaven: that humanity, destined as it is for this Heavenly infinitude, cannot be fettered nor bound down by the things of sense—that it must arise and shake off such fetters, asserting its Divine right to be free.

The Prayer-book of our Church recognises the great solemnity of the occasion of sickness very specially in these words:—

'... Now therefore, taking your sickness, which is thus profitable for you, patiently, I exhort you, in the Name of GOD, to remember the profession which you made unto GOD in your Baptism. And forasmuch as after this life there is an account to be given unto the righteous Judge, by Whom all must be judged, without respect of persons, I require you to examine yourself and your estate, both toward GOD and man; so that, accusing and condemning yourself for your own faults, you may find mercy at our heavenly Father's Hand for Christ's sake, and not be accused and condemned in that fearful judgment.'

The Rubric, furthermore, emphasises the great needs of the time:—

SICKNESS

'Here shall the sick person be moved to make a special Confession of his sins, if he feel his conscience troubled with any weighty matter. After which Confession, the Priest shall absolve him (if he humbly and heartily desire it) after this sort. . . .'

This quotation from the Rubric opens up a great vista of thought. We at once grasp some perception of the serious issues attendant on the opportunity which lies now to be seized by us. We see before us a new walk of life: we see how, by what Blessed Means, to secure the right method of advancing. Confession and Absolution:—then, according to GOD's Will and ordinance, the Reception of the Blessed Sacrament, with solemn and particular Intention! This is, undoubtedly, of the Will and ordinance of GOD for us. And it is then that in supremest measure Christ is ours. It was not alone the patient bearing of suffering that GOD required. It was such bearing as should of necessity lead to This.

And how great now is our patience! Even at the beginning of our illness we had gladly noted our growing power of forbearance. As one day, as one night, succeeded another, we found ourselves more able to lie still and endure our sufferings. We might be very weary each day, and each night, but the weariness altered, both in character and degree: and always it meant the nearer approach of Christ. And when we lay within His Arms, as it were, He told us what it was that we must do if we would have Him all our own. Some of us, perhaps, had not realised Him in our daily living; and so He gave to us this special chance of coming to know Him truly as He is.

Yes, it is our peculiar opportunity: this trial of Sickness. It may be a Sickness that will never leave us, it may be one that will last a long while, it may be but a slight and short lying still before GOD. But ever, in some sort, is it our opportunity of greater growth unto perfection. Discussed particularly, or treated briefly in wider sense, it matters not. The words which apply to one form of illness apply on most points to all others of its forms. It is GOD's calling aside of the life, that we may learn the beauties of patience, courage, endurance; and be brought under the influence of His Life.

A new call has come to us: a new consecration is upon us; a new dedication is required of us. GOD is teaching us as we lie here what life really means and involves to us:—teaching us through the disappointment of certain hopes, which has been so hard to bear, through the thwarting of certain schemes and ambitions, through the very arrest of our activity, our power of physical movement and action, that the true secret of right living is endurance of suffering, and reliance on Him for the solution of its purpose in life. He shows Himself to be *The Life* for Which all must strive. We are henceforth, indeed, to win souls to this knowledge; and whether it be by rising and going forth as new creatures, or as lying where we are with our fresh anointing upon us, concerns us not: only we are to be faithful to our anointing. We are now in special wise to hold high the censer of devotion, that its odour may

SICKNESS

reach to Heaven: we are to swing it to and fro, that the place where we are lying may be hallowed by its fumes. Now is our opportunity of grace, and we are to seize it with both hands, as it were. The incense of prayer and devotion is to be offered to GOD, in rich, in full, measure. In the intervals of such agony as may make definite prayer an impossibility, we are to pour forth our souls to Him in words of praise and adoration, in loving thanksgiving to Him for all that He has seen fit to send to us; and, on the other hand, to intercede, amid our earnest petitions in our own behalf, for others, for those laid by as we are, for those suffering more than we are, for sinners, for those who need our intercession in their behalf in any different way. And during the hours when our agony precludes definite prayer, the devotion with which we bear it and silently hold it, for, and with, the Blessed Master, is as beautiful to GOD, and as valuable, as positive, uttered devotion.

A still and patient service may we offer: a service so grand, so holy, that the Angels knowing it shall rejoice; and men, seeing the reflection of its beauty on our faces, shall be brought to find Christ as, through no ordinary active service of ours, could they have found Him. Self now has been purged: we have attained to that dismissal and entire effacement of self which means (as it leads to) absolute self-identification with Christ, and which causes the love, and the beauty, and the glory, which characterised Him on earth to shine through us, as earthly media of His communicated Grace and Life. On the face is seen a calm look of resignation, telling of joys willingly surrendered, and perfect—or almost perfect—peace and satisfaction gained : of a will laid down at the foot of the Cross and absorbed in Christ's, so that there can be no more struggle to be free from suffering. At the first, if there had not been actual rebellion, there had at least been faint-heartedness of such a kind as almost to approach rebellion. There had been a desperate clinging to the gladness and happiness of health, a dreadful shrinking from the visionary prospect of pain and weariness. But now the clinging is oftentimes rather to the suffering that has wrought such wondrous change in us, and the shrinking is from the busy, stirring, throbbing daily life that those in health must lead. There is work, beautiful work, we find, to be done where and as we are now ; there is happiness, there is a kind of radiant gladness even in it. We do not want to rise up and go out into the feverish joys and temptations that belong to ordinary living. Life now is rich and beautiful to us as we are.

But the will perfected in Christ does not yield to such desires and feelings. If with a tender Hand He bid us arise from our bed of sickness, and once more take our place amongst the strong and healthy ones, with something if not all of the old vigour upon us, then must we obey His Will. We have known what it is to surrender joys, and make them thus as 'garlands to hang about His Cross,' beautiful with the grand beauty of renunciation. We must now take down these garlands, and bear them with us ; and separating each hallowed blossom one by one, plant them where they may grow and make manifold bloom for Him, rendering His world sweet and fair.

That is one possibility. But there is an alternative, to be viewed solemnly.

Maybe we shall never go forth into the world again. Maybe the garlands will remain where we have hung them. They will not be given back to us on earth, but will be held there by the Cross of Christ until they shall go to form our crown beyond.

Then must we feel as one felt when he said :—

> '. . . All need of Action dies ;—
> Because GOD is ! and claims the life
> He kindled in thy brain ;
> And thou in Him, rapt far from strife,
> Diest and liv'st again.'[1]

From sickness and weariness of physical pain and inertion shall we go to the glorious life in Paradise, and the Light from the Unseen World here rests upon us day and night, as, holding ourselves up in loving, patient devotion to GOD's Will, we grow hourly more blessed, more ready for our departure.

[1] Dr. Mac Donald.

POVERTY

THERE are two kinds of Poverty. One of them does not rightly come under the head of this chapter, yet, as it is a form of trial and suffering, it may perhaps excusably be discussed here. And it seems best to bring this slightly alien point forward first.

It is natural Poverty, that state of Poverty into which many persons are born. And this is the Poverty, of course, which our Lord Himself knew; to which His Blessed Mother, most of the Apostles, and many of the Saints of later times were subject. It has been the lot, in fact, of the greatest who ever lived, and has thus been handed down to this present age bearing upon it a peculiar sanctity and an especial power of blessing. But there is still a possibility of adding to the holiness and beauty of it by the manner in which, under its trials, we comport ourselves. If we take it gracefully, as a Divinely ordained lot, as being GOD's Will for us at the particular time in which we find ourselves, and as bequeathed from a Divine and saintly experience, we may truly adorn the state; add our little quota to the splendour surrounding it. There is upon it a consecration grand and glorious indeed: still there is ever scope for a fresh personal adornment of it, and this is in our own hands, to be used, or to be neglected. There is within it an opportunity for affording grace and power of holiness; there is all the material for a gradual attainment of worth and strength of being, of a noble character and manner of living, such as no other path in life offers. And in our acceptance of the fact as it is in GOD's Thought lies the scope for our personal adornment of it, of its power to adorn us.

It is a simple fact—though so glorious a one—and it should be taken simply; without any attempts to hide it on the one hand, with no inclination to parade it on the other. If people, in their gracious kindliness, would alleviate for us some of its hardships and the suffering which it may entail upon us, then should we accept their aid, gently and thankfully. Never must we, however, seek such alleviation and aid, either by uttering distinctly our, perhaps great, wants, or by seeming to be distressed by our Poverty. It may not be done unless one dear to us, those dependent on us, are in some sore strait from which only we aided can deliver them, or if our own life actually hangs in the balance. If for the preservation or the salvation of life help is necessary, then our path of conduct is clear and open before us, and we can feel and think of ourselves as the poor of whom Christ spoke when He said, 'The poor ye have always with you,' commending them, as it were, to the care of His community of followers. Much of the 'Socialism' of the present day (though not happily, by any means all Socialism) encourages and fosters in its disciples a clamouring spirit which refuses to recognise the necessity of Poverty amongst us, and rebels against its application to themselves if it 'happens' to be their lot. Into the midst of such noise and clamour comes with a calm, still dignity this saying of our Divine Master :—'The poor ye have always with you'! And in it, if our eyes are not blinded, we see the truth that perfect equality of state will never be, and that Poverty continues side by side with worldly prosperity, a thing to be alleviated, to be aided, *but not removed.* 'The poor ye have always with you'; and our Blessed Lord would have it aided where this is possible. But ever must we bear in mind the holy counsel given to us indirectly from our Lord, through the medium of His saints. 'Receive what is given you with humility,' said S. François de Sales, 'and accept a refusal meekly. Frequently call to mind the Blessed Virgin's journey into Egypt with the Holy Child, and all the poverty, contempt, and suffering they endured. If you follow their example you will indeed be rich amid your poverty.'

It is possible to be very rich amid the direst Poverty, and we should surely be on our guard against such false and contemptible conceptions of it as cause it to be taken as an embittering affliction. Then truly are we very poor—and very miserable—and very small. But it is ever our own fault when such is the case.

'He and His Apostles lived on bread and fish, as spare a diet as poor men have now, or sparer.

'He was constantly journeying during His ministry, and journeying on foot. . . .

'In spite of penury, He and His were in the custom of giving something to the poor, notwithstanding. They did not allow themselves to make the most, even of the little they had. When the traitor Judas rose up and went out to betray Him, and Jesus spoke to him, some of the Apostles thought that He was giving directions about alms to the poor; this shows His practice. . . .

'He had no home. He was, when He began to preach, what would now be called with contempt a vagrant.

'Need I add that He had few pleasures, few recreations?'[1]

Yes, it is possible to be very rich amid our Poverty. The journey into Egypt, with all the consequent suffering, did but typify, was but in harmony with, the manner of our Blessed Lord's whole earthly Life. True, in that case there was not the 'journeying on foot'— the holy Mother carried Him as she rode poorly along the way, enduring the necessary privations and pain of the way. Still, there was the particular evidence of want and hardship that signifies Poverty. And it was ever so. We do not know that at any time of His Life our Lord suffered absolute want in the sense in which we often employ the word:—as expressing a state of starvation: but the lack of comfort and ease was His. Yet He was rich in the midst of the deprivations and want, and He thought of the needs of others.

[1] J. H. Newman.

And this spirit He bequeathed to His followers. 'Silver and gold have I none,' said S. Peter, 'but such as I have I give unto thee.' S. Peter, from amid the Poverty which at that moment was his, gave a better aid than a pecuniary one! And this reminds us that the higher aid should be ever readily at our command, though the other may not always be so. Still, usually there are possibilities of ministering to the wants of others even out of a very scanty store, and such ministration is valuable as the widow's mite:—the sum which seemed to our Lord more than the largest offerings made from well-filled stores.

Very rich amid our Poverty may we be, and therefore if by some sudden stroke those among us who had been in worldly prosperity are plunged into a state of absolute Poverty they need not feel as though all treasure and possibility of happiness had left them. This is the kind of Poverty which comes quite suitably under the head of 'Things New and Old'—the gifts, that is, from out GOD's treasure-house, the gifts held forth to one who is entering the Sanctuary of Suffering distinctly and markedly.

GOD's sudden holding out of Poverty! What is it? It is a gift new to the individual recipient, yet old as the first days of man. It means banishment from a life that was replete with delight and charm. It means— ah! more in little ways than it did in the first days of man. Life is more complex, more elaborate, now. Man is no longer a simple being with simple tastes. He himself is complex—he was, as we know, ever

POVERTY

complex in one sense; but this is an acquired complexity, unknown in the days when his natural complexity yet expressed itself simply,—and his tastes are unspeakably complex. He is a highly civilised being, and many of the marks of his high civilisation he assumes to be facts of absolute necessity, matters on which almost his very life depends. Sometimes, possibly, it occurs to us that humanity has *pushed forward* its state of civilisation, and reached a good deal not of Divine ordinance. However that may be, civilisation now—to use a homely figure—says:—'Yes, certainly eat, drink and be merry: eat of the very best and most delicate and most *outré* food, drink the very choicest beverages that can be found, enjoy yourself in such manner as is possible when you have a carriage to drive in, and some one at your elbow to do every little thing for you:—luxurious comfort throughout the time of enjoyment.'

Then into the 'joy' of such living a sudden stroke comes, comes to *us* we will say, and we find ourselves placed amongst that great crowd of toilers and moilers whose lot had hitherto stirred us, if not to pity and kindness, at least to contempt. We are now even as these. Our luxuries must go, our pleasures, delights, indulgences must be yielded. All must go: nay, have gone. And a hard lot stares us in the face. We know that henceforth for us will be laborious days, fretting cares, gnawing anxieties, wonderings as to whether the purse so far from full to-day will meet to-morrow's needs, or whether ere the day runs out it shall be empty quite. It is a bitter prospect, and one scarcely can be surprised that sometimes the heart grows bitter too—unless there is that large trust which will enable us to see through the trial, to the beautiful power at its core.

S. Francis said: 'If you are impoverished much or little by unforeseen events, such as storm, flood, fire, drought, theft, or lawsuit; then is the real time to practise poverty, accepting the loss quietly, and adapting yourself patiently to your altered circumstances.'

The difficulty is when people do not conscientiously strive to adapt themselves to their altered circumstances. Then they are not attempting really to 'practise poverty,' and they miss the very power that the trial contains for them. GOD, then, is not brought more nearly to them; nor are they in any true wise allied sympathetically to the condition in which our Blessed Lord as Man lived, and in which the Apostles and many of the later Saints lived glorifying GOD. It has been said that 'greatness is to take the common things of life and walk truly among them.' To seek to live luxuriously when the means to do so have gone were to render life one great denial and rejection of the truth; and if truth be absent from a life then must GOD be thus absent. But by honestly accepting circumstances, and striving to let the conduct of life be in harmony with such circumstances, there is introduced at once into the life the birth of a new power and a new beauty.

If it be given to us, then, to be enrolled suddenly amongst the 'poor' of the land, must we not set ourselves firmly to take the gift as it comes from GOD, allowing the true scope of its intentions towards us to have play? Too often people rebel against the so-called misfortune: murmur before GOD's Hand as He holds it towards them. Many of us do this, forgetting the old-time protestations of loyalty and fidelity, which we had thought should hold good for always. 'Although all shall be offended, yet will not I'![1] 'Lord, I am ready to go with Thee, both into prison and to death'![2] In our vauntingness we had almost echoed the impetuous cries of S. Peter; but when the test comes it finds us very much as that once great test found the Apostle. We fail as he did: though with a so much greater failure, in that our test is so much slighter.

A very slight test serves to overthrow our boasting, a very small trial offends us. And yet how angry we should be with any person who presumed to say we were not Christians in thought and word and deed: true followers of Him Whose Life, even as His Death, was one long patient Cross-bearing!

Should we not regard this new Poverty as a part of His Cross-bearing?—as being absolutely of it, whilst left behind for us to carry after Him?

If the state of Poverty now be ours we must not miss the opportunity of increased devotion to the Cross, and the Name of Christ, that therein lies for us. We must take the gift from GOD with two hands readily, trustful that all which shall follow in its train He will give us strength and ability, not merely to bear, but to sur-

[1] S. Mark xiv. 29.   [2] S. Luke xxii. 33.

THE SANCTUARY OF SUFFERING

mount, to His and to our own glory. It could not involve more to us than we can thus bear and surmount, else GOD would not have allowed it to us; for He does not see a bit of us and no more, a span of our life and not the whole. He knows exactly what we can do with, and what we cannot do with. It is all quite clear to His gaze. And so we must feel that this gift is ours because GOD knows it to be the very best thing for us: knows that by its power we shall learn our own powers, by the wealth of its beauty we shall be made richly beautiful.

It has been said that most of the beautiful lives and the fine works have been nurtured in a condition of Poverty. And we almost naturally look, now, to this state of being for the enrichers and the enrichments of the world.

> 'In palaces are hearts that ask,
> In discontent and pride,
> Why life is such a dreary task,
> And all good things denied.
> And hearts in poorest huts admire
> How Love has in their aid
> (Love that not ever seems to tire)
> Such rich provision made.'[1]

The very want and the deprivations of Poverty seem to impel the life towards, and to draw out from it the particular genius and goodness which are possible of realisation by that life. If it had not been for the Poverty which had stirred men and women, and made them thirst and long for something better than was then theirs, the world would be very much darker and poorer

[1] Trench.

than it is. 'By holding fast at home Christ's Truth in greater purity, by growth in love; by devotion deepened and increased, by more earnest and frequent communion; by a wider, more enduring, more steadfast unity; by being more filled with the Spirit; by being transfigured into Christ's likeness; by sitting always beneath His Cross; by bearing His burden; by learning to do common things in a higher spirit of self-sacrifice and grateful love to Him;—by those, beyond all other ways, shall we become able . . . to cast abroad a brighter light of truth, and to gather in more largely the fulness of the heathen to our Saviour's fold.'[1] In a state of Poverty, far more easily and thoroughly, can all these things be learned and done than in a smooth life of ease and plenty. The hardships and suffering accruing from Poverty act as a spur to the natural goodness and ability in a man, and make him look beyond common things to what should—must, he feels—lie beyond. Yes, the world would be darker and poorer were it not for the fostering arms of Poverty, in which men and women are held until they find their peculiar ideal and the particular ideal of living for them. And GOD would be further off from many of those lives in which now He is an ever-present Loving Power.

'The best good in the world,' has said Dean Farrar, 'has always been done by personal service, and beyond all proportion poor men have been greater benefactors of the world than the wealthy. Run over the names of all the world's greatest benefactors, reformers, poets,

[1] Bishop Wilberforce.

artists, writers, philanthropists, scarcely one among them all has been rich. Were the Apostles rich? What was the monetary value of S. Paul's cloak and parchments, which were all he had to leave? How much would any one have given for the sheepskin coat of S. Anthony, or for the brown serge of S. Francis, or the poor rosary of S. Vincent de Paul? Was not that saintly poverty one secret of Luther's power? Wesley only possessed two silver spoons. Would he have done more, or as much, if he had had ten thousand a year? ... " I have no time to get rich," said, with disdain, both Faraday and Agassiz.'

'No time to get rich!'—I have no time to do this or that because I am bent on getting rich! would be the true cry of certain among us: and these, very often, men whose incomes are large, and whose manner of life is luxurious. I must think of my children! they say. And so on, and so on: whilst GOD and the true good of life are forgotten, and the real purpose of Poverty in our living is missed.

If Poverty be given to us, what should be our bearing towards it?

We should meet its advent nobly and submissively: as being a part of that great Cross which Christ bore, and would have us bear with Him, seeing in it a fresh means of close union with Him, a power of growth for Him. Surely we will not 'deny,' nor forsake Him here? We would, instead of this, own, and devotedly follow, Him; and catch up and weave into our lives some ray of His Light and Glory.

And is it rash to affirm that those who really trust in GOD and live to Him will never come to a condition of actual, hopeless, unrelievable want? No; there is no rashness in such an affirmation. They may have to live hard laborious days, and yet have to deny themselves luxuries; but so had Christ to live, so had He to deny Himself. And even the thought of the children— if they are those to whom GOD has granted children,— dependent as they think on them, need cause them no undue weight of fear. For is not GOD 'in His heaven'? And has not He, Who knows all things, said: 'Take no anxious thought for the morrow'?

Thought there must, of course, be; but anxious, untrusting thought, no. Planning, wherever this is possible, there must be; but not such planning as shall exclude GOD from the life. Will not He Who sounded the depths of Poverty for our sakes, and was so loving and tender to little children, so guide thought, assist plans, further both, so that neither shall they come to want? Dreams of good education and of high places in the world will, perhaps, not be realised: their lives may have to be lived in very different fashion from that for which they had in fancy been predestined. But who are men that they should think to know the best? They, as Keble says,

> '. . . plant and build,
> Add house to house, and field to field,'

thinking that thus they are doing all that need be done and should be done, for their own good and the good of their children; and then if 'storm, flood, fire, drought, theft, or lawsuit' come, they lose faith and confidence, and believe that ruin of life has met them, and will enswathe all in its cruel folds.

Yet in such sudden Poverty a great lesson lies. It is as though GOD said :—See! I give thee that by which all that is fine and noble in thee may be called forth into active life; and on the strength, and by the use, of which thou mayest grow indeed akin to Me in thought, and word, and deed. And thus to thy children shall come a fortune greater far than any planning of thine own could give them. 'What I do thou knowest not now; but thou shalt know hereafter.'[1]

And if Poverty come to us, as it may, through one on whom we are dependent,—if it be the consequence of error, either by reason of the weakness or the sin of such a one,—there lies in it a special scope and power for good results to us. Perhaps we may, at the first, be inclined to think hardly and bitterly of him, seeing only his hand in the matter. We should, however, look beyond his hand to GOD's, which is at the back of it: rather indeed laid gently and grievedly on it. And then we shall find what a high and beautiful gift there is for us to take.

'The fault was not ours,' we say: 'why should the suffering be ours?' But there is, truly, a glorious network of thought around the question. So mysteriously blent are the error of one and the suffering of another: so mysteriously held within the great law of sacrifice, that the fault is seen and known by GOD, and the

---
[1] S. John xiii. 7.

burden of suffering borne, as being a part of personal redemption in Christ. Both are taken up and viewed in union with Christ's offering of sin in the form of sacrifice; and hence there issues a dual power of saving health, for the one in error, as for the one suffering from the error. Strangely involved and strangely blessed are the two; and grace flows from the sufferer to the errant one :—the endurance, our patiently offered life and will, serving marvellously for the removal of the load greatly oppressive to the transgressor. The suffering then is truly a part of the law of righteousness, in that it is vicarious suffering, undeserved indeed, and therefore undefiled; and it has thus a strength within it which no mere self-merited suffering could possess. Such a cross on which one is lying makes for the redemption of wrong in another; and the mind should hold vividly within it a view of the Great Cross with the Saviour of the world hanging thereon. One's fault —Another's suffering! We need not dream of injustice, nor rebel bitterly against the hardness of such a combination: the Cross explains it all. And during the days of toil, as in the nights of weary exhaustion with the toil, we can dwell upon This, feeling ourselves exalted in the accorded privilege of suffering so nearly with our Lord.

And should we not—if such a case be ours—lovingly forgive the transgressor his error, and remember always that if our trouble be great his is great also? The punishment is not remitted to him because we seem to be bearing it for him. We bear it for him in one way, but we do not take it from him. He has to suffer in his own right, and far more than we can tell. The fault was his, and, as he looks on and sees us bearing the consequences of it, the sense of his wrong-doing must ever be upon him, his pain must be far beyond words to express. Forgiveness should, truly, be very easy: resentment or hardness towards him impossible.

So, even here, with a great trust in the goodness and wisdom of the All-Father, should we go bravely on, knowing that one day Light shall dispel our darkness, Love reign supreme over Pain. Never should we faint nor be daunted, never appalled, at the weariness and the length of the way; but, holding fast by GOD and His Righteousness, advance to the very end. It may be groping now: some day there shall be fullest Light. Pain may hurt us now: soon it will be merged in Perfect Love. In all Poverty, through all Poverty—but most of all through undeserved Poverty nobly borne—we may grow towards GOD, and 'of a truth,' said the saintly Bishop of Geneva, 'he is very covetous to whom GOD will not suffice.'

MISCONCEPTION

'BLESSED, thrice blessed, are ye, to whom your Lord has fitted your cross, as He in His righteous but tender Love saw best for you. Blessed are ye, if ye but learn your blessedness, whatever cross by nature or by the order of His government He has placed upon you. Ye will not seek high things on whom the lowly cross has been bestowed. But treasure it up for yourselves in your secret hearts; there is no form of it which is not healing—bury it deep there, it will heal you, first through His precious Spirit, and when it has healed you, will through you heal others. Only yield yourselves to His Fatherly Hand Who gave it to you, to do to you, in you, through you, His loving and gracious Will. To be by suffering made meet for doing well, and to do well and suffer for it, and to suffer in order that we may do well, this is our calling.'

Dr. Pusey has, in these words, conveyed to us something of that beautiful spirit of devotion to the Will of GOD, which, finding its supreme expression in the Life and Death of Him Who was the GOD-Man, found approximate expression in the attitude of the Blessed Virgin Mary.

See! Far away, in a little Eastern town a girl is

kneeling—only a girl: not a mature, strong woman, able, as one would feel, to face and bear the world's obloquy and scorn:—a poor girl, alone, weak perhaps, unaided altogether in her solitude. And to her comes a strange messenger, with a strange message. Is it aught of which she has, in her life hitherto, had premonition? No, it is all quite new to her: it finds her unprepared by any special course of discipline for its reception and acceptance. Yet she kneels on—(Have we not a picture of her so kneeling:—a picture by a masterhand inspired by GOD, in which, in her blue and white robes, with the Sacred Dove hovering near, she is depicted as awed, puzzled, yet wholly submissive to the holy stranger bearing the white lily of purity in his hand?): she kneels before the messenger, and says in response to the message:—'Behold the handmaid of the Lord; be it unto me according to Thy word!' And then she goes forth to endure all that GOD's Will shall decree for her.

> Was the message strange and awful?
> Did her very soul seem rent?
> GOD had sent His Angel to her;
> Called her up the dread ascent.

And she arose at the bidding—she whom people are afraid of over-honouring!—she who was ordained to be the holy girl-Mother, to be blessed and honoured above the holiest saint who ever lived and sanctified the world by his or her saintly dwelling in it!—she whom painters have been inspired to apostrophise, representing her as Queen among women!—to whom poets have

MISCONCEPTION

sung of their sweetest songs, and musicians delighted to show reverence in melody! She whom we—we ordinary, commonplace people—put aside from our lives and our thoughts, our love and our reverence, as though it were crime and dishonour to ourselves to offer homage to her!—the Mother of our Lord!

Perhaps some time a call may come to us that will involve to us shame, obloquy, the world's scorn. Perhaps some such call has already been sent to us. If it has, if at some special moment of our lives GOD sent a summons to us to arise from a smooth path and go up a very rough one, leaving all we loved and knew familiarly behind us, ascending an untrodden way, forgetting, or forsaking, the old well-trodden track, turning our back on the peace of smiling knowledge, what did we do? Our call, the summons sent to us, could be but a very trifling matter beside the Divine call, the Angelic summons, in the far-off Eastern town.—Almost, indeed, one shrinks from introducing any purely human matter in sequence to that Heavenly theme. We are trifling beings, and our lives are trifling things, compared with any great saintly being and life: then how impossible of true comparison in any detail with the case of her so strangely blessed! Still her beautiful example is there; and did we, in our tiny measure, follow its single devotion to the Divine Will? This is what we have to ask ourselves. Perhaps our call came when we, through weakness of body or long-continued strain of some sort, were not so well able as, maybe, at another time we should have been to receive and obey it. Possibly, though we did try to receive and obey it, the flesh was so weak that it kept the spirit within us tarrying for a while. But surely we would follow when our Master called us to the conflict? Surely, when into our ears there sounded the echo of those words spoken to that other Mary, beloved by our Lord :—'The Master is come and calleth for thee!' we should rise up in willing obedience to the call?

Did we rise up?

Yes; in the end we rose up. We rose up and put forth ungrudgingly all the force of our feeble being into the working out of His purpose in the call. Only, we still were weak : we still feared, still shrank from and dreaded the possible consequences to us, ungrudging as we were in the devotion of our will to what we thought was His Will. He seemed to be asking of us that we should bear another's burden, perhaps : a burden not merely belonging rightfully to some one other than ourselves, but one in the bearing of which we should, we knew, be wronged and insulted, even by the person whose it rightly was. People would think scorn of us if we went forth thus : would despise us, shrink from us, condemn us as unworthy of their regard. It was a hard call, and our soul shrank away from it in horror: shrank away, yet—ah! no ; surely we did not grudge the bearing of the burden? Perhaps, just at first, we screened our eyes, and put out our hands almost in pleading that we might not be called upon to bear so much as arose in prospect to us : wellnigh revolted at the thought of it all, seeing the awful insults, the slights, the cruel, hurting wounds that would come to us. But GOD never asks of a human being more than he or she can bear, and even at such a moment as this trust in His Will and His guidance would support —did support—us?

Laurence Scupoli, who himself for many years lay under a black cloud of Misconception, said once: ' If you would enter by this gate of humility, you must toil and make every effort, especially in the beginning, to embrace tribulation and adversity . . . desiring to be despised by all, and to have no one who entertains a favourable opinion of you, or brings you comfort, but your GOD. Fix deeply in your heart the impression, that GOD alone is your GOD, your only Refuge. . . . And if some affront is offered you, be very glad of it, and bear it with joy, being assured that, because of it, GOD is with you ; and desire no other honour, and seek nothing else but to suffer for love of Him, and whatever may redound to His greater glory.'

' Be very glad,' ' Bear it with joy ': ' being assured that, because of it, GOD is with you ; and desire no other honour, and seek nothing else but to suffer for love of Him, and whatever may redound to His greater glory.' Perhaps we did not get so far as this counsel would have us go: perhaps we could not feel glad, nor rejoice: perhaps we found the stinging contempt of others hard to bear, and longed for comprehension at the hands of certain of our fellows, realising not the fullest comfort that the thought of GOD's comprehension should have brought us. Possibly to any one, at any time, this form of trial is a peculiarly hard test of glad submission. And yet how grand an opportunity it affords! How closely should the sufferer be drawn to GOD, to Christ, thereby! For our Lord ever suffered from this cross. It pervaded His whole earthly Life, and was there still at His Death—His Death on the supreme, visible Cross.

There is indeed a grand opportunity of Grace within such a trial: a grand possibility of embracing GOD's Will, of growing strong and beautiful by our submission to His Will. It is a mysterious, yet unutterably sacred gift; and if it be held forth to us we should strive to adorn it by a ready and even glad receiving. 'Be very glad': 'Bear it with joy.'—Strive to rejoice, when others use towards you injurious, reproachful, or contemptuous words; for a great treasure lies hid under the dust, and if you willingly accept it, you will soon find yourself rich, though the one who has enriched you be unconscious of the benefit he has been the means of conferring upon you.

And Epictetus has pointed out to us that if any one does us an injury, wrongs us in any way, it is he, not we, that is injured really, for he has been deceived and is therefore placed on false ground. He has followed a thing as it appeared to him, and not as it appeared—*is* —to ourselves, and it has led him into error. He, therefore, is the one to be pitied. 'Setting out, then, from these opinions,' he goes on, 'you will bear a gentle mind towards any man who may revile you. For, say on each occasion, *So it appeared to him.*'

And ever there is GOD's glory and the *Right* to be considered. And with this feeling we would unfailingly follow His leading, confident that there could be nothing for which He would not give us sufficient guidance and strength ; and that all, if we do but remain faithful to His help, must be turned to good. We may grow tired, and may, in our weakness and clumsiness, sometimes stumble over the ruggedness and unevenness of the upward track, but if our trust in GOD stands sure and fast we shall soon find that

'. . . pain and loss and grief
Are swallowed up in radiant victory';

and that the trial so hard to bear has turned to that special good :—the true meeting with Christ.

Meanwhile there is, during the growth of conformity and near approach to our Blessed Lord which thus goes forward as we ourselves advance on our rough path, the opportunity of becoming strong and beautiful, tender and more unselfish. There is the opportunity of learning by personal experience what difficulties may often accompany onward growth and advance : difficulties which had been beyond our powers to conceive. We thus attain gradually a habit of sympathy with others which hitherto had not had clear, definite place in our lives. We, maybe, had managed to feel for, and sympathise with, tangible, evident ills ; but for those vague, hidden trials which now we know may beset a life we had had no thought. Such things had been outside our experience. Though we had seemed to thrill and burn over palpable wrongs, we had really never

R

grasped the knowledge which we possess now of there being concealed wounds about a life that may render that life one long cross-bearing. With the new light upon us, however, we become able ever to remember the possibility of such being the case; and it makes us gentle and reverent in our attitude to people—for the sake of their 'possible' suffering. We fear to tread roughly on hallowed ground : to probe a wound which, though hidden, will be none the less sensitive, to speak hardly of one who, perhaps, is at that very moment bowed down by the weight of a cross which is his, and Christ's too. We learn much; but most of all we learn this lesson of true sympathy with other lives, this ever-watchful consideration of those with whom we come in contact. We become slow to judge, and lenient when we are compelled to judge : ready to vindicate, to uphold, to be merciful in thought and word and action. ' Only stand firm,' again says Laurence Scupoli—' Only stand firm, and do violence to yourself, and do not shrink from the pain which such a discipline will cost you.' And then its full power and blessedness shall come to us.

If we want to be tender and strong for others we must go through some such trial and discipline as He went through, Who was the tenderest and the strongest ever known. If we want to glow and burn with the Love of Calvary—that Love Which comprehended all woes—we must walk with our faces 'set steadily towards Jerusalem.' 'Let this be thy whole endeavour, this thy prayer, this thy desire: that thou mayest be stripped of all selfishness, and with entire simplicity follow Jesus only; mayest die to thyself, and live eternally to Me.'[1]

Then it is that gradually we find we have a new tenderness and a new strength; and that these enable us to do many things, to be of higher service, than had been possible to us before the trial came. A fresh power we have, and a fresh attractiveness. There has been a loss of physical power perhaps, but we have gained in spiritual and moral power. The old attractiveness of face, maybe, has gone, but a new attractiveness has nevertheless come to us. We find that people bring their sorrows to us more than they used to do; that children love us more than they did in the old days; that more frequently the nights come when we can say: To-day I drew a soul a little nearer GOD.

And is not all 'worth while' for such an end? Even if conceivably we ourselves could have drawn no nearer to GOD through this special trial, would not the thought of our power for others satisfy us for what we had endured? But we ourselves are drawn, must be drawn, nearer to Him; and for this, as for all else, there should be henceforth within the heart a deep and intense gratitude to Him for the whole of what He has given us to bear: a gratitude not less in that it is spread over this glorious new possession of ours:—this living, throbbing, burning passion of love for others. Has not life taken upon itself a richer meaning than ever it had for us before? Has not the world become to us holy ground, on which we shall tread always with soft

[1] Thomas à Kempis.

THE SANCTUARY OF SUFFERING

and gentle tread, fearing to introduce harshness into sacred precincts where only still and quiet reverence should prevail? Others' sorrows, others' trials, others' lives: they are all ours. We cannot tread roughly on such ground as this. It is all hallowed. And we pass about as humble ministers, bound to hold up in active love the broken, harassed, troubled lives to the Father in heaven, for the sake of Christ and the Cross to which we have been at last truly bound.

'. . . If the Cross be on us laid, and our soul's crown of Thorns be made,
Then, sure, 'twere best to bear the Cross, nor lightly fling the thorns behind,
Lest we grow happy,—by the loss of what was noblest in the mind!
Here—in the ruins of my years—Master, I thank Thee through my tears—
Thou suffered'st here, and didst not fail—Thy bleeding Feet these paths have trod—
But Thou wert strong, and I am frail; and I am man, and Thou art GOD!
How I have striven, Thou know'st! Forgive how I have failed, Who saw'st me strive!'[1]

As we look back on our striving, we may see that oftentimes we failed: that we might have done better in many particulars than we did, that here and there a ray of light was shed on the path of our advance and we did not see it, that now and then a stone was removed and we turned aside, seeking that very stone instead of accepting the smoothed bit of ground. We see many things differently now, and we know sadly

[1] Lord Lytton.

that we might indeed have 'done better.' Still we did strive. And ah! how we suffered! How tossed and torn we have been! What torturing days and agonised nights we have known, as the temptation assailed us to speak out, and so lay down our Cross, our burden; and, finding us weak, assailed us again, and yet again! How hard it was to keep silent when one little word would have cleared us! How fierce the struggle for stillness and patient endurance was! And others—How difficult they made it all for us! How they shifted and changed the position of the burden as it lay upon our shoulders, causing with each movement fresh agony to those already wounded shoulders! Perhaps they meant it kindly, seeing the weariness in our face, the lassitude of limb. Or perhaps they made the pain and suffering harder for us, because to them we seemed wrong, mistaken, guilty in our Cross-bearing. Only we prayed to GOD that *some* time they might know why it was that we were going along the way so laden and borne down, and why we would not move nor slip the burden from our shoulders—those shoulders so bent and bruised with the carrying of it. And at last, though most did not know, some did, and we were left in peace. And whilst conscious that throughout our earthly life the burden will in some wise lie there, our shoulders having grown so strong, and our souls so much more patient, than of old, we can bear willingly and gladly the weight that remains, and thank GOD ever more and more for His gift. We do not flinch now. We have learned too much to be capable of aught like this. We do but

THE SANCTUARY OF SUFFERING

strive with greater earnestness to walk aright, with Christ.

But it was hard to bear. We were conscious oftentimes of a weariness almost beyond our power to endure. We felt on some days, in some nights, that to-morrow we would lighten the burden a little: that we would not keep wholly silent. Perhaps when the 'to-morrow' came, we did say just one little word, and then we repented that word and sought to call it back and shroud it up in its old silence. And it could not be recalled nor shrouded. And in the efforts to do so we added to the former weight of our burden.

Ah! truly such a form of trial is difficult beyond most trials. But if the difficulty be great, so also are the value and the glory of it great. If it come to us at any time, we shall find the hardship, but we shall find something well worth the greatest hardship that could be ours.

Bravely, therefore, would we accept the conflict, advancing on the way where He leads. And though often, in our weakness and clumsiness, we may stumble over the stones and the ruggedness of the path, we shall see before us the 'fields of light and homes of rest, and the company of the Saints and the presence of the Angels'; and ever there is the beloved Master, holding high His Own great Cross. And we seem to hear Him saying :—
On this Cross I bore thee: bore thy pain, thy trial, thy shame; the wounds that hurt thee. There I blessed them and made them beautiful for thee. There I took them in My Arms and to My Heart; the Arms that

held thee, the Heart that bled for thee: that they might reap the healing and the salving which none but I could give to them. Bear a little longer: endure the pain and the struggle a short while yet. Let Me do what I will with Mine own.—Art thou growing weary? I was weary. Is the way difficult? My way was difficult. Is there no sweetness to compensate thee for all that is so bitter? I found sweetness in the thought of GOD: find thou thy sweetness in Me, Who am thy GOD. Do those for whom thou art suffering spurn thee, turn away from thee as they meet thee on the rugged path which thou art treading for their sake? Even so did men spurn and turn away from Me, as I went along bearing their Cross for them. Wait a little while; and then the struggle and the weariness will be no more for thee: only thou shalt have the rest and joy of work accomplished, duty done, GOD's Will fulfilled.

By taking up the 'mantle of affliction which Christ wore here, and left behind Him when He ascended,'[1] we grow into such conformity to Him that on us rests His beautiful Spirit of self-sacrificing Love, and we truly see in others' gain our own gain, others' safety our blessing, and find our highest satisfaction in the doing of GOD's Will. The difficulties of the way gradually become glories: the pain, the test, the shame of the way but so many aids to the finding of Christ. Christ hallowed all such things ' by enduring them as the Will of GOD'; and the hallowing is ever upon them, to be taken up by us and added to our own tiny hallowing:

[1] J. H. Newman.

by reason of the endurance of them as being the Will of GOD for us.

Thus we attain to the possession of such a trust as shall enable us to feel that whatever may come, either to ourselves or to others, is best, and will lead to some great end of living, even apart from—though this is indeed an errant phrase—the Supreme End, which is Christ.

'Apart from' Christ? This can never truly be. We are made His. We are drawn within the hold of His Spirit, our heart is welded to His Heart, our will has been taken up into His Will, until it is blent with His; so that now we may cry with a joyous ring of certainty: 'I am my Beloved's, and He is mine!'

LONELINESS

'I WISH you had dared to live alone with GOD for a few years,' Mr. Robertson said once to a friend whose far-offness from GOD at that time was disturbing him. And those among us who have lived in solitude with GOD for some while can appreciate the love of such a wish. When a sudden Loneliness comes into a life that has been peopled with beautiful personalities (and has had, perhaps, some special personality standing out conspicuously from the rest) it is a bitter stroke laid across that life. Yet a picture presents itself to the mind as one considers such a visitation, which conveys something of the significance of the trial.

We have seen a fierce rain-storm beat down upon the grass in our garden until it is laid flat upon the ground. Then, after a little time has elapsed, the grass rears itself in the gentle, still calm that has followed on the storm, and as the sun shines forth, blessing the blades so lately felled and crushed to the ground, we see that they are more truly beautiful and strong, because of that fierce storm through which they had passed.

Is not this somewhat akin to the process which goes forth in our lives when a storm of affliction passes upon us and seems to leave the life crushed and almost deadened? Is not even the period of still torpor rich in effect? Do not we, too, rise up afterwards in fresh vigour, and, shone upon by the Sun of Righteousness, appear beautiful with a truer beauty, strong with a fresh and enlightened strength?

Ah! We are reared so high that we see right beyond the limits of the borderland which lies between us and the great Unseen. And as we continue gazing there, the secrets of the Most High are whispered in our ears:—these ears so lately deaf in the torpor of our grief.

That time of torpor is, indeed, almost as a living death to us. It is a veritable benumbing of our faculties and powers. We have no consciousness of aught within us, any more than of aught without us, which makes life still 'worth living.' Death, of a kind, appears to have overtaken our actual living. Our continued power to breathe is but as a mockery: a misleading sign of something that does not now exist. We feel nought of that throbbing of a new life within, which is to render the old life so infinitely more grand than it had been. Yet it is there: it is only that in our present state we cannot recognise it. We are simply conscious of wretchedness. It is as though we had been drawn to some drear, waste place from which there will be no escape: where the wind howls and the rain sobs, and there is no sun, nor moon, nor light of stars to brighten it. We are there prostrate, dead worshippers of a grief that we would let master us.

But GOD will not allow us to stay where we are: He will not let the grief master us. By and by a tiny star will appear in the sky above us: a little 'shoot of everlastingness,' as it were, declaring the undying Love of GOD for us: a scintillating light which is to be to us what that wonderful star in the East was to certain of old.

How was it of old? Men were seeking a deliverer. Their faces were turned towards Heaven, watching for a sign which should lead to an answer and satisfaction of the great bitter want in their hearts whence had arisen so many sighs and prayers, not understood by themselves, but yet ever pointing towards the Ideal of the human race. Life had puzzled and distressed them, but they felt that GOD had an answer for them somewhere, and they sought it where GOD, they believed, was:—in Heaven. So, with their eyes upraised, they prayed and waited and were patient. And then at last a glimmer appeared to them, a star of bright light shone out. What was it? Was it GOD's answer? They would follow it, and find out. They were reputedly 'wise men,' and it seemed a peculiarly unwise thing to journey on afar at the bidding of—a tiny light! What would men, other men, those who had greatly esteemed their wisdom, say if they left all to follow this small scintillating light? Yet surely it had shone out for them, and they would go.

And we do not sufficiently appreciate the beautiful trust and faith of these men. If we did, we should find a store of strength on which to draw, and by which to be helped, in our special hours of need. Very frequently for us shines out a glimmer of light; but if we do not fail first of all by reason of our unwatchfulness, we fail subsequently from the fact that we do not trust nor believe in the slight evidence before us of 'things not seen.'

It is ever the venturings forth towards a vague prospect, not seen, nor felt, nor in anticipation understood, that lead us to Christ. That wonderful chapter —the eleventh chapter of Hebrews—in which occurs the verse containing the words quoted, is full of lessons to the soul on this matter of trust. But we are so familiar with it that perhaps many of us regard it as lightly as we do the account of the 'wise men's' confiding onward march. Then it is that we miss the richness of its bearing on our lives. They knew, those people of still older times, that GOD had better things in the distance for them, and they trusted and lived on, ever towards the Light that was to come. They saw not the full Light actually, but they saw as much as was needed for their ultimate realisation of 'The Light of the World.'

We can actually see, and grow to live, even on earth, in 'The Light of the World'; and it is the little scintillating light which appears on the horizon of our dull living that will, if followed, lead us to that great Light. Ever, if we did but know it, in the desert of our affliction, Christ really is very near to us: much nearer than He was to the wise men when the star shone out for their guidance: much nearer than He was at any time to the people of the still older days, when they trusted GOD, and went forth as He would have them go forth, do as He would have them do, live as He would have them live.

'We are too anxious about feeling good ourselves, to rejoice in His perfect goodness,' Dr. Mac Donald makes a character in one of his books say. And that anxiety is very frequently at the root of a good deal of the despairing desolation of spirit which may be ours after a 'loss.'

There is no doubt that, following on the loss to us of one, or of those, dear to us, which brings on the life such terrible affliction, there are stages. We are at first crushed; then a sort of despair comes, in which we wonder and question if we are not sinning in the torpor that has crept over us. And this wondering, this questioning, is, if we let it do its intended work in us, the glimmer of the star that will lead us to Christ. It is as the little scintillating light which the 'wise men' followed trustfully, and which led to That in Which lay the explanation of all life's trouble and mystery. They followed the star, and they found Christ. And this is what we have to do. Then we shall know why our Loneliness had to be, and wherein lies its real, true blessedness.

There are differences of Loneliness. There is a sort of Loneliness to which men are liable that does not necessarily follow distinct loss of another life, or other lives, that had had prominent bearing on theirs. It is the Loneliness into which many are born, in consequence of special gifts and powers that are in them, and which lead them on to a greatness, or at any rate some very special condition, of being, not possible to those about them. This, of course, has been experienced, and must ever be experienced, by distinguished poets, artists, literary or scientific men: men of genius, of whatsoever kind it may be. Then there is a solitude arising from the fact that a person may have found GOD in very early years, and feel ever the thrilling consciousness of a Presence with him that others do not perceive. The consciousness of that Presence makes for him a world, a realm, in which he moves alone, able always to commune with, and learn the secrets of, the Most High. Or a person may be endowed with an unusual tendency towards, and a faculty for, meditation, which draws him into an apartness from his fellows, who are almost entirely of a practical, active, turn of mind. In this apartness he finds GOD, and lives with Him in a sweet, holy stillness, approaching, perhaps, in beauty to that time spent by Mary of Bethany at the Feet of her Lord.

But to many, there has not hitherto been any marked Loneliness; and so GOD sends a Loneliness to them, a desolation in which the soul and heart must find Him, or else perish, virtually, of misery and despair. They had been living a conventional life where GOD could not really be found: had been living the kind of life well described as an 'official life with the Redeemer, and actual life with the world.' And they needed to learn the empty hollowness of such a life: its utter inadequacy to satisfy the real claims and aspirations of the soul. They required to learn the true greatness of soul, which ever points to the acquisition of Christ as an ever-present Fact of life—as indeed being *the* Life:—the End, the only possible Satisfaction, of all human longings.

'We are and remain such creeping Christians, because we look at ourselves and not at Christ; because we gaze at the marks of our own soiled feet, and the trail of our own defiled garments, instead of up at the snows of purity, whither the soul of Christ clomb.'[1]

Some of us, however, do not go so far as this. We are not even interested in our own progress: are not even striving to realise Christ in our daily living by moral, clean walking along the vale of life. The world is ever really in our heart, dragging us away from the Christ with Whom is being lived, at the best, an 'official life.' We call ourselves Christians. We actually go so far on Sundays, as we say the creed of the Christian Church, as to call ourselves Catholics; and the word Catholic implies that the entire being is Christ's. Some of us certainly would not apply to ourselves this absolutely self-committal term on the days when it does not occur to us to join in the Church's worship of her Lord: we prefer that negative description of ourselves which commits us to nothing—excepting negation! Yet on Sundays we do undoubtedly go so far as to pronounce ourselves members of the great body of which He is the Head; and we fancy that through our veins is coursing the Life-Blood of our Redeemer. But in reality He is not in our lives, and therefore the true object of life has not been realised. He beckoned the people of old to where

[1] Dr. George MacDonald.

they might find Him in lowly form, with the pressing burden of humanity upon Him. And this is what He would do in our case. It was devotion and trusting submission that made them follow the beckoning; and it must be devotion and trusting submission with us, if we would truly respond to the beckoning, and genuinely follow it to the designed End.

GOD in His Mercy, then, draws us into a place of new and special solitude, different altogether from the condition in which a soul naturally is placed, that in this region we may be brought to the realisation of GOD, and of Christ Personally. Either it is that our beloved are taken from our sight and consciousness of their presence, or else that we ourselves must go apart, must 'leave the beloved for the Beloved.' One or the other must be, and GOD knew it; foresaw, all along, the moment in our lives when this would be a necessity, and when it could be most productive of good result to us.

It is a bitter moment. It must ever be this. Yet what great things are to be accomplished in us! In this drear, waste place in which we are, where the only things of which we are sensible are the weirdness as of wind howling and rain sobbing, in which is darkness seemingly hopeless, will a sign soon appear; and we, if we are faithful, shall follow it and so find Christ. GOD will draw us on and on until we come verily face to face with Him Who is The Light of the World. In the old life this had been impossible indeed, but now it will be an actual fact. We had then had merely the faintest

LONELINESS

adumbrations of Christ; not Christ Himself. There had been a species of solitude in our life, arising from the inevitable fact that man is an individuality, one amongst many though he may be; and therein it was that the faint adumbrations of Him had been: but these were but as shadows cast by the Light. They merely foretold the eventual reaching of the far-off Light before us. We must actually be brought within the radiancy of the Light.

There is a wonderful tree which grows in India, known commonly as the 'Night-blowing Cereus.' When all the land is dark, enshrouded in deep gloom, when beauty seems gone and the glory of life dead, this tree suddenly puts forth a splendour of golden and snow-white blossoms, and makes a new radiance of beauty and living glory. It is like this with the soul that has been enwrapped in the darkness and gloom of desolation. Suddenly there bursts forth a form of life startling in its contrast with the pervading dark gloom, and the soul touches perfection: asserts its right of rich living amid the dull torpor of all around.

> 'Spirit of peace,
> O let me rest beneath Thy palmy shade,
> And trace in Thy clear fountain, calm and deep,
> Shadows of happier things, and the pure Heaven;
> Mirror of deep tranquillity, beyond
> The sweep of scorching winds and wintry cold!
> Or if not to that haven of Thy rest,
> Yet let Thy cheering beam, through the dark wild,
> Fall gently on my lonely path! and oh!
> When all around is dreariness and night,
> Let me not call it solitude, if Thou,

THE SANCTUARY OF SUFFERING

Light of the soul, be near ! And if the storms
Gather around me, and the water-floods
Roll o'er my soul, oh ! let no envious clouds
Hide from mine eyes that solitary star,
Rising in loveliness beyond the storm '![1]

When the star shines out for us it is the awakening within us of that glory of being which is to ensue from the first desolation of heart, soul, mind, life in which we were. There is within us then a sudden development of life akin to the bursting forth of the beautiful development in the Cereus tree. In startling contrast with the former unrelieved gloom is this new vigour and beauty of life proclaimed as born within us.

Is it not truly with us as it was with those of old ?— 'The people which sat in darkness saw great light: and to them which sat in the region and shadow of death, Light is sprung up.'

We have been in utter darkness, have been in the region and shadow of death ; and it has been a bitter time. S. Francis said that 'solitude without GOD was a living death,' and indeed we seemed even bereft of GOD. But now that the star has appeared and been seen by us, now that we have begun to follow its leading, how the darkness and dreariness seem fled ! How leavened all is with this light that shines ! How the new inner glory of being seems to redeem the gloom of its power ! How in our self arise—

'August anticipations, symbols, types
Of a dim splendour ever on before
In that eternal circle life pursues.

[1] Archbishop Trench.

> For men begin to pass their nature's bound,
> And find new hopes and cares which fast supplant
> Their proper joys and griefs . . . . . .
> . . . . while peace
> Rises within them ever more and more.'[1]

We advance then to Christ and find Him in the little Child of Bethlehem ; and we ourselves become as little children. And in the simple readiness to learn of Him there comes forth still, and ever, a greater growth and freedom of life, a simpler, truer expansion of the original 'touch of goodness' within us. We look 'beyond the shining of the furthest star,' and see ourselves become as Christ, in thought and longing, in bent of character and mind. Seeing Him as the Holy Infant in the poor stable at Bethlehem, our old attitude of life and being is changed ; and growing, by contemplation and study of Him there, into the similitude of a Child, we become susceptible truly of the reception into our being of the only Ideal by which we may be led to realise completely our own ideal. In some there may ever have been this susceptibility to receive Him : this gentle, childlike simplicity which thrills to the sense of His Advent and His touch on the life within. Some have ever been conscious of the light and joy of His Presence, and been open to monitions born of, and given out from, this Presence. But most of us need to be brought first to a 'region and shadow of death,' ere we can really be led to Him as He may be known, and must be known if perfection of living is to be realised. Thence we look up, and, from the great height and the

[1] Robert Browning.

remote distance where we had placed Him, is emitted a sign by the following of which we may lose our old artificiality of position, and gain the true position of near worshippers of the Incarnate GOD. It was into the midst of this artificiality of being that the heavy cloud of bereavement came and overshadowed us, seeming to plunge us into greater darkness and gloom than had ever been experienced by us. It was into the midst of our self-detached daily concerns and interests, our friendships and loves, that this cloud came, and seemed to make us hidden and apart from all the rest of life and being. And indeed for a while we do stand and remain apart from our fellow-creatures, apart from the actual stir and throb of living; and it is only when the cloud begins to disperse, and to admit of a glimmer of light being shed upon our eyes, that we see at all why we have been led thus apart. Then we find that the whole view and scene of life have altered.

We do undoubtedly, in our ordinary living, place Christ on an inaccessible height. We persist in thinking of Him as the remote Creator of the universe, instead of as the near Saviour of the world. We think of Him seated above in the Heavens, having the earth for His footstool, and forget that He is also the GOD-Man, Who went about the earth doing good, gathering up the weaknesses and infirmities of people into His own Being, even as He gathered little children in His Arms and drew them to Himself; allowing tears and beautiful, human love: drawing to Himself, in fact, humanity, with all its concerns and its needs, big and little, until both the bigness and littleness were lost in His great Heart of Love. We do not consider Him thus. We put Him far away, up above and apart from our lives, and allow others to take His rightful place beside us (in so far as they are able to fill this place). We are not real enough nor simple enough with Him : we carry our little affectations of humility and our conventionalities of thought even into this high and holy region, where we should walk as children, with all the trustful, daring naturalness of children upon us. We will not let ourselves know Him as He should be known. We say we are not worthy of so great an honour as to walk beside Him through all the common days. On such a special day as Sunday, maybe, we would try and draw a bit nearer to Him ; but the common days—the week-days,—when we have on our bodies our working-clothes perhaps, and in our minds our busy thoughts, and our amused thoughts even! Oh! no ; we could not think of His being with us, nor at all near us, at such times as these.

Yes, He has been too far off from us, and we needed to find Him as the little Child, as the tender Man of Sorrows, as the GOD-Man dying to redeem the world from its sin. We needed to be drawn aside from our fellows and our ordinary living into an apartness where a sign of Him might appear, by the following of which we might truly find Him. And then peace indeed rises within us more and more, and our whole life and being glow and burn with the radiant glory, the wondrous flaming, of the great
'Light of the World'!

LOVE

'ON our way to Paradise and Heaven all else must drop away from us, all else must be unlearnt, save only the love which we have felt or found:—that silent, hidden grace is the only thing in all the world of which we are quite sure that we can take it with us. . . . This is the great business and meaning of our life on earth: that we should more and more yield up our hearts to GOD's great grace of love: that we should let it enter ever more fully and freely into us, so that it may even fill our whole heart and life.'[1]

Love is indeed a gift of GOD, and it is the 'crown of humanity,' but it is not always an evident happiness to the person in whose hand it is placed. Sometimes it is almost at the very first a visible cross; and always the learning of it, and the circumstances and conditions surrounding it cost so much to the individual that the truest way of treating the subject is to include it distinctly under the head of GOD's gifts of pain. And perhaps nowhere in our life's way of experience can we have a more beautiful lesson and Divine message accorded to us than is accorded in the view of Love as

[1] Dean Paget.

pain; for then most surely do we come to realise the truth of pain being 'the very beating of the Heart of Love.' No life, we feel, can be really complete, no life's experience adequate, that does not contain the knowledge of what Love is, what it can do—is *driven*, by the beauty of its nature, to do: what purpose Love must serve, and what end it would gain.

Whether Love, then, cause us at the first joy or woe, whatever be the measure of the suffering it must entail, it is yet the most sublime gift that could be given to us. It is a gift right out of the Heart of GOD Himself, and it must bind us to the Higher Life as nought else could bind us to that Life. It will open our eyes, uplift our soul, awaken all powers of the soul. It will teach us the graces of patience, tenderness, and courage. It should strengthen and support us in the most difficult hours of our life: even that terrible hour when we have to use its power against itself.

Lacordaire, perhaps more happily than the generality of teachers, has discussed the beauty of Love. He says, however, that no man can really know what love is except by personal experience of it. And surely we know that no amount of talking can make the matter clear to him. He must learn what it is to be wrapped into a great, pure Love, which, filling all the recesses of his soul, draws that soul into a communion with the GOD of Love which elsewise were not possible. He must know what it is to be possessed by a visitant, seemingly of earth, actually of Heaven, that teaches him the absolute need of, and call for, the sacrifice, the complete surrender, of himself. 'He that shall lose his life,' said the Master, '... shall save it.' To lose one's life even in another human life is to find it :—to find it placed on the brink of the Divine Life, into Whose embrace the lesser shall be wholly drawn.

We must learn then by personal experience what Love is ere we can really reach to GOD and find our true and high selves. We must learn it through that exquisite pain of Love which leads to sacrifice as the only possible satisfaction of its own longings. A Love which has to lay itself down in another's being, impossible of content without the acceptance of the offered sacrifice, a Love which knows no happiness without that other's happiness, no rest without that other's rest, a Love which watches ever over another's life, yearning for its good, seeking for its perfect completion of life and being, is a gift right out of the Heart of GOD ; and it teaches us what GOD is.

Sacrifice is truly the language, the expression, of love ; and in Love is found the key to all beautiful sacrifice, the solution of its mystery and power. Thus does it reveal to us much of the Story of the Life of our Redeemer, in Whom Love was the supreme force. A man ignorant of the nature of all pure Love cannot really grasp the significance, nor indeed fathom the depths of the necessity, of the Incarnation of GOD, and the entire immolation of Himself. But, with the immolation of his own self on the altar of Love, is born within him a dawning recognition of those Great Mysteries which before had been so dark to him as to lose their power of influence in his life. Christ is thus brought near to him, and the grandeur, even as the need, of the Divine Incarnation and completed Sacrifice is clear before his mind.

'Love loves unto purity.' Love, in other words, must have the perfectedness of the beloved. 'As it was Love that first created humanity, so even human love, in proportion to its Divinity, will go on creating the beautiful for its own outpouring.'[1] And it can never be content with anything less than its own absolute self-sacrifice. Thus is it a training and development of the moral nature of man.

We want to represent Christ in our daily life. But in order to represent, it is necessary that there should be some resemblance of the representative to the one represented: there must be certain qualifications of office, certain points which make plain the suitability and fitness of the agent to his office. If we would represent Christ we must possess some correspondence of life and being with His Life and Being, some qualities which will render us appropriate as His representatives. And Love is the only thing that can really lead to this, for by it we see GOD and come to know Him as without it we could not do. We want to live as Christ lived: very well, then we must learn how Christ loved, for that is the meaning and the explanation of His beautiful Life. We must learn what Love is, the course that it must follow for the sake of the beloved. We must learn the true path to perfect sacrifice. It should

[1] Dr. George Mac Donald.

be nothing to us how great may be the pain of the Love that comes to us from out GOD's Hands: only we must accept willingly the gift that He holds forth for us.

There is a strong tendency in the human mind to regard special Love, peculiar attachments, as at least apart from, if not utterly antagonistic to, the spiritual life which we, as spiritual beings, are called upon to live before GOD. It is a tendency for which much might reasonably be advanced, but against which the expression of Christ's Life, revealed to us in Holy Scripture, reflected through various media, distinctly declares. And perhaps we never realise more clearly the fallacy of the arguments (indeed it is out of the question that we could realise this in any other way) brought forward in support of that theory, of the detriment to our spiritual life caused by the allowed entrance into the being of special Love, than when to us such a moment comes as that described by Lacordaire in these words: —'Two beings meet in the immensity of time and space. . . . They are united by a reciprocal preference which honours both.'

Love, leading as it does to sacrifice as its natural expression and end, is the only thing that will really teach GOD to us as He should be known. It is a holy, glorious possession that binds the life to GOD.

Yet men seek to kill Love: the Love whose power is just beginning to be felt within the heart, the soul, the mind.

Mr. Brinckmann gives us a forcible illustration of the lengths to which an earnest, well-intentioned man may, in his efforts to be rid of all that he takes to be a hindrance of his spiritual advance, go. 'There is an anecdote of an ecclesiastic,' he says, 'who said he was happy to have practised detachment so long and successfully, that he could thank GOD that he did not care for a single human being on earth!'—One is reminded here of the Pharisee, who out of the midst of his ignorant, proud egotism, thanked GOD that he was not as other men are. And there is borne into the mind by a natural sequence of thought the belief that Christ, were He now on earth in the same way in which at one time He was on earth, would say of some poor erring mortal, struggling humbly with — though bowed down by — the weight of a love that enchained his higher aspirations, and made him but see GOD dimly before him: 'I say unto thee, that this man went home justified rather than the other!'

'Human love,' it has been said, 'is the chalice which holds Divine Love to our lips.' Surely, then, it is to be esteemed and received? No human being may try to dash this chalice from his lips. To do that were to seek to desecrate Divine Love, and to overthrow the application to us personally of the great Law of Sacrifice, which finds its perfect expression in Christ's Love.

Ever must we remember that the Love which teaches GOD to us is holy: never to be scouted, never to be shrunk from, never to be feared nor fought off. No life can be really complete without it. Whether crucified and offered to the Father in union with Christ's Sacrifice, or allowed to dwell with us in its natural, full

THE SANCTUARY OF SUFFERING

livingness and beauty of tenderness, it yet must be allowed entrance into the being; for, so far from injuring advance in spiritual life, it is the mainspring and the quickener of spiritual living. 'It is better, a thousand times better, to have the hardest lot a man can bear: better to slave on day after day, and hardly to keep soul and body hanging together: better to carry a weary load of sadness or temptation ever dragging at one's heart: better to be alone, misunderstood, despised, and slandered: better all this with just the knowledge, just the quivering flame of love within one, than to have all that this proud world can give one, and to have no love.'[1] Without Love there were no bright thread of holiness drawing the soul on towards GOD, no true spark of Heavenly splendour to ignite the heart to a flame of Divine Love, no readiness of response quivering at the touch of GOD's finger as He lays it on the life to make it all like His. With it there is initiation into the mystery and grand complex power and significance of the Love of GOD Himself. 'There is nothing eternal,' says Dr. Mac Donald, 'but that which loves and can be loved, and love is ever climbing towards the consummation when such shall be the universe, imperishable, Divine.'—It *must* strive 'for perfection, even that itself may be perfected—not in itself, but in the object.'

Only the learning, the acceptance, of Love costs! It costs a good deal more than an unregenerate heart is always ready to grant. And perhaps this is why people, at times, try to drive it away as it is being born in their

[1] Canon Knox Little.

hearts. Perhaps it is not so much that they fear the possible detriment consequently to their spiritual life, as that, unconsciously to themselves, they are afraid of that close intimacy with the law of sacrifice which it will entail on them. Possibly they are attempting to preserve their easy, comfortable 'peace of mind,' which makes no great demands of them. Yet, the continued peace of mind were a paltry possession beside this great, grand messenger of GOD. And even the relative desirability is not a consideration to be weighed and measured when it is a question of receiving a gift from Him. If the being is regarded as GOD's—well, there *is*, in such a case, 'room for the creature to stand in'; and GOD's Presence, wrapping the lesser presence around with its glory, will draw both that indwelling presence and the other indwelt by it into a higher, purer atmosphere of living, wherein they shall commune with Him in truest correspondence of heart and soul.

Ah! if Love cost much, does it not yield much also? Does it not yield to its possessors a thousand-fold more than its cost? It does truly bring about a closer union, a more glorious communion, with GOD. It gives Christ to us. It is an illuminator of the whole life; so lighting the eyes of the soul that that soul looks out, and up, and sees GOD everywhere: it quickens, revivifies, irradiates with a Heavenly splendour the inner and the outer being of man. So far from making us love GOD less, it teaches us how more really to love Him. So far from binding us to earth and the things of earth, it sets free—or should set free—the wings of the soul, and makes us fly to Heaven, finding delight there in the revelation of things hitherto unseen and unknown. It makes us strong where otherwise we had been weak. It, infused as it is with the breath of Eternity, says to us, once fettered and dwarfed by the thought of this life as *the* life, great with a greatness of its own, yet ending when death shall claim it :—' Ye are now in Eternal Life!' It comes in the beauty of moonlit nights, it shines in the brightness of stars; it looks down from the blue of the sky, from the glad radiance of noon-day sun, and calls to the soul which we are before GOD :— Arise; shine with the glory of Heaven! It breathes forth in the flowers, the song of the birds, the myriad sweet scents and sounds in the world, and whispers to the heart :—Be holy and pure and beautiful, that thy life may be a link between Heaven and earth : that in all thy movements, thy ways, thou mayest preach Christ, holding Him up before men as the altogether lovely One.

Truly the lesser life is a part of Life Eternal, and the lesser love a part of Love Eternal. Love is ever saying :—I bind earth to Heaven. So ' we are never so near Heaven, we can never get so true a thought of what it is, as when some great glow of love is filling our hearts.'[1]

Love is the pre-eminent revealer of GOD and of the beauty of heaven, the surest bond of the seen with the Unseen, because it is the nature of the Divine Life and the life of Heaven. And by natural consequence it is

[1] Dean Paget.

also the revealer, and at the same time the illuminator, of our fellow-men. Without Love, therefore, we can know truly neither GOD nor men, heaven nor earth. It awakens in our hearts a burning, glowing 'charity toward all men,' a practical loving of our fellows: it unites the acts of earth with the Acts of Heaven, so that the whole earth becomes indeed 'encompassed . . . with the great girdle of GOD.' It causes our being to be in such beautiful harmony with the Divine Being, that at every vibrating touch there comes forth an answering chord of perfect music. No other love will really teach us what this special feeling teaches. There may, without it, be a certain love of our fellows, and a certain devotion to GOD, but neither of these can be the reality in our lives that this supreme love for a human being becomes.

There may be, as we know, a circle of persons dear to us, and they stand out very beautifully in our soul's life; coming to us in the rising of morn, the dying down of day, in the sights and sounds and scents that delight us. They even creep into, and grow to belong to, our life of union with GOD, enriching (if one may dare to put it thus) and fertilising this union by means of the special revelations that they make to us of the peculiar beauty of their souls. And there is ever the love of family and relatives, which also is education and development of the life towards GOD and the fulness of living.

Still none of this quite equals in force and significance —nor indeed nearly equals in this way—the special Love that exists between two persons brought together in the course of life by the providence of GOD, each of whom is to the other the only one who could stand forth in the Divine Presence within the being, girt about by, partaking in and (humbly it is said) adding to, and intensifying, the beauty and richness to us of this Presence. We may think much of, and strive greatly for, the objects of these other loves and affections, and may even become far more tender and earnest in our ministrations to them, and more gentle and humbly grateful in our acceptance of their ministrations to us. We may, and do, see more beauty in them by reason of the wondrous education of our inner selves wrought by the power of the special love. Still, what a difference there is! Tenderly affectionate towards, and anxiously striving for, them as we may be, there yet is not the power and significance in the bond—the varying bond—that holds our lives bound as there is in the (humanly) supreme Love. They do not become involved in the same way to us in the bright, glowing sunsets, the soft radiance of moon, the shining of stars: they do not speak to us in like voice in the song of birds, nor pass upon us the same sense of their presence in the delight that is ours when to us is borne the fragrance of flowers, the sounds in the air, the manifold charms of GOD's natural world, throbbing about us in its Divine beauty.

No; we love them with the love of which S. Paul wrote so earnestly: a love that is sympathetic—sympathetic even to scourging when this seems necessary,—tender, strong, mindful ever of their real good. We love them with a love that is not ignorant of pain: that has in it the pain of disappointment, of disagreement often; the pain of the fear, and then the actual realisation, of 'loss':—separation, by distance, by circumstance, by death. But it is not as that other Love whose very breath at times is pain : whose content can never be known without complete self-immolation : whose special office it is to make of our being a sanctuary, with an altar of sacrifice within it.

There is ever, here, an altar of sacrifice: there must be a pain insatiable until it has lost itself in the then known delight of realised sacrifice. There is ever, here, the going together to an altar of sacrifice, where GOD may be better served and glorified, where may be true connection with, and eventual participation in, the Sacrifice on the great Altar of oblation. Even if there be granted to us the humanly desired consummation of earthly Love, there is yet sacrifice required. Indeed, here is a perfect expression of Love demanding for its satisfaction the immolation of self on the altar of the beloved. This is the losing of a life in another, the merging of separate individualities in one individuality, the entire obliteration of a distinct self, described by Lacordaire as 'a fusion of two beings in the same thoughts, the same desires, the same wills.' It is then that human life is in beautiful, fair balance, in equipoise that points in faint measure to the sacrificial union existing between the bought human being and Christ, that figures in some dim (though infinitely unworthy) degree the marvellous union of the Holy and Blessed Trinity, fused, as the Eternal Three Persons are, in a Perfect Being and Life of comprehensive Love.

Truly, nought can teach GOD to us as special Love can teach Him. In the complete, mutual offering that Love involves ever in some wise, lies a means of intelligent approach to Him through renewed and repeated oblation, such as cannot be otherwise attained. In it is proclaimed the nature, somewhat, of Christ's Sacrifice—of the Divine Sacrifice viewed in its totality,—and by it are we led to this Sacrifice. We see that, by logical necessity, Love, finding its only perfect expression in sacrifice and sacrificial union with Christ, the sole stay of Love, as the true satisfaction of Love, must lie for us in the Blessed Sacrament, wherein are given the Body and Blood of Christ—the 'Lamb slain from the beginning of the world'—to the offered soul and body of man. Love points the way to sacrifice: is willing to lose itself in and for the life of another. In the Blessed Sacrament Christ comes, and says:—This is the Perfect Sacrifice, and the means of perfect sacrifice: lay the will and the being here before My Altar: receive the Lord of Life and Love. Die in Me and live again in Me, and then shalt thou find for thy beloved perfect Life, the crowning perfection of Love.

Love leads logically to the Perfect Sacrifice of the Altar. But there have been through its courses many phases, many stages, of sacrifice. First there have been sacrifices of thought, of time, of possessions: then there have been sacrifices of inclination, aim, personal, distinctive ambitions: finally there has been the fully recognised necessity for, and the absolute yielding of, self-sacrifice. And all these phases, these stages, involve to the individual pain :—not the pain of giving up, for in giving up is the only possibility of accorded satisfaction, but that far other pain of the insatiableness of the will to give, the ever increasing desire to give, set over against the limitations constantly visible to the mind and heart: the whole great sorrows attendant on the craving within us, which is ever seeking vaguely for a satisfaction that comes not.— And here there is in supreme measure the dread of separation:—so-called 'loss.'

So, Love we find indeed is pain, and only by its power and bearing toward us are we able truly to apprehend the great truth that 'Pain is' [of necessity] 'the very beating of the Heart of Love.' Interchangeably do pain and Love exert their office in our lives; and as each throb of pain signifies the pulse of Love, so does each beat of Love within us explain the mystery of pain. It is impossible to separate pain from Love, but we do not realise this until we have studied and grown to understand, by means of personal knowledge and experience, the nature and office of Love. Love *is* pain, and an enumeration of the 'Things New and Old' which are given to us in our Sanctuary of Suffering must be crowned with this revealing 'Thing,' Love. Else would it not hold together. And without consideration and inclusion of Love amongst the chief gifts involving suffering to us, we could not truly reach that awful agony :—the 'separation from,' the 'loss of,' one

—or of those—bound up with our earthly living and happiness.

GOD takes from us, either by death, or by some circumstance of life, one very dear to us. It may be a relative, a member of our actual family circle—a parent, a brother or sister, a child; or it may be that special *other* one who has at times made life almost a seeming completion to us. The circumstance of life which alone could sever members of a family, one from another or the others, would, of course, be in most instances distance: the going away to some far-off land. This is a heavy trial. Still it cannot approach in intensity of suffering to the individual, or individuals, that seeming severance by death, or that terrible trial which comes to two lives that had, in the mysteries of GOD's providence, become blent one with the other and both with GOD.

That is an awful trial: a far harder test of patient submission, usually, than the trial of separation (seemingly) by death. We had looked up from the midst of our happy love and seen GOD, as we fancied, quite clearly. And indeed He had been very clear to our gaze: only not clear enough. We had thought that the love which had come to us was to be with us, consciously to ourselves, for ever. It had brought GOD near to our life, and made that life doubly sweet and glorious; and we rested, sensible of a great content within our being. From the depths—or what we took to be the depths—of our heart and soul we had gazed Heavenwards, and cried in an ecstasy of praise: My GOD, how good Thou art! How beautiful!

Yet had we truly known GOD? Had we not rather formed a picture of Him in our minds which was not really GOD in the full beauty and glory of Being? We had caught a glimpse of Him as He is actually, and even the glimpse was so beautiful as to dazzle our eyes; but we had not learned GOD as He may be known.

We had had 'evidence of sorrow and joy, of goodness and of evil, of sin and of pardon, of despair and of hope, of life and'[1]—Ah! no; we had not had evidence therein of 'death,' or of virtual death :—a blow harder, indeed, to bear than the stroke of death.

'Seeing that I am composed of two parts, of soul and body, say which of them you love most, the body, or the soul?' said Savonarola. '... If then you love the soul most, why not look to the good of that soul?'

Do we do this enough? Do we always love the soul pre-eminently, caring little, comparatively, for the body which in some sort and measure reveals the soul to us? If we did, we should not feel so terribly the stroke of 'death,' or the blow of that which is worse than death. We prove the great defect of our love when we sink down, crushed and despairing, in the face of the removal from us of the seeming of what pre-eminently we should love. The soul may love the body, truly, by

[1] Rev. R. C. Moberly, *Lux Mundi*.

reason of its intimate connection with the higher part of the loved one, but it may not love that outer seeming first, or even equally—or nearly equally—with the higher part. The first care, as the real devotion, should be directed to that 'higher part' of any being: that spiritual essence which goes forth certainly through bodily functions, through speech and signs and movement generally, and therefore may rightly make the body dear to us. We may love the body because of the soul, in and with the soul, and so for Eternity; but we may have no separate love of it, no mere love of the body. And so, when either actual death, or seeming loss of the body—that is, loss of the bodily presence and nearness to us—intervenes in our life there should be no sense of the united life being marred:—the life that bears towards GOD. If death come, then our hearts need not be buried in the grave which receives the dear form of the one loved by us: there is nothing there that could rightly hold us. If separation between the complete living of one with the other come elsewise, then there need be no roaming discontentedly through earthly space, in a vain endeavour to touch a complete living: that were a waste of spiritual force, and an involved attenuation of spiritual life. We should, rather, in each case, mount in thought to Paradise— actual thought in the one case, anticipatory thought in the other—and find higher communion and better union than any of which we had had prescience hitherto: looking on, further, to that Realm wherein shall be physical being become spiritual, one, absolutely and indissolubly, with the spirit that had before quickened it, and only made its true beauty, its ordained dearness to us.

And yet to talk of physical 'being' at all! What an error this is! Physical 'being,' when the body exists only by the presence and the power of the indwelling spirit! It is an error into which one slips from carelessness, but how culpable is the carelessness which makes such a lapse possible! We need surely to guard ever our thoughts and our words, but perhaps we never need it more than in consideration and discussion of that life so mysteriously blended of soul and body, that points to a life without the body, and to the life of body and soul re-united and perfected into a full spiritual entity.

We should think and judge and love in the light of Eternity. And then when the 'seeming' of Love is removed from our daily path on earth we shall be able better to endure the shock, and to discern the high mission of it to our life. Such separation should be a crowning of the soul. The separation that is, in some measure, involved both in 'death' and in the removal by life-circumstance of the bodily presence and nearness to our personal life of one dear to us, should not be viewed as true, or final, separation: rather as GOD's 'best' for the perfecting of that beauty wrought already through the loving union of earth. Continued evident union here, or apparent severance, matters not as affecting the permanent reality of the oneness that GOD had brought about between the two lives. The death or the life-circumstance which comes to break the earthly bond asunder is but a messenger from the eternal shore bidding us arise to a more elevated, to a holier, condition of being than even that gladness of being which had been ours whilst the bond held.

And this gift of GOD to us, in the Sanctuary of Suffering, is a mighty gift even when the security of life and Love that seems to prevail in a home is rudely dispelled, and some loved member taken away—so far as bodily presence is concerned. A period of sorrow must ensue, in which no human aid can meet the needs of the afflicted. Perhaps some of us are apt to forget this, and to resent the stolidity which presents itself to our well-meant efforts at consolation. Yet how unlike GOD this is!—GOD, Who waits so patiently, and feels so tenderly all the while! How unlike the 'Man of Sorrows,' Who 'wept' when Lazarus was dead—wept, really, in unison with the bereaved ones! For the first few days a life, any life, almost, is stricken by the blow of seeming separation, and the only sense possible is the sense of desolation. But after these days, then should be the arising that is 'possible,' and which is of the Divine intention for us. Then should there be the glorious thought of the life in Paradise, the life of the soul set free; so that the whole being may be drawn into a new and beautiful knowledge of GOD, and communion with the Unseen. Does it not come, most often, on the day when the mortal remains are taken away from our neighbourhood? Is it not then that the spiritual life becomes truly clear to us? Many of us may awake before this. Many, perhaps, not quite then. But surely the awakening should not be later than this?

> '... Something to love
> He lends us; but when love is grown
> To ripeness, that on which it throve
> Falls off, and love is left alone.'[1]

And when this takes place, in whatsoever form or sphere of living, the wrench of the outer seeming from the inward reality signifies to the bereaved a separation of life awful indeed to contemplate. Happy the being that is not alienated even for a moment from the conscious possession of the Love that in GOD had been learned. But so rare is this, so limited in its suitable application, that it seems essential, when treating of 'separation' and 'loss,' to admit into discussion the inevitability of certain days of unrelieved desolation, and, as it were, rebellion, or sullenness, before GOD. It is really not often this, however, but rather a numbed condition of being into which at first the Light and Truth of GOD cannot penetrate.

'It is hard in this world not to dread meetings because of partings; greetings because of farewells. The purest joys are dashed by the foretaste of sorrow, the closest and dearest bonds have no assurance against the rude violence of death.'[2]

Yet, though we know this latter fact so well, we are rarely prepared in due manner for the reception of the blow of seeming severance. But, as the writer of the

[1] Tennyson.   [2] Baldwin Brown.

above passage continues, 'It is well. We would not live' [on earth] 'always; we would not take our fill of joy in such a world as this. Our hope stretches into brighter and more blessed regions, where those who meet have met for ever; where those who love need no dark warnings, lest love should grow idolatrous and write its epitaph. . . .'

Can we not feel that 'it is well,' when we reflect that this earth is peopled with beings whose Love is made to live on evermore in 'brighter and more blessed regions'? The death, or the stroke of earthly circumstance, that seems to part us from our loved ones, can have no power of real severance of one life from another. It does but form a fresh link and bond between us and the great Unseen World, where our hope, as the realisation of all fondest and highest hope, lies safe. If it be the white-winged messenger of death that has intervened in our life, his message is fraught indeed with Heavenly meaning for our present daily mode of living. As he carries the spirit aloft to the GOD Who had made it ours (in Him), there should be born within us a power of joy that nothing else could give, and a better apprehension of the truth of our life. The passing of the body from life to death, the flight of the spirit from life to a higher life, the eventual laying of the body in a tomb, the felt activity and reality of the life beyond the veil of sense, now possessed by the spirit 'departed,' do alike accentuate the fact that this life in its clear palpability is yet evanescent, whilst the glorious impalpability of the great Life beyond is the actual, the only sure Life. And then it is that there comes to us a strength that shall encompass our earthly living, and make it ever most truly a looking into the face of Eternity.

But if the seeming separation of one life from another be not death, but some earthly circumstance, some life-circumstance, there is still the great thought of the Life Beyond to uphold us, and strengthen and inspire us with Heavenly beauty of living. 'Those whom we love in GOD we cannot lose.'[1] Always it might be truly said : 'Not lost, but gone before.'

This gift of separation, in whatsoever form it may be, is GOD's gift, whereby we may gain in spirituality of living. It is better far that the body, the 'seeming,' of Love should be dead, and that we should live more truly as beings should who are destined for an eternal perfect spirituality of life :—better this than that we should have grown—as we might have grown—content with an earthly mode of life, and wanted not a 'higher self.'

GOD has given to us a blessed hope, which shall serve to keep our minds above the earth on which our little present part is being played. It is essentially of His gift that we should see Paradise and Heaven more clearly than before. We may pass along the earth thrilled with the sense of union one with the other and of both with GOD. Feeling within us the beautiful consciousness that neither in Paradise nor in Heaven will the bond of love be snapped, that communion and intercourse are possible when one is freed from the

[1] S. Augustine.

body and the other remaining in it, that that communion and intercourse will be maintained when both are freed from the body, and still more richly when there has been the putting on of the new body—the body so different from the earthly form which certain among us manage to regard as a 'casually adjacent fragment of the external world'!—Feeling all this when death has been the agent of apparent separation, are we not helped on towards a truer view of all living, a truer apprehension of the greatness and grandeur of life? And if it be not death, but a life-circumstance that has seemed to part us one from the other, may we not still look up to where, beyond the veil, all Love that is pure and true shall meet with its perfect satisfaction and crowning?

> "'Tis sweet, as year by year we lose
> Friends out of sight, in faith to muse
> How grows in Paradise our store.'[1]

'In proportion as we throw ourselves forward into that future, so our capacity for all that is most worthy enlarges. To live with an eye on the future is to make the present rich in action, and to free it from the paralysing effects of cowardice or fear. The human soul exiled from its natural home must lift its eyes above the mountains and see the morning dawn. We are looking, not at the things which are seen, but at the things which are not seen: for the things which are seen are temporal, but the things which are not seen are eternal.'[2]

[1] Keble. [2] Canon Knox Little.

VII
THE GREAT UNVEILING

THE GREAT UNVEILING

'To Christians, the bitterness of death is gone, just because Christ died and rose again; and they can hardly be said to die at all, but to pass from a less desirable scene of life to a more desirable.'[1]

This sentence states briefly what is surely the right guide in all our consideration of death:—the fact that in Christ, as by Christ, death is no longer bitter but sweet, inasmuch as it is the Divine path that we must tread to a higher, grander life: that its sting is gone, its nature changed, because He Whom supremely we love suffered it in His Own Person, and triumphed absolutely over its evil power, when, rising from the grave, passing through the gate of death, He bore into the highest Heaven a Perfect Human Life.

Christ has 'gone before': we may follow Him!

And do we shrink from following Him here?—we who, in fellowship of suffering, in communion of Sacrifice, have been made His? Are we afraid of following the Captain of salvation whithersoever He shall lead the way? Does there come a time when we would stay behind, because we do not know exactly to what,

[1] Canon Mason, *The Faith of the Gospel*.

and where, He is leading us? Have we not yet learned obedience?

Christ has 'gone before': passed through death, first into Paradise, then into Heaven. And we are on earth; on the earth that He sanctified by His visible Presence, that He ever sanctified by His invisible Presence. And we fear to leave it. To some of us it has grown peculiarly beautiful since we have seen revealed so much of its 'Mystery of Pain,' come to understand so greatly its burden of suffering: to some it has ever been beautiful and ever powerfully attractive: to all it appears real and sure and familiar. Many of us fear to leave it because it holds, we think, the lives of those we love. Some dread it by reason of the carelessness of their lives here. However it may be individually, the world taken as a whole either fears death or dreads the results from it to them. The earth and this life seem to them so real and sure, so comfortably familiar! And the great 'Beyond' is vaguely uncertain. People—the majority of persons—believe that they will live 'somehow' and 'somewhere': partly because GOD has made the fact clear to human consciousness by direct revelation, and partly through the indirect revelation conveyed through the media of earthly fluctuation and change, of the soul's sense of incompletion, imperfection, as pervading the whole scene and scheme of this, the earthly living. All around the human centre of life and beauty are signs of yearning for a 'blest new birth.' Even if GOD had not revealed the fact of there being a life beyond the Veil of sense, there would have been evidence of it in the surrounding elements of life. But GOD has revealed the fact, clearly, unmistakably; and no outer evidence—nor even the natural instinct of the soul and heart which declares the great truth—is needed as augmentation thereof. Still, quite surely, quite distinctly, the world, on which we place such firm reliance, does pronounce in favour of immortality. Life is replete with unanswered riddles, unsolved problems. Everywhere is imperfection; beautiful imperfection it may be, but still imperfection.

Mr. Greg said, in *The Enigmas of Life*: 'Every sort of beauty has been lavished on our allotted home; beauties to enrapture every sense, beauties to satisfy every taste; forms the noblest and the loveliest, colours the most gorgeous and the most delicate, odours the sweetest and the subtlest, harmonies the most soothing and the most stirring: the sunny glories of the day; the pale Elysian grace of moonlight, the lake, the mountain, the primeval forest, and the boundless ocean; "silent pinnacles of aged snow" in one hemisphere, the marvels of tropical luxuriance in another; the serenity of sunsets; the sublimity of storms . . .' But in all is there not the evidence of imperfection? Do they not, each and all, proclaim to our hearts and souls that there is something beyond this grandeur and marvel: something to which earth's most wondrous treasures are but infinitesimal? The things of earth are truly great and wonderful, so much so that they bear upon the face of them a high message of what reasonably may be; but in their limits and in their defects, their general distinct shortcoming, they add their evidence to human yearnings, to immediate Divine revelation, and point logically to a perfection ultimately to be reached. Nature's messages to the soul, the soul's own messages to itself, take up the Divine proclamation and say :— There is another Life, a perfect Life—' Behold, I make all things New.'

Signs of yearning for a blest new birth there are, and GOD has lifted for us somewhat the veil between this life and the new birth, and has so far drawn aside the thick folds that we have been enabled to catch many a glimpse of the true nature of the new birth, and of the new life to be lived beyond it. Yet some of us still say, with morbid, shrinking dread :—It is all vague to us. We cannot see, we cannot understand. We are afraid. We know not how we shall live : it is an unnatural prospect that is before us. No, we cannot understand.

> ' " *Anima Mundi,*" of Thyself existing,
>   Without diversity or change to fear,
> Say, has this life to which we cling, persisting,
>   Part or communion with Thy steadfast sphere?
> Does Thy serene Eternity sublime
> Embrace the slaves of circumstance and time?' [1]

The discipline of life has not done much for us if we cannot get any further than to question thus. The various experiences of earthly life should have led us to a different mental plane from this. If we have been advancing in growth towards Christ, if we have 'put on' Christ, if we have partaken of Him in our earthly living, surely we should have learned much of the Great

[1] Lord Houghton.

Beyond, and should be able to look with glad eyes through the folds held aside by the Divine Hand, and see and understand something of the Life in store for us. Perhaps it is the 'Intermediate State' which most perplexes us and daunts us. Yet, has not life's course taught us that all true living is thought-living:—that we are, ourselves, actually 'Thought'? Need there then be any insuperable difficulty in the way of a clear conception of a life in which spirit lives apart from a carnal covering? apart from a body? It is strange to us? Yes, in measure, it is strange; and some of us are such veritable human beings, so hampered by the body, that the Thought which truly we are cannot assert over us its appointed sway. We bow to the demands of the body and refuse to let ourselves perceive the might of the invisible force within. We are almost as vague—some of us—as is the epitaph on a certain great Professor's grave. We may live: we may not live:—it almost amounts to this; despite revelation and the promptings of reason. Ah! it is very uncertain, very conjectural, and this life, at all events, is a fact beyond the possibility of doubt.

Many questions arise before us and array themselves in a garb of terror to us. And most of us do indeed fear to contemplate our 'end.'

Yet, is this earth so sure that any one need cling so tenaciously to the thought of it? Do not its very fluctuations and changes speak otherwise to our souls? Are we not constantly being informed, and reminded, of the mutability, the uncertainty, the precariousness of all that is of earth; and having our eyes led to gaze beyond the earth for sure stability, lasting firmness? As a lecturer said in London recently:—' There is no *terra firma*!' The tremblings of earth's surface, the subterranean disturbances, the seismic 'shocks,' are surely all messages of the earth's liability to change, of the fact that for permanence we must look far, far beyond our present home.

Still we are afraid of the 'intangibility' on the other side of the great Veil. We are practical, material beings, we say, and no faculties at our command are adequate for our grasping of the reality of that spirit-life, there to be lived. What will it be like? How shall we manage to live away from our familiar earth, parted from our familiar bodies? How can life be regulated and maintained without a body to act as a vehicle and supporter of the spirit?

In a quite useless and unnecessary way we perplex ourselves over the Great Unveiling which is before us: forgetting the happenings of our earthly life's course, which have revealed to us so much, which have brought us—or should have brought us—so closely to GOD that spiritual things should stand in our eyes as the Real, and mere physical things as the dream and vision, the rather intangible prelude, of the Real!

How is it with us here?

> ' We are spirits clad in veils;
> Man by man was never seen;
> All our deep communing fails
> To remove the shadowy screen.'[1]

---

[1] Cranch.

But, 'In proportion as the perfect obedience of the Life of Christ comes, through humility and prayer and thought, to be the constant aim of all our efforts: in proportion as we try, GOD helping us, to think and speak and act as He did, and through all the means of grace to sanctify Him in our hearts: we shall with growing hope and with a wonder that is ever lost in gratitude know that even our lives are not without the earnest of their rest in an eternal harmony: that through them there is sounding more and more the echo of a faultless music: and that He Who loves that concord, He Who alone can ever make us what He bids us be, will silence every jarring note: that our service too may blend with the consenting praise of all His Saints and Angels.'[1]

This we have as our prospect, and we call it an intangible unreality!

'Has not the soul in view, as a *practical reality*, an unbounded and unimagined future? Sometimes it seems like a dream, sometimes very awfully near the present; but it is *always a certainty*, though always beyond the reach of exact knowledge.'[2]

We know not, truly, what life will be to us beyond the Great Veil, but we may know this: that it is 'a practical reality,' 'a certainty,' though it lie outside the range of exact knowledge. And when it seems to us as a dream, it is that we indeed are living in a dream-world: exalting fleeting trivialities into the rightful position of permanent facts. We need to alter our focus of

[1] Dean Paget.   [2] Canon Knox Little.

vision, and almost to echo the words of Ignatius Loyola —'How mean and low earth seems when I contemplate the things of Eternity!'

Yes, we need to have our focus of vision different from what it has been: as a cause of terrified, bewildered questionings. The experiences and the discipline of earthly life have markedly failed in their allotted purpose to us if we are dim-seeing, unbelieving, here, in this supreme respect. We should have learned the grand truth that the spiritual element of all living is the preponderating element.

We not only fear the strange, 'vague' nature of the Life beyond our present sphere of living: we dread its loneliness. We shall go away, we think, such human spirits; so tenderly loving our beloved on earth, so bound up with them: and the vast realm to which we go will be the vestibule of Heaven! Shall we not be overpowered by its magnificence, and conscious of a desolation not known on earth?

But, though we pass from earth, shall we have passed from our beloved? We had been spirits clad in veils on earth: when we leave the earth and the earthly veiling, shall we be severed from the spirit—or the spirits—still veiled thus? Is everything now so separate, so far-off, that there can be no communication between the living in Paradise and that on earth? Does GOD cease to bind hearts together? Does He break the bonds that had united lives in the earthly time? Are the relations between soul and soul so changed when death intervenes between the common life of those, one with another, living in communion and intercourse on earth, that the tie will seem snapped? Will there be no communion and intercourse between the two worlds? When the to-days, the yesterdays, the to-morrows, have dropped from us, and time as we had known it is not, shall we be quite cut off from their life; living a life so different from theirs that there can be no sympathy, no comprehension, between us? We know that it will be a higher life (when we think definitely of it at all), because it will be lived more nearly to GOD: within actual sight of the Beatific Vision, we believe. But, despite our love of GOD, shall we not be lonely, afraid, conscious of a desolation we had not known on earth?

Yes, it is natural to most of us to have a certain dread and fear of death, beneath which we cower away from the thought of it. But to some the temptation is to long for death, seeing in it, not only the passage to a higher life, a life of greater nearness to GOD, and of freedom from the thraldom of the flesh, but further, a release from the ills, the sorrows, the afflictions generally of this earthly life. And it is here that one feels S. Paul's attitude towards it to be of such peculiar value and significance for us. 'I am ready either to die or to live,' he said—To live is more profitable for you: I will live.

S. Paul's whole attitude in the face of death is indeed a grand lesson to us. If it be difficult to keep our thoughts in due check and balance as we contemplate that which means the unveiling of the spirit—viewing the question of life or death, the facts of life and death, taking into consideration the opposing desires and longings that beset us at such a moment, the alternating dread and fear, now of death, now of longer earthly living, under which we groan in cowardly fashion,—S. Paul's comportment comes to us as a Divine message and instruction. In the ecstasy of martyrdom saints have, as it were, gladly seized death with both hands, rejoicing to be counted worthy to endure torture of death for the sake of their Crucified Lord, the Captain of their Salvation. S. Polycarp, with the flames forming an aureole around his head, looked up praising and blessing GOD for the honour bestowed upon him. S. Agnes, the girl-martyr, 'went joyfully as in triumph' to her martyrdom. Many of the saints of old not merely rejoiced in the agonising death that came to them, but even courted it. But it is not in these cases that we must expect to find our special lesson, but in that of the great Apostle himself. Of him we read that he was simply ready to die or to live. 'To me to live is Christ, and to die is gain!' But he was willing to wait for the gain, because he wanted to please GOD, and he felt that his longer presence in this world would be of service to his fellows, for GOD. It was needful for others that he should live yet a while with them in bodily nearness. GOD had taught him this in his hours of prayer and communion with Him. And so he lived on, his life a grand offering to GOD in this willing service of his fellows: and when death came to him it found him prepared and ready—and still, at the age of sixty-eight,[1] so full of zeal for the souls of all men that

---

[1] According to S. Chrysostom, in the sixty-eighth year of his age.

THE GREAT UNVEILING

he converted, it is said, on the way to the place of his execution, three of the Roman soldiers that were leading him there.

We have another beautiful lesson in Epictetus. Epictetus, the slave, the man fast bound in chains, his flesh full often rived and lacerated with these chains; the man, as he himself said, 'naked, houseless, without a hearth, squalid,'—this man regarded life and death as GOD's, to be endured nobly for Christ's sake, and as seeing in them a means of glorifying Christ. He lived on in happy content, blaming nor questioning GOD nor man; only preaching the beauty and the worth of life because it is the gift of GOD, and of death because it leads to Him. 'I must die. But must I then die sorrowing?'—'I am always content with that which happens; for I think that what GOD chooses is better than what I choose.' Thus he rejoiced in life whilst it was his, and only met death willingly, because when it came he knew that it was what GOD had chosen for him as being best at that time. This was the echo of the spirit of S. Paul, the brilliant logician and rhetorician, found in the life of a poor, humble slave; and it reaches us now, in these days of contemptible scepticism and cowardice of mind, as an echo of a time when men, though burdened with a flesh that meant to them, perchance, not only ordinary sorrow and pain, but the further ills of shame and disgrace and contumely, yet lived on in that flesh grandly and mightily, without seeking, or even desiring, deliverance, because it was the most glorious possible condition of being for them, having been 'chosen' for them by GOD: reaches us as an echo, and a terrible reproach. Epictetus, with his suffering body, seeming to him a weight carried about by the soul, stands forth a splendid example of the power of the belief that 'the spirit of man is the seat of his personality;' and a proof that in feeling the truth of the scientific dogma respecting the correlation and preservation of force there lies a sure rest for man. The old stoics—although they might word it differently—felt the truth of this dogma, and looked to the time when the supreme force in them should be living independently of the body, as to the equation of many knotty earthly problems. Marcus Aurelius regarded the 'divinity' within him with particular care and reverence, and from him, even—nominal Christian though he were not—we can glean words of wise counsel and assistance to us in our attitude towards death. And Seneca, also, bestowed great thought on the hidden 'force' within his earthly being, and looked on hopefully to the larger freedom he should enjoy, considering death as merely the way to this larger freedom.

The unveiling of the spirit:—the freedom, the true emancipation, of that in which and from which all true life is evolved, all true beauty issues! What a sublime reflection it should be to us Christians! We are not seen here, we are not known: even to our nearest and dearest our best thoughts are but half-revealed, if they be revealed at all. The very complexity of our being baffles real knowledge of us, though the anxious learner be allowed by us the freest possible access to the

THE GREAT UNVEILING

'divinity' within us. The special supreme 'force' in us, whose eternal continuance is so sure a fact, cannot express itself clearly; and as each 'force' is peculiarly and distinctively a person's own, no reliable data can be had from one, for the other. We are 'lonely' here, if we would but recognise this truth. We think of loneliness in the Great Beyond, when we are 'parted' from our loved ones on earth, but we lose out of sight the solitude in which, in varying measure and intensity, each person walks through his, or her, earthly life. None is really known nor communed with in the body as knowledge and communion can be 'Beyond.' And are there not times when the pathos of this touches us deeply; and unconsciously, perhaps, to ourselves at these moments, we humbly utter the cry: 'How long, O Lord? How long?'

A very complex being is ours, and, at the very best, a very germinal being, full of 'infinite possibilities' and potentialities pointing to a higher life, fettered now, and hindered ofttimes, by the body. And the sigh of the spirit after perfect holiness and completion goes often forth in troubled yearning. Not merely does the body hamper the spirit-life on occasions, but it is a troublous element to us in itself. It is very liable to pain and disease, filled sometimes with rending, tearing agony (which, again, hampers the spirit, in many cases), and growing weary almost beyond endurance: seems in fact, just what Epictetus described it as:—a weight carried about by the soul!

The Mystery of Suffering! Has it, at times, oppressed

us? And then again, has so much of its might and beauty been revealed to us that we have longed for a further revelation of its majesty and glory? Are we here led to *desire* death, not simply as a passage to better life, but as the supreme agony of all the suffering we have endured on earth? Some of us, possibly, arrive at this wish, this feeling.

Yet, is death, of necessity, the supreme agony? Is there not a good deal of delusion on the subject of the departure of the spirit from its body? There may be agony preceding the actual dissolution of our complete earthly life, and we know that in many cases it is so. But it is not inevitable. 'We are, perhaps, too much in the habit of thinking of death as the culmination of disease, which, regarded only in itself, is an evil, and a terrible evil.' That is one way of viewing the subject. 'But,' Dr. Mac Donald goes on to say, 'I think rather of death as the first pulse of the new strength, shaking itself free from the old mouldy remnants of earth-garments, that it may begin in freedom the new life that grows out of the old.'

And this, after all, is the thought with which we should be filled. There may be great pain heralding the approach of death: there may be scarcely any, or actually no, pain announcing its advent.—For do we not constantly read and hear of, and actually witness, deaths that have come gently upon those being called away; gently, without tumult, distress, or great disturbance? Do not doctors and hospital nurses tell us that the more common form of death is that best described as 'a gentle passing away'? The present writer was told by a nurse that in the whole course of her hospital experience she had only seen two 'hard' deaths. Does not all this point to death as being generally not that which so much involves pain and physical suffering, as that which is the reliever of pain and suffering? And by our common experience are we not shown that, as has been said, often there is not even an immediate precursor of suffering, but that the prelude to death, as the actual death itself, has been painless, free from marked suffering? Weakness, lassitude, exhaustion of the body, lethargy of the mind, maybe, have been present; but only these. And they could not rightly be classed as marked suffering:—rather as the calm succeeding to that storm and stress of suffering which may have been endured during the term of earthly living.

We fear death, we fear longer life: and by either we are wronging the spirit within us, and failing to observe that submission to the Will of GOD to which the happenings of our earthly life should have led us. Personal trial is the key-note around which may be gathered a harmony of beautiful devotion to GOD, but this harmony of devotion is not there if we fail to confront death with a peaceful equableness of mind, regarding it as our 'best' from GOD whensoever it may come: whether it come quickly, or tarry long.

It is truly the discipline of life, the sorrows and agonies of life—the numberless sacrifices offered in union with Christ's supreme Sacrifice, the constant offering up of His supreme Sacrifice in Holy Communion with Him—that bring about this equableness of mind. And it is the only acceptable position in the sight of GOD, the only preservation of the due balance of the great issues of life and death, the only 'looking unto Jesus' which makes of our human life a reflection and expression of His Life, and a holy preparation for a sanctified death. Walking hand in hand with Him along our earthly *viâ dolorosa*, we should come to possess that facing of a foreknown and fore-accepted death which marked His earthly Life.

And always must we remember that death is the passage to truer life. It means the unveiling of the spirit, the 'soul,' in which has lain our real life here. It means the larger freedom and emancipation of that part of us through whose powers we have felt, thought, loved, yet so often been misunderstood in the feeling, thinking, loving. It means the freedom, most truly, of our real life.

And is not death most truly 'swallowed up in radiant victory'? 'Death hath no more dominion' of its own. It is subjugated by Him Who bore it in His Own Person; and, through it, went first into the 'Intermediate State,' then into the Highest Heavens.

A SOUL SPED TO THE UNSEEN WORLD

'PASSED into a higher life!' What a pregnant phrase this is! With what strange import it sounds in our ears! How the heart and soul within us are stirred, quickened, awaked to new vitality! Some one with whom, perhaps, we had been quite familiar has, we hear, passed from us, gone with the flitting cloud-forms, whose vanishing we had been wont to watch, gone away into the great Unseen World ; and we are still on earth. With what mingled feelings we are filled! Perhaps another friend—a friend yet on earth, before us, in the body—has come to see us, and has told us the news with a sad shake of the head, and in an awed tone of voice, as though some terrible calamity had overtaken that one with whom both had been familiar:—'Poor fellow!'—'Poor woman!'—with some such phrase is the announcement completed. Or perhaps this is said : 'How sad it is! And he—she—so young, too!'

Does it not flash across the mind that this is a strange way of speeding a soul to Paradise? Mingled feelings there may be in our hearts: but not surely a sense as of the happening of a calamity to the life removed from us, the life we had studied and known familiarly? A tangle of thoughts may be in our minds. Our friend has truly gone out of the feverishness of this life, with all its cares, its beguilements, its perplexed questionings ; gone into a great calm world, where the 'murmurs and scents of the Infinite Sea' make a beautiful music and sweetness, in which the earth-weary soul may find rest. It is well for him—for her. Only there will be no more ordinary meeting and intercourse for us. All this is at end, and we think sadly of how many opportunities we had missed of adding beauty and pleasure to that life when it was on earth ; of how many things we might have done and said, and yet had not done nor said them. And now we cannot repair the breach, cannot supply that void which we seem to see in such startling clearness before our mind's eye. Perhaps the one ' passed into a higher life' had been especially our own: had been that *other one* whose life was above all others bound to ours, and we are conscious of not having fully discharged the trust that, in bringing about the union of lives, GOD had given to us. And if so, the first pain must be awful.

But even then, lovely and tender thoughts may fill our minds ; and surely opportunities of future help may arise in prospect ? It is the soul, the spirit, which is the real ground making intercourse and communion possible, and the soul of our beloved is not harmed, nor is it fettered, nor dwarfed. We shall be able still to hold intercourse one with the other. The bond that unites for all time—or, in more correct expression, beyond all time—can never be injured by the death of one's body. It is a seeming severance : not an actual one. Have we not learned to look thus upon death, the death that in one sense comes between two lives? The original bond still holds: it is a permanent fact in the life of both. Nothing can do away with that old time when each had seen in the other the scope for a perfect satisfaction, the capacity for yielding completion of being in a Heavenly union. Even if unreal words and cruel deeds, yes, and miserable, wronging thoughts, had intervened and caused a coldness here, deep in the heart of both lay always the sure knowledge that each was the other's absolutely for ever. Sometimes, perhaps, the revelation of this consciousness had been held back, but none the less was it there, influencing and guiding the lives of both. Does this count for nothing now that the blow of 'death' has fallen on one of the lives so bound? Do these lives seem to the one remaining on earth as apart as they had often seemed to general onlookers? They had met, possibly, as apparent strangers, and those about them had accepted them as such. But they in their hearts had never been strangers. An electric current had ever been ready to pass from the inner being of one to the inner being of the other. Mysteriously the bond had held them:—Just a look in the eyes, the sudden sound of the voice, a movement of the hand, of one or the other, an almost nothing, sufficed always to remind them that one day they should be together by Divine right, as they had never been together here, even at the closest moments of their lives. They might utter little platitudes around them, and remain silent (so far as words go) to each other; might

x

appear indifferent to, and actually unconscious of, each other's neighbourhood: but all the while the bond had held them close, and communion had gone on.—Why? Because 'the seat of a man's personality is his spirit.' Because the spirit is supreme in any life. The little look, or sound, or movement, had truly been due to the bodily faculties; still it was the power of the spirit, the soul, the immortal essence, within the body, from which the current of love had gone forth from one to the other. If it had been sound or sight that had conveyed the feeling of undying love within the being, what matter? The soul is really independent of such aids to communion. It was the spiritual part of the being from which, into which, the love current had passed, and the body, in either case, had played so small a part in the intercourse and communion of one with the other, that it was but a slight step to the higher touch of spirit upon spirit which had been felt when there was no bodily nearness of the two lives. This *had* been felt and known, and why when one spirit loses, for a time, all bodily presence and accompaniment, should the one still clothed in the body feel as though separation, severance, impossibility of communion and intercourse had come? That mysterious magnetism, that undying sense of union, was a fact of the spirit, not of the body; and of what did it speak if not of a union and communion of life, even if one (or both) should be out of the body? The force exercised, as the effect produced, had ever been of the spirit, in whatever circumstances the bond had been felt and recognised: why should the spirit suddenly become less mighty, less near, because bodily essence is missing? Each is the other's wholly, and each supremely GOD's: because one has gone into greater nearness to GOD—even if the change involve loss of bodily functions—need there be loss of spiritual power of communion with the beloved on earth? No; the force of love, the power and effects of the Divine bond, still hold the lives together: still mean communion and intercourse, and opportunities thus of grace and help accorded to each, for the other, *under GOD,*

'Blessed and happy dead!' said one who is now enrolled amongst their number. 'In them the work of the new creation is wellnigh accomplished. What feebly stirs in us, in them is wellnigh full. They have passed within the veil, and there remaineth only one more change for them—a change full of a foreseen, foretasted bliss. How calm, how pure, how sainted, are they now! A few short years ago, and they were almost as weak and poor as we: harassed by temptations, often overcome, weeping in bitterness of soul, struggling, with faithful though fearful hearts, towards that dark shadow from which they shrank. . . . Let us be much in thought with them that are at rest. They await our coming'[1]

Thus may we think of our beloved:—as awaiting our coming! But meanwhile union and communion are not suspended, though one life be in Paradise and the other on earth. There is no longer any possibility of earthly meeting and earthly intercourse: still there is the possibility of that spiritual 'talking,' that soul-communion,

[1] Rev. H. E. Manning.

which, needing at one time aid from the body, had gradually been growing independent of the body. The physical vehicle had been necessary once: it is not necessary now—though one of us still abides in the body. It had led the spirit of one to the other, but now that they are united, they need no such means of intercourse. The Angels will watch invisibly over the tomb that is to hold, or that now holds, the body of the 'departed' spirit: the same Angels, perhaps, who bore the spirit aloft to Paradise. The troubled surging of life has no power now to disturb the peace of that life 'blossoming as the rose' in the garden above. There are differences, alterations; but nothing has 'happened' to create severance of union between the life in Paradise and the life on earth. Both are very near each other. And the meeting of spirit with spirit—though one be still 'clad in a veil of earth,' and the other but enveloped in some vague, almost impalpable, covering, spiritual and not bodily—is a real fact, making the living on earth far more beautiful and holy, from its wonderfully close connection with the great Unseen World, in which perfection is so much further advanced than here.

And are we not called up in thought higher than this, even? Is there not flashed into our mind, more clearly than ever had been flashed before, a vision of the fully perfected Life? Do we not see ourselves adoring the Crucified Lord in His immediate Presence, bowed down before the Throne of GOD, and receiving into our hands a crown of pure blessedness? Do we not see ourselves shining with a Heavenly splendour, enjoying the wondrous delights made possible by completely expanded powers, enlarged capacities; finding in each other beauties never dreamed of here, knowing each other and loving each other, as never had we known and loved each other on earth?—superlatively happy before GOD?

Ah! surely, glorious thoughts come to us; and, bound as we then are to the Heavenly life, we should grow beautiful indeed for GOD. There should be in us a greater power for sanctification of the whole being, greater strength of goodness, more intense devotion, as, gladly surrendering to GOD our beloved to the purely spiritual life beyond the great Veil, we follow there in humble meditation, and grow to look clearly into the Heavenly Life, where we may see our love perfected, glorified by the perfection of union with GOD in Christ.

'So they two went together!' May it not be a perpetual going together in glad and holy sacrifice, of will, heart, spirit, longing desire? Should there not be born solemnly in the mind the full truth of that old going together, when one was to offer up the other in submission to GOD's decree? 'So they two went together.' Was only one to be held up to GOD? No, both were to be offered, though in different ways. In each case self was to be given up, and that meant a freeing of the real life, the true spiritual life, from earthly bondage and corruption. *So they two went together.*

Body, soul, and spirit; heart, affections, desires: all must be offered up in holy oblation to GOD. All are ours that we may give them to Him, and have them gradually perfected by Him. With each of us there is the same demand, from each of us is to be held forth for Him a complete offering. We may not shrink, we must not strive to hold back: all must be given up when the summons comes. Prince and peasant, peer and pauper, all are alike in this respect: absolute offering of the whole being must be made in ready obedience to the Divine Will. Each and all of us must submit to the white-robed messenger bearing the Divine message in his hand. Each and all, with our several capacities and our varying opportunities, must arise and go forth, uplifted in devotion and glad obedience to GOD; feeling, by the inspiration of His Presence with us, that neither here, nor in Paradise, nor in Heaven beyond, can there be true consciousness of separation of souls bound in Love, but that 'in the heavenly courts' love shall receive its crown of rejoicing, and lives welded on earth be bound afresh, and ever anew, in the Eternal Love of GOD, and make perfect praise of Him in the Divinely blent life.

What does Dr. Pusey say in such connection? He teaches to us surely the beauty and truth of holy love: represents such love as living always. He says it shall 'live on and shine on in the heavenly courts when all riches of this earth shall be dissolved; yea, when what is now of this earth, but from our Maker's Hands, not from our marring of His work, shall be transformed into the glory of Christ.' And towards this we grow, in glad, buoyant hope, which itself is a purifying unto perfection: the perfection that awaits us of high union and communion, now made clear to our spirit's gaze.

Beautiful and holy indeed should life now be to us, as we look beyond the Veil and picture the glorious, new living there. Gone into the nearer Presence of Christ has our beloved; into the realm where His Spirit went when the marred, worn Body was lying at rest in the grave. It is a glorious vision for us. Our eyes and our life had been gladdened by the presence with us and the love of our beloved, but what was such gladdening compared with this soft, intense glow of happiness that comes over us as we picture to ourselves the new life into which has been taken the spirit so dear to us? We are left behind 'sorrowing' in a certain sense, and we know that moments, hours, nay, even days perhaps, will come when the sorrowing will seem the chief thing in our minds. Yet we know also that these need not hinder communion with that undying, loving spirit whose mortality is laid in a grave. We know that the infinity which marks real love must necessarily reach far beyond the confines of earth. There has been seeming separation, but it is only seeming: there is no actual severance of life. There is suffering; but we look beyond the suffering, and dwell happily on the present unequal union of spirits: seeing in that a sign and proof of the higher union to be ours when we too are out of the body, of that highest union that we shall know when there has been the resurrection unto Eternal Life of the forms laid in a grave, and we live as spiritual beings, with all our higher functions and powers developed to full perfection. We seem to see even Heaven opened, and amid thronging Angels, in the presence of Saints and Martyrs, ourselves glad and perfect before GOD : in new forms which yet bear likeness to the old forms in which we had first seen each other, with a new love which yet is akin to the old love : knowing as we are known, blessing and praising GOD ; thanking Him Who had robbed death of its sting, and the grave of its victory over us.

INTERCOURSE BETWEEN THE SEEN AND UNSEEN WORLDS

DEATH, truly, hath no more dominion. Those who die, die to Christ. Those who pass from us simply go nearer to Him. 'To be with Christ is life,' said S. Ambrose, and where Christ is there is His kingdom.

In the learning of this, our great lesson of death, lies the secret of union and communion with those whose life is being lived beyond the Veil:—those who have put off the covering of sense, and have thus become both independent of, and impossible of, communication with us, under the ordinary means of communication used between people living in the flesh, under this personal veiling of sense. They, in their fleshly developed life and spiritual being, they in their nearer Presence of Christ, they progressing—as humbly we trust in GOD—unhindered in acquisition of holiness, are living a better life than ours, even at our best. Yet they are not perfected. They, having died, have died to Christ; having passed from us (on earth) have gone more nearly to His actual Presence: but they are not, we believe, actually *with* Christ. The Saints of old, the glorified Martyrs, might speak as S. Paul spoke of being with

THE SANCTUARY OF SUFFERING

Christ after their death; but we are not as they: we die, we pass from earth, and we are nearer to Him than we had been when on earth; but we dare not think of His actual, closely visible Presence as being possessed and known, realised absolutely, by us, until after we shall have been through a course of preparation and higher development in the 'Intermediate State.' The best among us is not perfected in this life: the worst among us — Ah! what a reflection is here forced upon us!

Those who leave us have put off with the flesh all that concerned, and was involved in, the flesh; they are living a holier life than we are living; they advance towards the acquisition of absolute perfectedness more quickly and directly than we can advance: but, as the hymn tells us, they are

> 'Still with us, beyond the veil
> Praising, pleading without fail.'

They are not only, in their higher condition of being, praising GOD: they are pleading to Him also. And what does this not say to our hearts? We prayed for them, we pleaded with them, to Him, when they were on earth: shall we suddenly stop our habit, because they have gone from our earthly range, our earthly sight—or the possibility, at any time, of earthly sight? Shall we remove from their spirit-life our own spirit-life, merely because now they have put off the body in which the spirit had tabernacled for a while? It was with the spirit that love and communion of the best sort had been given out, felt, held. Are we going to strive to raise a barrier, obstructing spirit union : to cut off—if that were feasible—our real life from their life? Shall we speak with unnatural, bated breath of them, as though all with which they were now involved were too remote from our conceptions, too far off and vague, for us to feel that we have any hold upon them at all? Shall we get so far as to manage to speak of them naturally, in our ordinary tones, evidencing the firm reliance that we have on the revealed truth that they are living a quite simple, real life, and yet not get far enough in our belief to know that we may do more than just speak thus of them? Have we learned so little of the power and reach of love that we do not know its capacity for bridging all seeming gulfs between the lover and the loved? Has the ardour of our devotion to GOD, in itself, not taught us this great lesson? We have truly grasped much of the beauty and the sense of necessity that exists for love and love-union, but we are not putting our quickly acquired knowledge to usury, to even mere good use, if we have not grown to understand the office and scope of such love and love-union. The love felt on earth was but a prelude to a union where love should be triumphant over every obstacle that might arise and confront us. The lesser love whose quickening, stirring breath had seemed to breathe into us anew of GOD's very Life, the Love Which He is, should surely have led us on to see that no power on earth, no, nor in the heavens above, could separate, could deaden, could interfere actually with, the life of one and the other bound in love. Its beauty and necessity! Ah! have we not realised its true beauty, the ground on which its necessity reposes? In the old days, perhaps at times we had feared that it might outrival GOD in our hearts and souls; but if we had cast it adrift we should have lost something of GOD. Love taught Him to us: not only drew Him more and more within our being, but caught us up, body, soul, and spirit, more, ever more, to His Life being lived 'Above.' It had been sent—as holy love is ever sent—to make GOD and a Heavenly Life increasedly ours; but it had been sent to make GOD and a Heavenly Life ever increasingly ours, also. We must not forget this. We must not fail, from want of due thought and care, to seize any fresh opportunity that may present itself to us of adding to the closeness of Divine, of Heavenly, union.

And such an opportunity arises when the human loved life is taken from us to the Unseen World. Some of us fail indeed to discern the opportunity; some fear to seize it, perhaps by reason of old prejudice, possibly from a lack of that study of genuine, authenticated Church History which sets forth clearly, not merely the privilege, but the duty, of richly seizing this opportunity.

Life is far too great and widely complex a thing to be dependent on the flesh for its maintenance in any true wise, or to forfeit its right to sensible, conscious, active living. Because the spirit has on earth expressed itself in matter, there is nothing that should lead us to believe in the ceasing of spiritual expression when the spirit is freed from matter, from material form. Rather should we be able to understand, from the many experiences of earth, that the life of a materially freed spirit would assume to itself fresh power and mode of expressing thought and affection, truth ; and be sensible of certain desires that in the old dual life had not been present—or if present, in so slight a measure as to call forth no more than a faint, indescribable wish or expression of a wish. The spirit's freedom from a bondage that, after all, was but an earthly bondage must involve a larger growth, an extended consciousness of want, of not yet completely realised ability, of a coming short that in the old life had not made itself really felt to any serious degree. The sense of vast complexity, of diverse purposes, must be augmented rather than lessened in the new living, and this freshly aroused feeling will surely be accompanied by an intensity of longing difficult to still. Awaked to the consciousness that there are possessed faculties and powers hitherto unknown, or but partially known, the spirit must be sensible of non-satisfaction, of a yearning for the perfect satisfaction which is seen dimly as existing for personal realisation.

And how is the want, the earnest longing issuing from this want, to be met? Is it to be left simply and trustingly to GOD? But this is not what we had done in former days. When we knew of some longing desire on the part of those we loved in any way we sought for satisfaction for them by joining our prayers with their prayers to GOD. We took them to GOD, as it were, and asked, and asked again and still again, that they might have their heart's desire. We spread their want before Him, and beseeched Him to supply it for them if it would be well for them to have it supplied, if it were of His Will and His Purpose in their lives. Sometimes we knew exactly what they wanted, sometimes only vaguely; sometimes we only felt that they would like us to pray for them. However it might be we did pray for them, by night and by day. We never failed them. It depended not really on their asking us to do this. We knew that they would like it. If we were asked, we not only knew that they would like it, but knew further in what way to direct our petitions; but if we were not asked, we still had the knowledge that it would be welcome to them, and we directed our petitions in such manner as to be quite sure that we were praying good and right prayers in their behalf. And ever it was that the more love there was in our hearts the more frequently were we in prayer over them—though indeed our habit of prayer had not limited itself to those whom we loved specially : it had been applied to every one, for 'all sorts and conditions of men.'

And now! Now that death has come, we pray no longer for the one whose body is dead? although our love still burns steadily on?

> 'They whose course on earth is o'er,
> Think they of their brethren more?
> They before the Throne who bow,
> Feel they for their brethren now?
>
> We, by enemies distrest—
> They in Paradise at rest;

> We the captives—they the freed—
> We and they are one indeed.
>
> One in all we seek or shun,
> One—because our Lord is one,
> One in heart and one in love—
> We below, and they above.
>
> Those whom many a land divides,
> Many mountains, many tides,
> Have they with each other part,
> Fellowship of heart with heart?
>
> Each to each may be unknown,
> Wide apart their lots be thrown;
> Diff'ring tongues their lips may speak,
> One be strong, and one be weak;—
>
> Yet in Sacrament and prayer
> Each with other hath a share;
> Hath a share in tear and sigh,
> Watch, and Fast, and Litany.
>
> Saints departed even thus
> Hold communion still with us;
> Still with us, beyond the veil
> Praising, pleading without fail.
>
> With them still our hearts we raise,
> Share their work and join their praise,
> Rend'ring worship, thanks, and love,
> To the Trinity above.'[1]

Beautifully does this hymn set forth the communion possible between departed spirits and those still living on earth. Nowhere, perhaps—outside the Holy Scriptures—have we a clearer lesson on the state of those 'passed to a higher life.' They are still with us: we

[1] *Hymns Ancient and Modern.* Hymn 538.

remain with them. Their worship of GOD goes on in the courts of the Unseen World: our worship of Him is to be blent with theirs. They partake in the special Service of the Lamb slain from before the foundations of the world: we uplift our partaking in this Service; and there is received by us an increase of holiness even from the association of ourselves with them in the Service. They are serving GOD in work as well as worship: we may add our work, and join our special work, to theirs.

But the spirits departed, whilst being 'at rest,' are 'pleading without fail!' What does this imply if not that they have felt, recognised, want of some sort? Is there not a great vista of thought opened out to us? a vista into which one is so fearful of placing obstructions where they should not be, that one hardly dares to specify the nature of the work that we may add to theirs, the pleading we may make our own—for and with theirs?

The Church tells us plainly that we may join our work with the work of 'departed' spirits, and leads us to plead for and with them. But are there boundaries to this work and pleading? Are there limits? 'The Spirit bloweth where it listeth.' It may be borne into some hearts and souls that they may do much, and see no boundaries, no limits. The Spirit-bearing Church teaches all not to be fearful or unbelieving, but to follow the spirit's instincts; to obey the monitions, the inspirations, to them of Divine Love, guiding and ruling as is best for the individual bent and capacity. It is

THE SEEN AND UNSEEN WORLDS 337

not easy soon to place sure lines of limitation. It does not seem as if the GOD of Love could be quick to resent any efforts in love's communion and intercourse in the behalf of the beloved : nor could we conceive of GOD as being jealous of our possible interference in His supreme work, His labour of Eternal and all-knowing Love for him, or for her. GOD was glad that we should work with Him for our beloved, for any life indeed, when the life was being lived on earth : would He be likely to repulse us if we continued this little work now that it has been taken from the earth, and has still great needs upon it that we may somewhat touch? We cannot raise the dead soul to life again. But can we not, by love's efforts, in Divine Grace, relieve and lighten the weight of intense yearning which must be going forth from a soul newly awaked to a sense of its shortcoming of true and perfect life? And who shall ever dare to say when a soul is dead, any more than he shall presume to say that GOD would not have us strive *always*, for any vanished being?—we in our poor, halting measure, with our eyes seeing only part of a way, our minds grasping little of the whole great Law of Life and Love.

Work, truly, may we with the spirits 'gone before': plead with them, and for them, surely should we. How can we tell what force our prayers may have? We do not doubt the force, the power, of human prayer and spirit-pleading when the objects of such prayer and pleading are in the body: why should we begin to question the worth of such human strivings now, and here? Love had led us to work for them thus when they were on earth — our specially loved ones, our beloved in GOD. Prayer had gone from our very souls in behalf of those for whom we had no special, distinctive love. Shall our love not impel us to do still for our beloved what we had done for those whom we had not especially loved?

Ah! everything, the whole course of ordinary living, not only the Spirit and the Spirit-bearing Church, leads us on to conscious intercourse with those we love beyond the Veil, leads us on to continue the old loving labour for them: points us to the only possible satisfaction of our love, the only Divinely willed end and object of earthly affection. They, in the great Unseen World, have longings, want, desires; they are not yet perfect in growth and acquisition of holiness; there is to them still a Beyond.—May we not assist them by our prayers to the attainment of their satisfaction:—the satisfaction that is GOD's Will for them? And shall we, in this service of them, not find joy and greater nearness to GOD? Because their satisfaction is GOD's Will for them, there is no need for us to stand apart and let GOD only give it to them. We might have argued in this way when they were on earth quite as reasonably as we should if we began to argue so when they are beyond our gaze. They were going towards satisfaction then, and it was GOD's Will that they should have it: still He permitted us to help them on towards their goal. Will He cease to permit such assistance now that the lives can be no longer viewed by us?

What can we do for our beloved? How can be maintained the continuance of love-union which GOD delights in? How can we serve and work out the Divine Purpose in the beautiful human love that is existing, and will always exist, between us? What would GOD have us do?

S. Ambrose has told us. S. Monica, S. Augustine, have told us. Many have told us. But most of all, can we not maintain inferentially that our Blessed Lord Himself has told us?—that S. Ambrose, S. Monica, S. Augustine, and all others who so clearly taught in the early days of the Church the beautiful lesson of communion, and the maintenance of Divine union, with the 'departed,' were but teaching what they had learned from their Master? May we not feel that the Church, in whom has been placed the safe keeping of all Truth, teaching to-day, as she distinctly does, the duty and the privilege of this means of intercourse, is merely handing down to later generations what she ever taught in her early days as a part of that Truth given to her by her Head? When Dr. Pusey—that close student and able exponent of Church History,—and not only Dr. Pusey but all other faithful and loyal upholders of the pure doctrine of the Church, tell us it is right to adopt and practise this beautiful means of intercourse, that it would even be 'against the nature and instinct of true love' not to do so, we may surely feel that this is an utterance of the Church, the keeper of Divine Truth? We doubt, we fear, we argue, and some among us would assert that to 'pray for the dead' were a positive sin against GOD. Yet how lacking we must be in the knowledge of the Truth if we stand up and aver that prayer for the departed is wrong! Nay, how illogical we must be! For logic leads undoubtedly to such belief as that held by the Church in her earliest days, taught by her still in these later days. The Church, counselling and blessing us, teaches us to say morning after morning, as the weeks and the months and the years go by :—' Most humbly beseeching Thee to grant that, by the merits and Death of Thy Son Jesus Christ, and through faith in His Blood, we and *all Thy whole* Church may obtain remission of our sins, and all other benefits of His Passion.' She would draw us on to include in our holy, prayerful offering and sacrifice all those departed in the faith. She still holds the old belief that they not without us will be made perfect, and that in our interwoven and blended living we must pray with, and for, them ever to the Father. She still sets forth in the special Service of the Lamb slain from before the foundations of the world the great truth of our acceptance in Christ, and would show us that the chief efficacy of prayer lies in the fact of its union with the Great Sacrifice of the Word.

The Word, the expression of the Divine Mind! ' We . . . bless Thy Holy Name for all Thy servants departed this life in Thy faith and fear ; beseeching Thee to give us grace so to follow their good examples, that *with them* we may be partakers of Thy heavenly Kingdom.' The Word, offered in the general, universal behalf, to the Father, for the expiation of each sin repented of, binds in closeness of union and communion those on earth with those in Paradise, and tells out to them the glorious power of sacrificial intercession, of service blent with that Divine Service commemorating and extending the Sacrificial Offering on the Cross, in the *whole* Church's life :—'That we and all Thy whole Church may obtain remission of our sins, and all other benefits of His Passion!'

In the holy Service of the Altar, when glad Eucharist is blent with penitent, faithful offering of Sacrifice in communion with His Blessed Sacrifice, does the Church teach us first, and chiefly, to hold up prayer and intercession for the departed in Christ. But she does not limit us to this one form of intercourse with them. In the *Benedicite* we sing to 'the spirits and souls of the righteous' that they would bless the Lord: 'praise Him, and magnify Him for ever.' We hold forth praise and thanksgiving to GOD, ourselves, in the words of Saints departed, placing ourselves quickly in humble communion with the great life of the Unseen World. We pray constantly for the good of the Catholic Church: part of which is on this side of the veil, part of it beyond. All this the Church counsels us to do, and blesses us in the doing. And she does not, in any place of her appointed book of devotion and directions, exhort us to confine our intercourse with the departed members of the body to services therein publicly held. She does not forbid us to pray for, and to have communion with, them in private: in our own secret chamber, our solitary walks under the broad blue of the heavens, in the stillness of evening when the earthly light is dim and the Unseen World feels very close. She does not bid us use only her words for those departed from the earth: she leaves us quite free, at liberty to word our prayers and our communings for ourselves. (And she even leaves us free to ask that they may pray for us.)

'At rest' our beloved ones are: we know this. Yet may we certainly ever feel that there is a certain coming short of perfect rest; and trust that the prayers offered up individually and collectively in their behalf may serve in some way to make the perfect rest nearer to them. We may always pray for rest for them, our beloved borne from our sight. How did S. Ambrose put it? 'Give perfect rest to Thy servant Theodosius, that rest which Thou hast prepared for Thy Saints.' Safely may we pray thus for our beloved:—that they may have perfect rest.

S. Monica, before her 'passing away,' desired that prayers should be offered for her rest. She gave no injunctions, her son says, concerning such things as her burial arrangements, but 'desired only that a memorial of her might be made at Thine Altar.' And he goes on to say:—'May she rest, then, in peace together with her husband before and after whom she never had any. And inspire, O Lord my GOD ... my brethren ... that so many as shall read these pages, may at Thy Altar remember Thy handmaid Monica, with Patricius.'

THE UNITED LIFE BEYOND THE VEIL

S. AUGUSTINE, indeed, teaches, in his exhortation respecting his mother, S. Monica, more than the lesson of intercourse and communion, and maintained union, between those in Paradise and those on earth. He conveys to us the beautiful belief, held ever in the Church, that in the Intermediate State there is intercourse, communion, maintained union, between the disembodied spirits. 'Together with her husband'! What does this not say to us?

> 'Love strikes one hour—Love ! Those *never* loved,
> Who dream that they loved once.'

In the glorious continuance of memory, there in the Great Beyond, will lives find rich delight in the old love whose higher life now has been realised.

'The ties of earth, O doubt it not, live on there, for these ties are the creation of GOD, and those whom He thus binds together are joined in an union which cannot be broken save by eternal death. But if these ties live on, in those who possess individuality and consciousness, and the power of mutual recognition, then we have the assurance that the redeemed in Paradise have sweet intercourse with each other. . . . Think, then, of their joy. . . . And as thus thou thinkest let thy heart beat high with the joy of sympathy as thou realisest the sweet intercourse they enjoy whom thou hast lost from earth.'[1]

The blended life there! How glorious must it be! We know here something of the beauty of such intercourse and communion: we know what it is to love in GOD, to think as resting in GOD, to behold beauty as in Him. But here the body fetters us. It gives to us many freedoms and means of intercourse? Yes, it does this; but yet it fetters our true freedom, it hampers our highest intercourse: it oftentimes places GOD further off from the life we are living, rather than brings Him more within its grasp. But there it is truly life lived always in GOD.

And is there nothing in the Intermediate State to take the place of, and answer in another and better way, the purpose here served by, the body? Did not the old Fathers of the Church preach that the soul in Paradise might be so enveloped that, though its freedom would be unchecked and unhindered, it would be capable of demonstrating and expressing its individuality and its power of receptivity in a dual way? Dean Luckock, in his beautiful work on the Intermediate State, has put this idea very forcibly before our minds. He acknowledges the great difficulty which many persons have in conceiving the possibility of there being mutual recognition—with its consequent intercourse and personal communion;—but says that he thinks

[1] Canon Body.

much of this difficulty would be removed by believing what certain of the Fathers most distinctly upheld, that in the state intervening between bodily life on earth and the completed spiritual life in Heaven, the soul is in spirit-*form*:—that is, that it retains some clear and unmistakable likeness to the personality which the body on earth went, in some degree, to support and show forth to those who loved that soul. In the primitive days of the Church this belief was very generally held, and we are sure that the days when the Church's doctrine and belief were the purest, the most closely allied to that teaching which had been given to her by Christ through the infusion of His Spirit into her, were those early times. But even if to some minds the evidence for such belief having been then clearly held and taught is inconclusive, there remains the mighty fact that in Parable our Lord conveyed distinctly to the minds of His listeners the truth of the power of recognition, and the consequent intercourse and personal communion, between souls in the Intermediate State. And He taught it, too, by His Own going to 'preach' to the souls 'in prison.' What had been the use of preaching to souls deadened into unconsciousness and dull inertness of being? Where would have been the good accruing from such preaching?

Life in the Intermediate State is not, cannot be, a virtual cessation of being, a loss of power, vitality, true livingness. It is—we are, by all study, by the facts and experiences of our life here, but supremely by the teaching of Christ, driven to believe it—an increase of life, a new quickening of power, a more intense living. Personality is absolutely indestructible. Memory, consciousness, thought, peculiar bent, special and individualising quality of soul:—all these are impossible of eradication. What a person is here on earth, that must he be in the Intermediate State, for the personality of a man is really his soul; the image of GOD in which he was made, and which with him is different, in some way, from that in which all others appear. The power that bound lives here must bind them still, and ever: the fascination, the delight, the peculiar joy of communion, felt between souls here will be felt there and always; for the cause and the ground of all this are of GOD and immortality. The love of those who loved, who thought and felt, ever in GOD must live on an actual, blessed reality, transcending infinitely all mere earthly delight of love, all mere earth-bound conceptions of such delight.

For what is the delight of love there? It is the seeing, not only the soul in a greater purity and holiness than any which earthly life had made possible, but the wondrous attainment of, and progress in, a beauty of living never dreamed of in that old time. Streamed over by the radiancy of light from Heaven, within view of the Beatific Vision—though not yet in actual realisation, and the immediate Presence, of the Vision,—how glorious indeed must the souls in Paradise become! Quickened anew by the now unhindered operation in Grace of the Holy Spirit, cut off from the 'body of sin,' the temptations and infirmity of the flesh, how freely must the Life of GOD be working for the perfection of souls!

Ah! we shall see each other as never here had we seen each other; shall love each other as never here had it been possible to love each other. 'Our GOD is a revealing GOD'; and though the complete revelation of one to the other, as supremely of GOD to each, can be only when He has raised from the grave of the old 'seeming' an absolutely real true body with every detail perfect, yet there will be revelation almost dazzling in its clearness and its beauty. There, in Paradise, is, and will be for us, a simple life of mutual revelation of GOD and of each other, grand with the inseparable grandeur of simplicity, and exquisite in its growing conformity to the Divine Life of Heaven. For it is an outer court of Heaven, in which souls are being sanctified and strengthened for the realisation of that which is within Heaven itself. It is a rest, a great, beautiful place of refreshment, a still pause in the midst of a Life never-ending. It is just a going to perfection.

Yet how full must this Life be of a certain gentle activity of livingness! Think of the soul going on unto perfection and the realisation of complete life:— how its range of vision, its capacities and powers, must be extending and increasing, the more nearly it advances to the actuality of the Beatific Vision: the living immediately in the Presence of GOD! 'Come ye apart and rest a while' has sounded, as of old, in the ears of His loved ones; but the rest is that rest of harmony of surrounding, perfect fitness of strength and vigour and ability of being for the particular task required, of cessation from all wearing distractions, all sense of fatigue as belonging to work done, all the agonies, the sorrows, the distresses, that had seared and lined the old life: the rest of conscious acquirement of much that in the old life had beckoned the soul on, yet seemed to hurt it by the opening up of a great vista of possibilities, far-off, vague, in a way impalpable to the then natural powers of acquisition.

> 'All we have willed or hoped or dreamed of good shall exist,
> Not its semblance, but itself; no beauty, nor good, nor power
> Whose voice has gone forth, but each survives for the melodist,
> When Eternity confirms the conceptions of an hour.'[1]

'Perhaps many have felt—I have often—that there are occasions in which the sense of the beautiful in nature becomes almost painfully overpowering. I have gazed on some very lovely prospects, bathed perhaps in the last rays of the evening sun, till my soul seemed to struggle with a very peculiar undefinable sensation, as if longing for a power to enjoy which I was conscious I did not possess, and which found relief only in tears. I have felt conscious that there were elements of enjoyment and admiration there which went far beyond my capacity of enjoying and admiring.'[2]

Such pain will in Paradise be gone, but will there not be a species of suffering? Something akin to the high suffering of earth? It is not a complete state: though powers and abilities be increased and strengthened, they are not there in perfection of growth. The state

---
[1] Robert Browning   [2] Edmund Gosse.

of disembodied spirits is a high state, but not the highest. In that solemn hush, that placid advancement in growth, there will surely be still a sense of imperfect condition, a longing to attain something not yet fully acquired? Perfect satisfaction cannot come until life is complete in the new heavens and the new earth. Then surely can it only be that we thoroughly realise 'all we have willed or hoped or dreamed of good'; then only can it be that to us has come the perfecting of our power to enjoy and to admire.

We must believe that in that progress through a comparatively high state of life into the superlative state, there can but be partial satisfaction of the soul's whole desire; and we must further feel that, in order to attain complete development of life, there must be the presence in the life of that which pre-eminently binds it to the Life of Christ. In worshipping the Lamb slain from before the foundations of the world, as the holy 'dead' are revealed to us in the pages of Holy Scripture as doing constantly and most chiefly, will there be, could there conceivably be, apartness and exclusion from the great Law so intimately bound up with the Sacrifice of the Lamb? Would not this be inconsistent with all that we have learned of suffering in itself, and as finding its ultimate solution and end in Christ's Sacrifice? The merits of suffering were derived from Christ: the nature of suffering is absolutely of the Nature of Christ, redeeming by its power that which had been degraded in man, marred, hurt by sin. To worship the Lamb, in union with the faithful com-

THE SANCTUARY OF SUFFERING

pany of striving men and women on earth bowed down before GOD's Altars there, to look to the Lamb as still the Holy Means of sanctification unto perfection, to be singing ever there the 'Song of the Passion'—does not all this point to the logical necessity of the continued presence of something akin to the 'suffering' we have known on earth, allied to it in closeness of union, developing all life submitted to it, supremely by reason of its alliance, its inherent oneness, with the sacrificed Lamb of GOD? By the knowledge we have gained of the true significance and beauty, the true power and worth, of 'suffering,' are we not led up to a firm belief in its prevalence in some form, and some degree, in the life beyond the Veil? The purging and right development of our life here had been carried forth in suffering, and in the permanent union thus effected of the human life with the sacrificed Divine Life. It had bound us to Christ, and in Christ we found the one possible Means of growing satisfaction of the soul's whole desire. It is all part of an unbroken Law :—the Law of development by suffering, into and through union with Christ, brought about, and in some measure even on earth realised, by participation in the actual Sacrifice of Christ, the offering to the Father of a Perfect Life, lived triumphantly in man's marred flesh.

Some sort and degree of 'suffering' surely there must be! Are we not constrained to feel that it is an inseparable accompaniment to the life lived in the Intermediate State? and that its agency is almost as complex as we have known it to be in the life on earth

THE UNITED LIFE BEYOND THE VEIL 351

—though not needing to fulfil all earth's requirements? Say that, after that particular judgment to which each soul is summoned, and must undergo, when it leaves the body in which it has lived such an errant, imperfect life—even at the best—on earth, a sentence, blessed indeed and most merciful, has been passed upon it, and it goes into the bright abode of Paradise:—is it perfect? Have there been no sad and painful revelations made to that soul? As it came face to face with its Judge, seeing Him in His Perfection of Holiness, has no rude shock come to it? Seeing the past life without the glamour of low understanding cast over it, the dim realisation of what it was that GOD had asked when He asked for holiness; seeing the thoughts, the words, the acts, the daily conduct and intercourse, of the life lived out, will there be no experience of new sorrow, new knowledge painful in its awakening? Seeing the love of GOD, the wondrous Self-devotion of the Christ Whom we had truly believed to be GOD, yet so dimly and feebly seen and loved, will there not be bitter remorse, grieving penitence, a great longing for a pureness and beauty of living which may in some measure repay that Self-devotion? and will not this lead to an ever striving for perfection, in which we must still suffer, still be unsatisfied?

We have already reviewed the probability of this great sense of incompletion and non-satisfaction. But is it not well to consider it here, especially, as going to form somewhat the material, and groundwork even, of a system of growth and development which, describe it as we may, is a purging, a discipline of soul; and—though the word 'Purgatory' has come to be regarded as a distinctive term of one branch only of the Church, and to be shrunk from as involving heresy and abuse of a great truth—truly a condition of cleansing by means of suffering? Through misconception of the tenor of the twenty-second Article of our Church, people have, in these latter days—following, of course, on the breach of communion in the Church,—grown to view with horror any mention of punitive discipline in the Intermediate State: and indeed if, through imperfect consideration of the point, punitive discipline is thought of as virtually the same as that punishment by material fire, which came to be taught as the state of the departed soul, and from which purchased 'Masses' were supposed to be instrumental in rescuing the soul, one cannot wonder that people start aside from the thought with horror. Yet, is it not a simple misconception of a beautiful truth? When we read of a pure saintly soul (according to our ideas) like John Keble expressing the deep thankfulness which was his—especially during the year immediately preceding his death—that there was appointed a time of 'preparation' of the soul after death, for the perfect life to be ultimately lived in the actual, positive Presence of GOD, we should surely be ashamed to find ourselves dreaming of entering Heaven in the same state in which we leave this earth. Truly, the main settlement of our destiny must, we feel, be effected at that moment of our particular judgment, which follows on the departure of the spirit to the

THE UNITED LIFE BEYOND THE VEIL 353

Unseen World; but as has been forcibly said:—'Though the tree may *lie in the direction* in which it falls, there is much of shaping and carving for the Master-Carpenter to do upon the tree before it is fitted to be a pillar in the heavenly Temple.' And the very best who leave this world leave it with many defects, imperfections of growth, upon them. Is it not, then, indeed a comfort, that all should sacredly guard, for us to be able to feel how unmistakably Holy Scripture and the Patristic writings, even as the Church throughout all ages, teaches this doctrine of progress unto perfection as being involved in our Faith?

And for those who, having lived consistently and firmly unto themselves here, thus die unto themselves, may we not feel that there is still a system of discipline possible? Of the souls so seared and defaced by sin that to our eyes the image of GOD in them has seemed obliterated, may we not trustfully think as being in the Hands of GOD? May we not commend all to His infinite Mercy, knowing full well that, though He may chide, though, in the perfection of His Justice, He must have the uttermost farthing of transgression paid *somehow*, He yet will remember the Sacrifice of Himself, and view the degraded life from the standpoint of the Cross whereon He had gathered to Himself just such hurt, marred souls? For them, as for those who have striven, with hearts filled with love of Him crucified, to serve Him throughout their earthly living, there will be particular judgment; and GOD alone knows what that judgment shall be, and how every palliating circumstance and difficulty of their life here will be taken tenderly into account, and seen in its true bearing on the life so degraded. Further, He alone can know the full force and extent of that purging as by fire—though not purging *in* fire—to which, in varying degrees and manners, all shall be lovingly submitted. That some shall leave their particular judgment condemned, we have our Lord's Own authority for believing; but this condemnation means but an initial sentence passed on souls who have certainly forfeited their right to be with the 'saints' departed in the Lord and blessed by Him yet whose punishment may work for them in ways not comprehended by man, nor capable of even approximate measurement according to the ordinary standards of man. 'After death the judgment,' when man shall receive in proportion to his deserts the chastisement of his sin! And sadly as we know that to some this agony of suffering must be actually the foretaste of final suffering, we still can never know who these are; and in the case of the worst life we have witnessed we may surely pray, and pray on :—'The Lord grant unto him that he may find mercy of the Lord in that Day'?

'In the place where the tree falleth, there it shall be' is often quoted as though it clashed with this doctrine of possible growth unto perfection after death and the particular judgment of those souls who, self-harmed, are sentenced by the Divine Judge to a place of 'torment.' But (changing somewhat the metaphor) may we not bear in mind the comforting thought that there where the tree lieth, the wind of GOD's Mercy blowing upon it, the rain of His Love watering it, the tempest of His Justice—or, as we term it, 'wrath'—stirring and bracing it, may work for the better growth of that which had seemed cut down and dead? May there not be a purifying, cleansing, bracing, which shall serve to awaken the original touch of living 'goodness' implanted in the human life when GOD had made it go forth from His Life? And, by placing it before, and gradually in communion with, the Sacrifice of the 'Lamb slain before the foundations of the world,' may there not be brought about in many souls, seeming to us utterly lost, perfect redemption and sanctification, actual glory of being?

Who shall presume to limit in imagination GOD's agency and the means of His work for such souls? As we cannot tell the nature nor the extent of His chastisement of souls in the Intermediate State, so we cannot tell by what manifold means He may work for their redemption? If, as we firmly believe, souls retain consciousness, power of recognition and intercommunion, may it not be that the happier souls may influence the others, and draw them on towards a greater nearness to Christ and the power of His Sacrifice?

However these things may be, we know that 'GOD is Love,' and that He died that all men *might* be saved; and that those poor souls who shall be eternally banished from His near Presence and consequent Bliss of Life can only be in that banishment through their own deliberate will. We think of such souls with terrible pain and sadness, and only ever touch upon the question of their state as being bound up inevitably with all discussion of the great issues of life and death. And any thought may surely be softened by a trust that GOD's cleansing and purging, His discipline of souls in the Intermediate State, may so mightily work for the benefit of such that the end may be in many cases far other than that which presents itself to the mind as the natural probable result of their terrible degradation of life. The glorious worship of the Lamb, going forth perpetually in the courts of the blessed resting spirits in Paradise, may, for all we know, draw the distressed souls into a sufficient nearness that, catching something of its significance and power, they may see in their awful suffering the possibility of alliance with, and participation in, the Sacrifice offered for the whole of humanity. So of none should we think definitely as 'lost.'

And in those courts of the blessed, will there not be a 'purging as by fire,' though in a much lesser degree? Would they not even ask that it might be so, had not Christ declared it for them? In the intense longing to be like Him, with which the clear sight of Him must have filled them, will they not long for that which they knew had in the old time brought them closer to Him? Will they not wish to suffer in some wise, so that they may, still in union with Christ's Sacrifice, grow perfectly into conformity with Him? They must be in bliss, because they have been face to face with Christ, because they continue in His near Presence, because ever before them is He seen as the known End of their life, because they love Him consciously as their Pos-

THE UNITED LIFE BEYOND THE VEIL

sessor, and with a love dimly like unto His; and they must be in tender, beautiful happiness because with them are those loved in Him and for Him, and because they too are seen clearly and truly, revealed to them as indeed eternally theirs and eternally theirs *in Christ.* But alike must they suffer, though the suffering be not what we consider suffering; save, perhaps, in those sublime moments of our life, when we love it and bid it stay with us so long as there is aught in us that GOD would have removed, and that He knows will yield to its cleansing power.

Being bound up still with the Sacrifice of Christ all must suffer; but to real love there is no pain in such suffering, and the blessed departed will so truly have learned the lesson of the gloriousness of sacrifice as being the expression of love, that, bowed down before the Lamb slain, they will be experiencing the highest bliss of which the imperfect soul is capable. They will realise, then indeed, what had been faintly foreshadowed in those moments of their earthly life, when they saw in suffering the bond of union with Christ, and loved it as the revealer and the giver of His Life.

The bliss of the departed in Christ must indeed contain a strong admixture of suffering; yet, with the will working in perfect harmony with the 'law of creaturely perfection,' and desiring above all things the realisation of perfection as being the only true answer to the Sacrifice of Christ, the only possible avenue to Him as the End of life, there can be nought of the sense of pain as pain, but only a rapture of being, compared with which all earthly conceptions of happiness must pale into dull insignificance.

There is, we may firmly believe, rest and peace: a stillness undisturbed, unbroken, in which GOD's Voice can be ever heard, GOD's Presence ever consciously to the individual near. Not at first may this be assured, but soon such peaceful stillness must ensue. And as the Holy Spirit works within the soul, and its enlarged and expanded faculties yield an ever-growing content to the possessor, fresh grace and power will be acquired in large measure, and the bliss of conscious union with GOD be intensified a thousandfold by the glorious happiness which each experiences in the witnessing of the new beauty of the beloved in Him, seeing in this the highest response to the old love which had yearned for and sought its perfection. Seeing each other as wholly Christ's, and discerning and reflecting Him in fresh and peculiar manner, they grow ever more and more toward Him; and their joy in each other thus, so far from hindering the acquisition of holiness, aids its advance. Each has for the other something of Christ to reveal and to give out: each ministers, therefore, to the other's perfection in Him. Each, revealing and giving some touch of Him to the other, draws out new beauty, fresh power, additional grace and glory of being; ever towards Christ. It is a steady, calm, active growth unto perfection, in which souls loved and loving on earth exert—or exercise, rather—that force of influence so strongly felt in the old days.

There are those, we know, who aver that it is pure

speculation to say that this influence of soul upon soul will be a factor of the life in the Intermediate State. But surely it is, again, a logical necessity, following on the continuance of consciousness, memory, power of recognition and intercourse, *love.* How could these continue, and personal, interchanged influence be absent? How, with the soul's enlarged grace and strength of life, could one soul fail to make itself felt increasedly, even, on the life of another soul? Everything necessarily points, not merely to a continuance of the wonderful power of personal influence, but of a developed influence. The real strength of influence here depends on the unseen life in the human being: comes from that hidden power and vitality which we call, perhaps, 'grace of character.' It flows out from the soul, and draws us to it, unknown to ourselves very often. Dr. Wendell Holmes used to say that a man's personality and power of influence extended far beyond his outer being, and were really, in a way, independent of this external being. And, after all, he was but stating the simple truth that the real part of us is spirit, 'soul,' and the real living the communion of one spirit with another. The hero of one of George Mac Donald's novels describes the fact of his always remembering each person, whom he met even casually, to his being careful to preserve a recollection of the spiritual relations existing between him and all others of GOD's human family. 'As far as I can help it,' he says, 'I never have any merely business relations with any one. I try always not to forget that there is a deeper relation between us.'

And this deeper relation being purified and intensified in the Intermediate State, involves an increase of personally interchanged influence. It had ever been the basis of intercourse. The silent going forth of soul-power, the touch of one soul upon another, the recognition and using of the special force of attraction which had lain in one soul for another, the sense of sympathy between, and comprehension of the particular working of, one soul and another which make of human beings affinities in Christ, and go to constitute a foundation of holy development and perfection of being,—all this is of the spirit. It is an extension of the holiness of GOD within and about us, a gradual resolving of chaos into cosmos, a bringing within the range of Divine Perfection that which, tainted by sin, had been antagonistic to GOD; and it reasonably prefigures and leads to this belief of the increased influential power in the Intermediate State. The bodily functions do not always lend themselves to ordinary spiritual manifestations, and only too often actually cripple and wrong such attempted manifestations. Furthermore, the spirit freed from the body is in conscious possession of greater faculties than had been realisable in a bodily condition of living, and must therefore have much more to tell and give out than had been the case in the old earth days.

We cannot reasonably conceive of the life beyond the Veil as being a life where personal influence can be absent. We are, on the contrary—as we find from one touch of thought on the subject—driven to believe that, when freed from the body, the spirit's range and force of influence will be expanded and intensified. So when we speak of the death of some great and brilliant servant of GOD as a 'loss,' we surely are culpable to a degree. We say of a Pusey, a Liddon, a Church:—How sad that such as he should be taken from us! How much he will be missed!

Is it not an error, both of imagination and of speech? Are we not most carelessly overlooking the ministry unto perfection in the Unseen World? It is truly a grave error when we speak thus. Their influence here had indeed been considerable, but is this the only ordained sphere for great work? Had their labour whilst here in the body been merely wrought by, and through, the bodily functions with which they had been endowed? Was there nothing that served to raise our thoughts to a higher work that they might be called upon to do:— beyond this earth? Had it been simply work of uttered words, of acts, of bodily presence?

No, there lay behind the bodily action an unseen power which can never die, whose influence, remaining still with us, filling up to us that void which the removal of their physical presence in our midst had at first caused, must now be exerted upon the lives being lived in the Unseen World. And we must feel that in that other sphere of living, their influence and their work of grace will be higher and nobler and more blessed than was possible here, when the physical part of their being did not always serve to keep true and pure the soul-power exercised by them, but even hindered at times the flow of progress and development that might issue forth from their souls.

Nathaniel Hawthorne has put very well the difficulty and the risk inseparable from the usual method of human intercourse; the interchanging—or attempts to interchange—thoughts and ideas. And he gives us his opinion of how this difficulty and risk should be faced and met. 'If at any time,' he says, 'there should seem to be an expression unintelligible from one soul to another, it is best not to strive to interpret it in earthly language, but wait for the soul to make itself understood; [and were we to wait a thousand years, we need deem it no more time than we can spare.] . . . I have often felt that words may be a thick and darksome veil of mystery between the soul and the truth which it seeks. Wretched were we, indeed, if we had no better means of communicating ourselves, no fairer garb in which to array our essential being, than these poor rags and tatters of Babel. Yet,' he adds naturally, 'words are not without their use, even for purposes of explanation—but merely for explaining outward acts, and external things, leaving the soul's life to explain itself in its own way.'

We know, of course, that not only have words, here, their use, but that they are absolutely indispensable, in the first instance, for the conveying truth from one soul to another, or others. Only we further know that, as we advance on our way towards the purely spiritual life which awaits us beyond the grave, we become more than independent of this means of intercourse, this method of conveyance of the truth in us, and love to rest in the silent expression of thought and feelings which souls give forth to us—insensibly to themselves sometimes, but always powerfully and inevitably. There is a great deal, ever, in the soul, of which verbal expression cannot be made; and in the attempt to make such expression as may be possible, a person may very often do considerable wrong to the beauty and grandeur truly resident within him. And the wrong may be aggravated from the fact that those to whom the attempted revelation is being offered have not advanced so far in spirituality as the intended revealer has advanced, and so there is obscurity and misconception sad beyond the power of words to tell. In the wholly spiritual state, obscurity and misconception give place to clearness of vision and comprehension, and in the rapid growth and increase of soul-power there goes forth an increasing general power of receptivity, in which can be laid many beautiful truths and impressions that had before been impossible of acceptance and realisation.

So we come to see the natural inevitableness of personal influence in the 'Beyond,' and even before our death have some idea of the richness and glory of such influence as must there be exercised. So it grows, surely, beyond the question of probabilities that we should grudge to the souls living in the Unseen World the felt presence of saintly and generally powerful personalities, whose departure from the earth signifies some measure of loss to the persons remaining on earth. So, too, are we able to conceive a fragment of the glory of that union and communion which must exist between souls specially bound in love, and in which can be no marring of maligning, wronging words ; where the heart, knowing its own truly, and seeing ever into the innermost life-recesses, is caught up into GOD, and enabled to live unhindered the dual life ordained by Him.

So growth goes on : so are united in communion and blessedness souls redeemed from evil. So, we must not forget, are united the seen and the Unseen worlds : so, by prayer and offering in the Blessed Eucharist, sung in the Presence of GOD and the lesser presence of worshipping Angels, are lives fitted, in their several varieties of growth and beauty, for the moment when the trumpet shall sound, and GOD shall call from the uttermost parts of His realm all the souls of His creation to His Judgment Seat, and shall apportion to each the due measure of bliss—(or of that woe which, self-entailed, a soul virtually *asks* GOD to give it).

And then shall our elect stand forth, and with us be perfect to GOD. They shall re-meet us after the Divine Judge has passed His sentence upon us, and be bound up with the life to be lived eternally in the new heavens and the new earth.

'Think what it will be to us creatures of sense, children of time, victims of custom, slaves of habit, to live in conditions where these are utterly swept away ! Think how blessed if there be to us places and conditions where all that has been best and beautiful, truest and most pure, all that is loftiest and most elevating, without danger of the depressing influence of sloth, without fear of our low views and earthly tendencies, shall be ours irrevocably and for ever! In sin or worldliness well may we fear a future in which this miserable self, from whose thraldom we long to escape, might be stereotyped for ever; but in penitence, in efforts towards true life, in our better moments and higher hours, how stimulating, how consoling, how elevating to feel sure that what is good and blessed and true, high and tender affections, noble resolves, holy purposes,—that these have their true power in an eternal future, and that that future is ours!'[1]

'Think what it will be to us to meet again in joy . . . : to see that the grave hath yielded her spoil, and that the warm flesh, and the flitting colour, and the breathing life is again restored to that cold and solemn spoil of humanity, which we in tears consigned to the dust from whence it came; to press to our hearts those living forms which last we reverently coffined ere they were removed from beyond our sight; to hear again those accents of joy and greeting which last sounded in our ears as heart-breaking farewells, or pious commendations of the soul into the hands of the GOD of the spirits of all flesh.'

So Bishop Forbes has written. And is there not conveyed through his words a wondrous message to all sorrowing hearts? We know that on this earth, in this present sphere of men's living—which so dimly and faintly prefigures the great life to come—though love is a beautiful gift, and may reveal GOD more clearly and

[1] Canon Knox Little.

fully to a human being blessed by it, there is peril in it : peril involving to every person to whom the gift comes a reverent, careful guarding of the treasure, and sometimes a purging of it as by fire, that the dross which has been allowed to accumulate about it may be removed. We have seen people beaten down, tyrannised over, subjugated wholly, by some special love of a human creature : losing their strong manliness, their conscious hold upon GOD even. We have watched people degrading from the life they had been living in communion with GOD, simply by reason of an overmastering love which had taken possession of their being. GOD had been divorced from their life, so far as they could accomplish this :—there had been sundering of spirit from Spirit, rejection of Divine advances still, and ever, being offered to their souls. No violence had been done to the intruder when violence should have been done : the struggle for supremacy had been a poor, feeble attempt to preserve an impossible position : a state of temporising with the adversary, and a prompt yielding to the proposed terms of agreement ! It was a perpetual striving to love out of, apart from, GOD. The soul is truly made for love, but it is not made for such love as should be a factor set over against GOD : only when we love unto purity and perfection of being can it be the spiritual agent in the life of man that GOD designed it to be. In the great Beyond where we shall exist, first as spirit independent of physical form, then as spirit enclosed in a spiritual body, with all functions and powers transformed, perfected, glorified with the glory of Christ, our Risen Lord, we shall understand better the love of GOD in which He interferes between an unworthy love-enslaved life and the love-conqueror, seeming to slay the latter—for the former's sake. For such the message of Bishop Forbes's words has peculiar significance. GOD in His Love had taken away the object of love from the man's life; for he had not been worthy to retain it—perhaps, indeed, the object had been unworthy: but from the grave (figurative or literal) in which had to be laid the form of the love, arose a spirit capable of perfection; and in the dawn of higher life that spirit shall be met and acquired, and the man grow towards GOD in the gradual realisation of its new life, wherein, resting on the clouds of Heaven, it is carried to the Arms of Christ and receives its consecration.

'To press to our hearts those living forms!' There is, inevitably to us all, dearness of the form surrounding, and being in intimate, dependent connection with, the soul; and sometimes there may have been such attractiveness of form, of feature, that the body has been dear to us by reason of its own beauty, and any stroke—a less stroke than actual death—that seems to rob us of its power to attract is felt by us as a terrible blow. But, any way, the form is dear to us: through speech, through general bodily functions and actions, the soul has gone forth and met ours.—In love's early days, in fact, these would be the only means of our getting at the soul of our afterwards beloved;—and so, whether inherently attractive or devoid of natural beauty and grace, whether robust and full of youthful, passionate life, or feeble and filled with age's approaching torpor, it is bound up in our thoughts with the soul of our love, and we love it, of necessity, unto Eternity. And the resurrection to Life Eternal of the form of the beloved will be a part of that marvellous rapture of joy that we shall experience before the Throne of the Lamb, slain, yet there in Perfect Form too. It will not be the old body, but it will bear distinct, unmistakable likeness to the old body: it will be a long cherished physical being become wholly spiritual, grown into complete accord with the high, pure spirit within, yet still the form of the beloved.

And there, kneeling in adoration before Christ in His Perfect Humanity, glorious in His Fulness of Being, shall each see reflected in the other something of His Grace and Beauty, and love anew the old pain and sorrow that had led the way to Him. Each, embathed in the Glory of the Beatific Vision, shining forth in a full perfection, shall worship, and give thanks to GOD with the entire being; as, with a love undying, he beholds the regenerate life of the beloved, and discerns the glory of the path of suffering along which, with weary feet and drooping head, the old dear form had so often trod. Knowing now all, as he sees all, most chiefly will he love the beautified evidence of pain written in the new beauty before his eyes.

Seeing clearly our elect, clothed upon, yet perfectly revealed and declared by the body so clothing, we shall all surely understand the Mystery of Suffering: shall understand indeed the full meaning of the old life, with its details of discipline and painful trial.

'To be with Christ is Life, and where Christ is there is His Kingdom:' and in His Kingdom we know no special, holy love can be lost, nor fail to meet its perfect satisfaction and crowning. Gone then will be the sorrows of earth, the agonies, the distresses, the doubts, the questionings. Merged in a glorious reality will be the former shadows and adumbrations of the truth of love. And blent with this will be other loves—covering, we feel, the needs of those whose hearts had longed for union with us, whilst we had not known reciprocal longing,—each perfect and all-sufficing, giving gladly to the delight and happiness of every object claiming it, yet interfering never with, nor detracting from the perfection of, the special love of loves, nor with the supreme love of GOD. No love will be grudging nor unwilling, but all will be rich and bountiful, poured forth for the completion of each single life in the One Great Life of GOD.

In GOD, truly, shall we all live; from Him draw ever fresh beauty of being: yet, beholding one another in the glorifying Light of His Presence, loving one another with a love perfect as the life and being are perfect, we shall feel that the general consummation and realisation of perfect love, one of another, is a large part of the glory of Heaven. 'GOD above everything!' would we still cry. But we and the beloved, made glorious in Him, with our fully expanded powers, our freed and completely enlarged minds, our supernatural forces and modes of expressing thought and feeling, shall surely be within ourselves as without ourselves a sanctuary, enclosed by Him, from which shall ever go forth such splendour of worship and melody as shall cause the whole new heavens and earth to echo and re-echo with the praise of His Name.

'What I do thou knowest not now, but thou shalt know hereafter.' Even the love that GOD gives to us here we know not fully, but this we shall truly know hereafter. When we kneel before His Throne and receive from His Hands our crown of perfection, we shall realise the part that love had played in our earthly life, and reverence it now, as, welded in a love pure as that of the Angels, we take up the New Life and find it to be—all Love!

With these lines would one wish to speed a soul to the Great Beyond :—

' Out of this vale of tears,
O Christian soul, depart !
From wearing pains, and haunting fears,
And griefs that rend the heart !
Accept this sentence of release,
That speeds thee forth in solemn peace, . . .
To broadening light and deepening rest
Till Heaven shall make thee fully blest ! . . .
   O crown of joys ! no more to stay,
No more to take thine own wild way,
No more the Friend of friends to leave,
No more His patient Spirit grieve ;
What promise sweet or boon secure
Can match these words, I make thee pure ?
So now—let Him arise, and put thy foes to flight ;
For thee this day let Paradise fling wide her portals bright . .

> To GOD Who made thee, GOD Who bought,
> And GOD Whose Grace thy cleansing wrought,
> That hell no part in thee should claim,
> Go!—in the all-victorious Name!"[1]

And if, by GOD's goodness, the soul is able to receive that strength for the journey imparted by the final bestowal to it on earth of the Body and Blood of Christ, and the body—the dear 'form'—shortly to be laid in a grave, be sanctified by the Supreme Means of Grace, then how wonderful is our realisation of the life into which has passed (or is passing) the soul, and how clearly do we picture in our minds the re-united life of soul and body perfected in Christ. The visible, tangible partaking of Him seems to affect and intensify more than aught else could our power of spiritual sight, and quickly we follow in thought the sped soul to the new life.

May GOD grant to each one of us, at the moment of our departure from earth, such strength and refreshment! May the soul and body thus be blessed and sanctified, and the sorrowing hearts left behind be enabled to rise in quick thought to Paradise, and see the freed spirit praising and adoring GOD in the Higher Sanctuary, where from all shall truly go forth the outburst:—

> 'My GOD, *Thou* art all Love!'

---

[1] Canon Bright.

Printed by T. and A. CONSTABLE, Printers to Her Majesty
at the Edinburgh University Press